The Primal, The Modern, and the Vital Center

A Theory of Balanced Culture

In a Living Place

Donald W. Oliver,
Julie G. Canniff, and
Jouni Korhonen

Volume Seven of the
Foundations of Holistic Education Series

Foundation for Educational Renewal
P.O. Box 328, Brandon, VT 05733-0328
1-800-639-4122
www.great-ideas.org

To the Domus at 18 Willow Street
Concord, Massachusetts

TABLE OF CONTENTS

Part Five: An Organic Theory of Place and Culture

Part Six: Reconsidering Prospects for Change

Introduction

This book is a critique and reconsideration of our modern way of life and more particularly about three places we inhabit there:[1] the corporate place where many of us work; the nuclear family where we live our private lives either alone or with partners and children; and the complex of "middle level" local places such as extended families, mutual aid/support groups, neighborhoods, and civic organizations.

The first place, the corporate organization, is generally defined physically by brick and glass and concrete office buildings, factories, warehouses, malls, convention centers, large parking lots and garages, etc. Within these corporate places the dominant activity is disciplined work organized by a hierarchy of executives, supervisors and managers who oversee the efficient production of goods and services to be sold in the market place.

The pressured business characteristic of the corporate work place has also entered the lives of children. School becomes more exclusively efficient and structured to prepare children for regular bouts of testing. They are required to spend increasing amounts of time writing, calculating, researching in front of the computer. Recreation becomes the serious business of organized "play" in games of soccer, football, baseball, swimming, or math Olympics, or drama and music competitions or workshops on how to avoid premarital sex and drug addiction.

The second, or family place, is something like a homestead used as a sanctuary to separate us from the utilitarian logic of the corporate work place. While the activities of the family in an earlier phase of the technological revolution were largely domestic chores and the nurturance of family members, this is less so today. More recently it has become more like a managed place into which we schedule all the busy fragments of a consumer centered way of life.[2] These scattered fragments include: taking children to fast food restaurants, shopping in the mall, seeing doctors and dentists and hairdressers, taking brief vacations at theme parks, going to church or temple, cooking on the grill, watching TV, writing e-mail on the net, and doing much driving about.

The third or middle place is really a complex set of places somewhere between the corporation and the nuclear family. It is here that diverse individuals and families and groups come together face to face over sustained periods of time to make a viable neighborly, economic, political, and civic culture. It commonly includes a variety of more specific "places"—local stores, shops and studios of trades people, artisans, and artists who build and repair and decorate our homes, family gardens, local restaurants and coffee shops, street corners and parks within neighborhoods, and civic places where one may learn the stories that tell us about each other's lives and where we talk through and negotiate in rough and tumble ways our mutual problems.

We will argue in this book that these "third" or middle places are essential to provide what we consider the preconditions of civilized life as they affect the other two places. They are also the preconditions for our effort to define and make possible a "genuine"[3] or authentic culture reflecting the fuller potentialities of our human nature. It is for these reasons that we refer to these middle places as the "vital center" in our title. We are not suggesting that these third places, or vital centers, replace corporate organizations or families (or whatever other places we inhabit). We simply need them to teach us something about how to engage in the creative, continuous, improvised process of culture-making without the corporate pressure to manufacture or market products.

Today many of us find ourselves spending less time in these third more informal neighborly places. The result is the loss of much of the vitality that comes from regular contact with neighbors and friends who, over generations, may create hospitable settings wherein people can simply be themselves. For, we imagine, it is in these middle places that we are in some degree significant not because we have power or money or a special occupational status but because we are known by family and friends and even by some cranky or hostile neighbors who understand at some level the importance of the place we and they share together.

THEORETICAL OVERVIEW

At a more theoretical level, a central project of this book is to analyze and discuss how the serious and chronic problems present in our modern societies[4] might be reframed so that we can better understand—and perhaps change—the "places" and the cultural patterns that define these places. We begin this task initially by critiquing and reconsidering a number of dualistic assumptions implicit in our modern understanding of such categories as reality, culture, individuality, human nature, diversity, and place. More specifically, in Part Two we move from a dualistic subjective vs. objective view of reality to a reality that comes into being as a subtle, continuous, emerging process in which we participate. In Part Three we move from a human nature vs. culture duality to a view of human nature as providing a range of potentialities, some of which particular societies enculture, actualize, and express as stable patterns of a common life. In Part Four we move from an individual vs. community duality to a view of community as an organic "natural" unit of social being with its own integrity composed of individuals, each of whom is seen as a unique and significant "person" defined in part by the individual herself and in part by one's participation in the culture of the community. In terms of place we move from the public corporate place vs. the private family duality to stress the importance of mediating institutions that may be connected to the corporation and the family yet have their own integrity—that is to say, middle level places which are neither public nor private but rather, in some degree, a fusion of both.

THE PRIMAL, THE MIDDLE, AND THE MODERN

Beyond our attempt to clarify and reconceptualize these problematic dualistic constructs, we go on to present a second thesis: Namely that creating an authentic or "genuine" contemporary culture requires that we move toward enculturing and expressing in some degree the balance and fullness of our humanness by taking into account the legacy of our primal to modern biological and sociocultural evolutionary history. One way of introducing and illustrating what we mean by "primal to modern evolutionary history" is to describe briefly one of the more significant sources of our biological nature, the human brain. One aspect of our brain is that it consists of three interconnected sub brains: the old so called "reptilian" brain, the newer paleomammalian or limbic brain, and the most recently evolved neomammalian neocortex. Hampden-Turner describes the dramatic consequences of having this layered three part "triune" biological structure as part of our mammalian heritage.

The older [reptilian and paleomammalian] brains seem involved in the ancestral lore of the species, i.e., hierarchies of dominance-submission, sexual courtship and display.... defending territory, hunting, hoarding, bonding, nesting, greeting, flocking, and playing. The [modern] neocortex, in contrast, seems more adept at learning new ways to cope and adapt. If the [older] limbic system is removed in monkeys ... they cease to resemble monkeys in their behavior. The whole capacity to imitate the monkeyish style is lost; all rituals cease.[5]

Generalizing from the behavior of monkeys, we would infer that we humans would lose much of our "humanish" style or humanness if we did not express in a balanced way elements of our older biological capabilities with the more modern ones. From this point of view it would seem desirable that we construct a range of "places" that allow us to act out a rich and balanced repertory of primal to modern cultural patterns. Thus to be "human" in this modern way requires that we live in places and cultures that allow us to express more fully such mammalian human impulses as empathic bonding, community building and ritual making as well as our relatively modern cognitive capacities for planning, coping, and creating complex forms of language and technology. Likewise we maintain that it is essential that we sustain not only our rich older social forms of nurturing, bonding and caring but also our older archaic forms of social organization such as the extended family, the neighborhood, and local modes of civic cooperation where these forms of empathic bonding can be transformed into stable cultural patterns. We would stress that these earlier primal human gifts need to be celebrated to balance modern corporate places which tend to enculture casual and transitory friendships and calculating self-interested individuals bound together by formal contracts and legal arrangements.[6] These neurological aspects of our nature and their relationship to culture are introduced and discussed in Part Three.

We optimistically assume that humans are drawn toward this fuller, organic layered wholeness which moves them to include and express the broad range of primal to middle to modern cultural potentialities inherited from their evolutionary past. However, we also acknowledge the sobering historical record which tells us that humans often exhibit the somewhat perverse and self-destructive tendency toward inventing and getting "stuck" in stressful and unbalanced cultural patterns that overemphasize or shortchange essential aspects of their nature. Greed, selfishness, cruelty, and envy, for example, are also potential elements of our nature, these can surface as dominant cultural patterns when not balanced with the natural sympathies that spring from the physical contiguity involved in community building which connects kin, spouse, friend, and work companions in a common life. In Chapter Two we discuss this human tendency toward making what we call "cultural errors." Here we warn that after enculturing dysfunctional, stressful errors, communities or societies may not repair them without difficult and painful trauma — or at times, without avoiding the eventual decline and dissolution of the society itself.

In Part Five we move on to a systematic normative theory of place and culture in which we integrate the evolutionary elements of our theory within a functional view of human nature and culture. Here we suggest three major overall cultural functions required for human societies to adapt and survive. These functions include 1) economic and environmental functional patterns, e.g., the range and level of technology, vocations, divison of labor; 2) social and political functional patterns, e.g., forms of bonding and cooperative behavior, power relationships, forms of reciprocal obligations, etc.; and 3) functional patterns used for meaning-making and communication, e.g., unconscious dreams, rituals, stories, interpretive science and philosophy, etc. We then organize and relate our primal to modern places and our primal to modern cultural patterns within the framework of these functional categories.

Below we present Table 1 as a kind of graphic gestalt to describe the complex connections among the elements of our theory; that is to say, the primal to modern dimension, the historically evolved dimension of places, and the three functional categories with examples of the more specific cultural patterns they suggest. While we do not expect the reader to fathom at first glance the information summarized in Table 1, we reassure her/him that these ideas are developed and explained in Part Five. We would also emphasize what we think is the most important message communicated by this complex theory: namely that it puts substantive flesh and bones on those rich but slippery metaphors such as "balance," "holistic," and "organic" which can usefully be applied as norms to compare the quality of life in the various places in which modern people live.

Table 1. Functional Cultural Patterns Across the Primal-To-Modern Dimension and their Relationship to Levels of Place

Primal	Middle Level	Modern
Wilderness — Household — Village — Native Town — Corporate/Commercial		

Environmental/Economic Cultural Patterns

A Sense of Place

Deep Sense of Connection	Flexible, Highly Mobile

Types of Vocation

Hunting-Gathering	Artisanship	Entrepreneurship	Engineering

Level of Technology

Hand Tools	Animal Power, Artisan Tools	Water/Steam	Fossil/Atomic

Social-Political Patterns and Forms of Bonding

Forms of Bonding and Social Glue

Kinship/Mating	Friendship	Communal Cooperation	Contract and Self-Interest

Sources of Power, Control, and Decision Making

Age, Size, Competence	Relational "Power Within"	Economic "Power Over"

Cultural Patterns of Meaning and Meaning-Making

Conceptions of Personal Identity (Being)

Implicit Within Kin/Place/Vocation	Based on Education/Corporate Success/Power
Participation of Self-in-Community	Importance of Individual Self-in-Corporation

Time

Dream Time/Linear	Organic/Seasonal/Cyclical	Linear/Progressive

Qualities of Experience

Primacy of Myth, Metaphor	Pragmatic Problem Solving
Narrative, Story	Secular Feasts
Sacred Ritual Embedded in Everyday Life	Games
	Mass Media

SOME RISKS, LIMITS, AND HAZARDS IN OUR HOLISTIC THEORETICAL ENTERPRISE

THE USE AND LIMITS OF ABSTRACT LANGUAGE

It is obvious that the complexity, level of abstraction and "objective" impersonal academic language reflected in much of this book present us with something of a contradiction in making our case for the importance of local culture. Local is commonly associated with the concrete and the provincial rather than with more cosmopolitan abstract ways of knowing used by elite professionals. Our theorizing might well be seen as celebrating a way of knowing used mainly in the cultures of corporate institutions. So one might ask: Where do we stand when we use this more abstract academic language to advocate greater recognition of the importance of local places?

In responding to this question we would refer to the writing of Christopher Alexander in the field of architecture whose work perhaps bears most closely on this issue. Alexander describes his effort to create (or discover) a simple universalistic language (what he calls a "pattern language") by which to frame the art of "building" for those who would live in local or village-like places.

As he says,

> towns and buildings will not be able to come alive, unless they are made by all the people in the society, and unless these people share a common pattern language, within which to make these buildings, and unless this common pattern language is alive itself. In this book, [*A Pattern Language*] we present one possible pattern language.... You can use it to work with your neighbors, to improve your town and neighborhood. You can use it to design a house for yourself, with your family; or to work with other people to design an office or workshop or public building like a school.[7]

In Alexander's terms, the challenge of finding a language that, when applied, will bring local places, buildings, and cultures alive is central to our project. Intellectual and commercial elites who plan and construct "major" buildings or public monuments often have little or no contact with "local" cultures or people except in so far as "locals" may actually do the physical building or get in the way of their grander plans. Moreover these are the same elites whose voices provide the social, educational, architectural, economic, and governmental policies which often receive little input from the voices of those people whose major civic concerns bubble up from the ground of their everyday lives. In most instances, elites identify with the economic forces of modernity which use the language spoken and written in corporate business, government, media, schools and universities, and R&D centers. So while we confess that the level of abstract and systematic (albeit sometimes vague) language we use to describe our "non-dualistic organic, holistic, multilevel theory" sounds somewhat inaccessible and elitist, we hope that at some point it can be translated, reworked, and used to strengthen our concern for sustaining and building local places and in forging a more positive connection between the local and the corporate.

A NOTE ON THE INTERACTION BETWEEN CONVERSATION, DIALOGUE, AND WRITING

As indicated above, this is a book about the primal to middle to modern dimension of our human nature and the places and cultures we create to express them. Two of our central arguments then follow: first, more authentic cultures are those which allow for the balanced expression of these various levels of our humanness; and second, modern societies which tend to ignore or suppress our more primal and middle level human qualities in favor of more "progressive," advanced technical ones may prevent us from attaining a fullness in our humanity. Stated this way the reader is likely to ask: What do you mean by primal, by middle level, by modern, by genuine or authentic culture, by human nature, by progress, etc.? And we immediately feel thrust into the academic game of spending the rest of our time and space cleaning up our language before we can begin a conversation about the topic under consideration. While we do define many of our terms, their meaning, we think, is mainly expressed in the many and various contexts within which we use them.

Ironically, these same theoretical terms—primal, middle level, and modern—might also be applied to the modalities by which we might try to communicate these issues. So, for example, we might communicate our ideas in a more primal way by creating and acting out dramatic rituals. We might use middle level modes of communication by telling or singing stories followed by conversation and dialogue. Or we might (and do) use a modern mode of communication best desdribed as carefully crafted written language in which the goal is universal, transcultural, depersonalized clarity and minimal ambiguity.

If it were possible, we would choose a "middle level" style of communication, i.e., story telling and the understanding and interpretation of story through conversation, dialogue, and the negotiation of ideas. But, quite obviously, we are here using a technical modern genre, i.e.,expository academic written language. So the expectation is that our writing will be focused and reasonably precise, which is not always the case. We imagine that we then hear such haunting questions over our shoulder as: What is modern, etc., etc.? We want to say in response: Modern is contemporary. Modern is the historical period from Columbus to the present. Modern refers to the more recently evolved organisms on the planet. Modern is defined in the first chapter of our book largely in economic and technological terms. The opposite of Modern is the way "primitive people" once lived and some still live. Modern refers to the way most people who may read this book live. Or we may hear the question, "What is 'genuine culture?'" We want to say genuine culture is one in which the patterns of action and meaning reflect the fuller and more authentic qualities of our human nature. But then the reader may ask, "What is authentic and what is human nature anyway?" And so on and so on.

So here in the beginning we want to confess that we would have preferred that the medium for this work were "middle level"—that is, face-to-face story telling, conversation, dialogue, and various degrees of somewhat systematic philosophizing. But then the obvious retort: If that's what you want, what then is the point of writing it out rather than telling it? Our answer: We see written work of this kind mainly as a prelude for a way of describing how we look at the world which may promote and provoke future stories and conversation. The purpose of using this type of written constricted language is to communicate as best we can the plausibility and seriousness of some issues so that they will not be dismissed before we can move on to discuss and talk about them.

The writing style we use is a mix between journalistic commentary and philosophical analysis, both of which we couple with illustrative findings and insights from essays and empirical research found in academic studies. Our intention in using these sources is less to provide evidential support for "provable" claims and more to elaborate and clarify positions that we assume we and our sources share. In these terms we obviously admit to using mostly "friendly" sources.

But whatever our style of language or use of sources, we must admit to constantly feeling how often and how close we come to the edge of sounding either too convoluted and complex or too simplistic and strident, either of which may dampen our credibility and prevent future conversation and dialogue with the reader. And we constantly wish from moment to moment that we could actually see the reader and work on these problems together.

THE PROBLEM OF VOICE:
GENDER, AGE, AND INTELLECTUAL TRADITION

We acknowledge that the issue of "voice" is important and note that our language is not only elitist but also predominantly "yang" or male, at least in source and style. We would qualify this by suggesting, however, that the yin and the yang of our thesis is quite balanced. To celebrate the critical importance of local homesteads and communal places and the social relationships and qualities of meaning central to these places moves us toward actions and activities in which women and men have been mutually engaged from time immemorial—activities such as raising children, growing gardens, building and maintaining homesteads, caring for the old and the infirm. This argument is developed with compelling clarity by Hilka Pietila in Chapter Nine.

We would also point out that the issues we raise run perilously close to highly charged matters of diversity and oppression related to gender, race, and ethnic minorities. We have only touched on these issues in order to keep our project within manageable limits. In Chapter Seven, however, we do deal directly with the genesis of social class oppression. We have mainly chosen to continue the line of work carried on by a limited group of seasoned insightful scholars who have, over the past seventy years, worked on the interconnections among culture, community, and modernity. While these scholars are transdisciplinary in orientation, their most common academic fields revolve around anthropology (and more specifically theoretical normative anthropology), process philosophy, and intellectual history. All have made contributions toward presenting their disciplines as fields of moral philosophy.

These figures have inspired us with their bold and often unconventional ideas. They have had the courage to see the roots of modernity as fraught with long-term revolutionary possibilities for good and for ill rather than simply as a somewhat bumpy trip to nirvana or as a perennial sump of exploitation and oppression. Nor have they inspired us to dance around the black hole of post modern thought. If our writing in any way distorts, vulgarizes, or diminishes this unique intellectual "tradition," we would prefer to blame it on our impulsive misreading of elements of their vision as we sit on the razor thin edge of what is certain to be an uncertain and revolutionary new century. Each day, as we look at the dizzying rate of technological and social change, we find ourselves living between feelings of exhilaration and terror, which does not always make for a balanced judgment in these matters.

A CAUTIONARY NOTE:
WHO ARE WE SAYING IS MODERN?

There is an an ambiguity running through our work regarding who we are "accusing" of being modern.[8] This is not the same as suggesting that we define modernity or being modern in various different or ambiguous ways. We think we state pretty clearly what we mean by "modernity" or "being modern" in Chapter One. In answer to the question "who do we think is modern?" however, we admit to a lack of clarity. At this point we would suggest that in some sense most of us writing or reading the kind of material in this book are implicated. We the authors are in most senses modern, although we may not have started out that way. You the reader are probably pretty modern. Most of our friends and relatives are probably modern. Anyone who has lived in what might be considered a "modern" society for a generation or two, is probably quite modern. If, however, in the course of one's lifetime, one has lived in a more "primal" or "traditional" or unconventional society for any significant period of time, s/he might very well look at this work in a fundamentally different way from those who have been more or less "modernized."

PASTORAL UTOPIA OR DEMONIC DYSTOPIA:
TWO VIEWS OF THE LOCAL PLACE

An issue that commonly arises when anyone celebrates "localness" is the charge that s/he may be unrealistically naive and romantic about such places. The vision of some kind of pastoral paradise that is available to humans is probably as old as "civilization." This vision runs the gamut from Adam and Eve in the Garden of Eden where all needs were taken care of by the bounty of nature (and the grace of God) to Thoreau's experiment in primal living on Walden Pond. We confess to having been contaminated to some degree by this pastoral vision, although we are probably influenced more by our own collective personal experience living within real local communities.

We well understand that local places are far from exempt from the pathologies that infect the human condition. We believe only that this level of social organization is a necessary but certainly not a sufficient condition to move in the direction of a humane and decent society. In our discussion of the requirements for a balanced culture in Chapter Ten this argument is worked out. At this point, however, we would make two comments. First, local places can and do develop destructive cultures. They may, for example, lack adequate resources to meet many of their essential needs for survival and end up fearful and suspicious of each other as well as of outsiders. We would note Banfield's study cited in Chapter Fourteen of a small Italian village in which an "amoral familistic" culture of suspicion and distrust among families reached the point where the lack of mutual cooperation led to unnecessary and continuing poverty for all. Or local peoples may have difficulty recovering a sufficient degree of mutual trust after having lived through destructive acts of conflict and betrayal. We would note the communal paranoia in the small Puritan community of Danvers, Massachusetts which, in 1692, was wrecked for a time by the notorious Salem witch trials spawned by greed, fear, and conflicts over the ownership of land.

Second, we would emphasize the fact that our concern for sustaining the integrity of local places is not set within the context of a relatively isolated rural society but rather within a modern technolgoical-industrial world where all must compete to survive the growing force of cosmopolitan corporate organizations. It is likely that what people in and out of local places have most to fear is less the ghosts of internal provincial suspicion and conflict and more the domination and "takeover" by these corporate forces. Our sense is that in our current situation, intolerance and coercion are as likely to come from corporate officers and lawyers as from the internal irrational dynamics of local bullies and bigots.

However there is a final point we would state without qualification. We should not underestimate in any way the importance of the vision and energy required to create institutions to protect the fundamental rights of unpopular individuals and groups from being abused at all levels of society. Would that we had a Universal Declaration of Human Rights including both economic as well as political and legal rights coupled with trustworthy and humane institutions to enforce them in a compassionate and equitable way world wide! Were there such institutions, the hope of protecting local peoples and local places and local cultures in a more diverse and pluralistic world would be immeasurably strengthened.

NOTES

1. A more complex understanding of place and places is discussed in Chapter Nine.

2. For documentation regarding the stress associated with work and overwork in modern American society see Juliet Schorr, *The Overworked American* (New York: Basic Books, 1991).

3. The term "genuine culture" is used by Sapier referring to the more integrated communal face-to-face way of life of early Native Americans as contrasted with the segmented lives of modern Americans after the industrial revolution. The term is discussed in Chapter One.

4. The obvious context of this study is the United States. However, we see the modern economic globalization process as rapidly taking over much of the planet. This does not mean that all the nations of the world will come to look like the United States. We assume the rich-poor pattern will continue and become exacerbated. It will probably mean only that most nations will attempt to imitate the modern cultural practices of places like the United States.

5. Charles Hampden-Turner, *Maps of the Mind* (New York: Collier Books, 1981), 80.

6. Competitive professional sports might be given as an example of primal-modern balance. Here there is a mix of high level physical-mental activity in the process of performing deep primal rituals organized by the ultimate in contract-based corporate management to sell products. What is left out, of course, is voluntary middle level communal engagement and participation. This would also apply to much modern entertainment.

7. Christopher Alexander, et al., *A Pattern Language* (New York: Oxford University Press, 1977/1979), p. x.

8. We admit to characturing in some degree the condition of "being modern." However, we are constantly surprised at the casual assumption by those among whom we live that the condition of life in modern America is either a universal norm or even should be a universal norm.

PART ONE

THE ERRORS
OF
OUR WAY

CHAPTER ONE

Modernity, Progress, and Balance

In this book we critique a process, "modernization," and a social system, "modernity," in an effort to rethink two of their central cultural assumptions. The first assumption is that the progressive nature of modernity through continuously advancing technology, mass production, and the commercial exchange of "products" resulting from this technology will benefit humanity at the expense of diminishing primal and more traditional cultural patterns.

Our purpose here is to reconsider this assumption and argue that an adequate society is one that sustains important traditions precisely because they tend to nurture more primal qualities in our human nature and connect these qualities with the modern. We define "primal" and "modern" in both evolutionary-biological and cultural-historical terms. So patterns of human biological potentiality such as mating and nurturing and raising the young we consider "primal." Similarly, we consider socio-cultural patterns developed earlier in our history such as living primarily in complex interdependent face-to-face social groups as "primal" also.

We argue that modern societies understate the importance of expressing a broad and adequate range of our human potential. Within the dimension of time, for example, humans can construct culture which includes a sense of linear time, cyclical time, seasonal time, time as eternity, and the sense of timelessness. It is clear that modern societies often function largely within the framework of an impatient sense of present-to-future linear time while more traditional societies celebrate a broader sensibility in the ways they experience time. Or, within the dimension of social structure, we know that people can build societies with cultural patterns and places that include nuclear families, extended families, clans, local villages, native towns and cities, corporate work-centered institutions, and large commercial industrial urban centers. Modern societies function largely within nuclear families, corporate work-centered institutions, and commercial industrial centers while more traditional societies nurture life in extended families, local villages, and native towns and cities.

Although modern societies claim that they provide a great quantity of choices, these choices are narrowly defined—as "good" jobs or products or services. In reality, modern people actually lose such fundamental cultural choices as the primal biological senses of cyclical and seasonal time or the feeling for one's native place, or the plausibility of maintaining social bonds across generations. Such choices are too costly for many modern people because they violate the basic logic of the modern system which reduces almost all choice to a single common denominator—money. Within a commercial market economy, it is "uneconomical" (or culturally dysfunctional) to expend the time to sustain the bonds of extended kinship or communal friendship. Such bonds would require direct human contact and a stable connection with place, and this restricts one's ability to compete in the market place for favorable educational slots or jobs.

The second cultural assumption of modernity is its approach to the problems it spawns. We see modern societies as continuously engaged in creating new and more powerful forms of technology that radically change how people live. These changes are attended by a backwash of chronic problems which it attempts to solve superficially, one by one.

We see this approach to problem solving as grounded in a relatively unreflective and ahistorical faith in the same process of pragmatic engineering and education that created both the changes and the problems in the first place. So modern societies attempt to progress and to solve problems by first inventing new technology, and second, by constructing highly organized and narrowly focused educational, therapeutic, or "work" programs to "fix" deficiencies in the minds or behavior of those who cannot quite "adjust" to this new system. Then they seem unable to reframe ways of dealing with these problems within a more deeply grounded understanding of the human condition.

Once having questioned these aspects of modernity, we are moved to reconsider, in some fundamental way, the problems that beset our contemporary world. We stress that we are not seeking solutions at this point. We are seeking ways to shift our thinking away from framing the challenges of modern life solely in terms of how fast can we make our way into a future of material affluence, high productivity, human convenience and personal comfort. We would redefine "progress" in more complex, ambiguous terms as the adequacy of and balance between deep traditional or primal cultural patterns within a society and our modern capacity for discovering through science and technology new ways of meeting our needs for comfort and survival. We argue that human quality of life must consist of a balance between traditional cultural patterns and the "progressive" novel cultural patterns generated by what we consider the more modern institutions of contemporary society.

Tribes, Villages, and Modernity

In contemplating the global landscape at the beginning of a new millennium there appear to be only three major types of human societies left on the planet. One type is the remnant of tribal societies in places like New Guinea and Brazil, most of which have been destroyed over the past two centuries. A second type is the more extensive remnant of archaic cities and agricultural villages left from feudalism—perhaps the most common form of human association over the past 5,000 years of human history. The third type is the growing industrial metropolitan society we call the modern world or what we refer to here simply as "modernity." This typology is, of course, an oversimplified sketch of the global scene, but our purpose in this chapter is to give the reader an overview or sketch rather than a detailed picture of the way humans have lived over the past few millennia.

Today, the remnants of tribal societies are in various stages of disintegration and transition, moving inexorably into modernity. With respect to feudalism, there are still a great variety of agricultural village-based places left in the world, many of which are no longer controlled by feudal landlords (and some of which never were). In its time, however, feudal institutions were world-wide and many of them have been carried over into contemporary modern institutions, e.g., in the idea of sovereign nation states or state governments which stand above any kind of local polity, or the pretense that there are somehow radical differences in the quality of humanity between an elite versus common people. This is particularly evident in the perpetuation of aristocratic bonds among the rich and powerful on broad regional and geographic lines, and in the creation of elite institutions, e.g., exclusive colleges, clubs, charities, churches, etc., to assure or at least encourage intermarriage among the privileged.

Feudal institutions presumably grew out of arrangements whereby a military establishment was created to protect the land and property of stable human cohorts which had shifted from nomadic hunting and gathering to farming on more permanent settlements. The military bands eventually worked out "contracts" whereby vulnerable villages could avoid destruction and looting in exchange for "protection." Eventually the military bands created an elite or class-based "noble" hierarchy which came to live a less hazardous existence within protected (often walled) urban environments (the preindustrial city) supported and controlled by a retinue of clergy, military, and servants, as well as by merchants, tradespeople, and the like. In the surrounding countryside agricultural villagers continued to live, contractually obligated to support those in the city with farm produce, indentured labor, and, when needed, a conscripted military force.

This feudal urban/village complex is what Western historians and their readers came to call "civilization." It is associated with the high culture present in archaic preindustrial cities and the maintenance of imperial cultural-ethnic-religious identities grounded in widespread sacred locations. It was and is still associated with the sharp distinction we make between "high" and "low" culture meaning more "refined" and affluent urban cosmopolitan peoples versus the poor urban servant class, and the rough agricultural village or peasant class.

Then some five hundred years ago the seeds of modernity sprouted in the form of a radical new approach to human inquiry in what we now call "science" and the transformation of that science into a marriage with a dynamic technology. The modern system has been developing rapidly ever since, stimulated by the industrial/technological revolutions in Western European countries, the creation of highly specialized units of production and consumption—corporate business, the factory system, mass migrations from farm to city as well as from poorer regions to richer regions, single crop agriculture and monoculture in harvesting from nature, wage labor, and dramatic changes in the use of buildings and space.

Socioeconomically this new system resulted in a sharp decline in the peasantry and nobility and created new classes of people: entrepreneurial capitalists, professionals, a wage-based middle class, an industrial proletariat, and an underclass of the segregated poor. Ideologically it meant a radical shift away from religion, which provided meaning in the culture, to a dependence on sophisticated science and technology to create a cornucopia of material goods and services. The idea of a "successful life" was transformed from fulfilling obligations to the gods and one's kin and friends to the accumulation of material wealth by working to maximize one's own comfort, convenience, and self interest.

MODERNITY'S GLOBAL PROMISE: PROGRESSIVE EVOLUTION FOR ALL

While the planet has been making a rapid transition from tribal societies and preindustrial and feudal societies to Modernity over the past few hundred years, the current revolution in the West went into high gear after World War II. At this time (in the 1950s and 1960s) scholars and policy makers in the United States and in other Western countries became convinced that this new consumer driven "modern system," in one variation or another (socialist, fascist, welfare state, free market, etc.) was destined to become the future of the modern society. These same policy makers began to use terms or categories like "first, second, and third world," and "developed" versus "underdeveloped" nations, later changed to "developing nations" to soften the pejorative connotation. At the time it was assumed that everyone would soon come to understand that this modern economic, technological and ideological system (and some variation of an accompanying political system) which had transformed much of North America, Europe, and Japan was superior to previous systems. Because of the seeming inevitability of technological progress, it was also assumed that all human societies would eventually imitate countries like the United States in having or striving for material abundance as the center of human life.

This more general global effort to imitate modern societies also included embracing the myth of progressive evolution or adaptation constructed by Western societies over the past 150 years. This myth tells the story of a human race which has embarked on a trip toward something close to utopia over the past ten thousand years. (In the past hundred years or so these utopias have been featured in various world's fairs and, more recently, in Disney-type theme parks.) The "story" describes how humans have moved from what was earlier called a "savage" or "barbarian" existence through a horticultural phase, through a feudal agricultural/preindustrial urban phase into a modern industrial phase, first at a national level and more recently at a global level.[1]

While our American passion for Modernity has been sensed and to some degree lived for the past hundred years, one consequence of the scientific revolution was not clearly envisioned by most Americans. In 1945, after the awesome achievement of releasing and "controlling" atomic energy, the "developed nations" appeared to accept responsibility for modernizing the whole planet. Some brief quotations coming out of this time period illustrate the bold thinking of modernist thinkers of these times. One article in an anthology on "social evolution and development" is modestly entitled "The Socio-cultural Development up to the Present Time and Our Place in It." Here R.F. Behrendt succinctly lays out the modern progressive theory and history of cultural evolution throughout human history:

> In the cultural development of mankind up to the present, we can distinguish three large phases.[2] On the whole we find that man's ability to exploit and dominate nature is enhanced in the course of the development of the three phases of culture. Hand in hand with this goes a continuous development of the division of labor and thus an extension of the spheres of economic, social, and intellectual relations within which interdependence of all participants prevails. What is most impressive here is, of course, the rapidity with which the speed of this development has been increasing in the last centuries.... Only 300 years ago men were threatened with death at the stake because they claimed the earth revolves around the sun. The last 30 years since Einstein's theory of relativity have widened our astronomic horizon more than the preceding millennia.[3]

In the third phase of this odyssey (which, in this work, we refer to as "Modernity,") Behrendt lists its major characteristics: "long term gainful employment" seen as the major purpose of life, "replacement of ... magical, mythical, and traditional methods ... by rational impersonal matter-of-factness," "high grade mastery of nature," a population explosion and massive migrations of people all over the planet, and shift from inherited privilege to privilege based on merit.[4]

Inkeles and Smith produce a somewhat similar but more comprehensive list of characteristics as the world moves from phase two (a "traditional" or "feudal" phase) to phase three. Their list then identifies those personal qualities needed for effective functioning in a complex modern society, including:

- Openness to new experience
- Readiness for social change
- Growth of interest in and opinions about a broad range of issues
- Acquiring facts and information to support opinions
- Orientation to present rather than past time
- Concern with efficacy and control over one's environment
- Concern with planning and public affairs
- Trust in large scale institutions
- Valuing technical skills
- Valuing distributive justice
- Educational and occupational aspirations to get ahead
- Valuing universal dignity of all
- Understanding the processes of modern production[5]

It should be added that Inkeles and Smith generated their definition of Modernity not only from presumed personal qualities needed to function in a modern society, but also from observed shifts in deeper institutional patterns and arrangements, such as:

- Kinship and family ties considered either as an obstacle or victim of modernization
- Equal rights and opportunities for women in the work force as well the pressure to exercise birth control and restrict family size
- Diminished religious practices and commitments
- Diminished respect for and responsibility to the aged
- Engagement in the larger political process
- Participation in or exposure to communications media
- Consumerism

- Social stratification and role differentiation based on merit and ambition rather than hereditary habits
- Commitment to outside work and the work place over family, religion, friends, etc.

Especially interesting about these lists is the "progressive" language in which most aspects of modernity are expressed. Rather than seeing modern cultural changes as including possible tradeoffs among conflicting dispositions of human nature or even including negative adaptations, they are implicitly understood as clearly moving toward a higher quality of life. Thus, from the modernist point of view, traditional peoples left over from earlier forms of society are required to "overcome" the unfortunate tendency of hanging on to irrational or maladaptive patterns of their previous cultures—a phenomenon that came to be called "cultural lag." In general, neither Behrendt nor Smith and Inkeles deal with the possible compromises or the "giving up" of significant positive aspects of traditional cultures in this journey along the road to Modernity, e.g., the loss of deeper spiritual sensibilities, long term loyalty to kin and friends, reverence for the environmental integrity and sustainability of place.

THE PROBLEMATIC NOTION OF PROGRESSIVE EVOLUTION

A more radical response to the various problems of Modernity is based not on the search for technical solutions to each separate crisis that emerges, but rather on a reconsideration of the theory of progressive biocultural evolution itself which Modernity simply presumes. The fact is that our underlying genetic makeup, which has evolved over millions of years, currently carries with it both very old and stable limbic mammalian tendencies as well as our relatively newer neocortical capacities for the unparalleled creative symbolic inventions and problem solving that we associate with "progress." And although these two characteristics of our nature are integrated biologically, we continue to have, to some degree, a schizoid nature.

Our multi-level biocultural tendencies are further complicated by the fact that the disparate qualities of our nature are distributed with varying strengths across individuals within the species. So different individual humans have differing balances of primal to modern tendencies and deal with these balances and imbalances with mixed degrees of success.

With such variability in our makeup, how does one compare our capacities for love and compassion versus our capacities for inventing novel technology within the framework of progressive evolution?

Our hypothesis is that it is essential to see successful human adaptation more in terms of *balances* among our various potentialities (obviously our social-rational ambivalence is not our only "problem") rather than simply as the fullest expression of our modern (rational, technical, linguistic) capabilities. Nor is this capacity for balance necessarily "normal" for humans—that is to say instinctively "wired" into our underlying biocultural pattern of adaptation which must express itself in the way we create and expand societies or civilizations. History suggests that humans tend to construct increasingly complex technological and social organizational systems which finally get "out of control," i.e., transcend the primal mammalian capacities for exercising adaptive humane moral responses and restraints. So as humans we have the capacity to organize vast numbers of people and develop technologies to extend our powers almost beyond our imaginations, yet when we transcend the boundaries of simple face-to-face societies in very substantial ways, we seem unable to limit the excesses and abuses of this technical power.

Excesses in human violence, for example, happen when those who have overall technical control are no longer in direct contact with the violence itself. Technical advances in weaponry speak to the point. The new rifled guns of the U.S. Civil War, the new machine guns and poison gas of World War I, the new fire bombs and atomic bombs of World War II all testify to our ability to terrify and destroy others through mass violence when those who give the orders are not so directly involved. (We would note that dictators, presidents, and generals rarely risk their lives in mortal combat.)

Likewise, technical and symbolic capacities give modern people incredible powers of communication. Simply consider the effect of advertising or demagoguery to influence and deceive crowds of people through the impersonal medium of electronic mass media. Remarkably, most humans have an instinctive sense of fairness and justice. Still, this sense of fairness is increasingly subverted as people are required to live within impersonal corporate forms driven by impersonal and abstract power carried out by impersonal and indirect communication (like "messengers from the king" under feudalism or orders from the CEO in the corporation, or directives from the principal in a public school). Honest, authentic face-to-face communication may not be necessary in the short run, but in the end it is a requisite for a compassionate and balanced culture and society.

SYMPTOMS OF A CHRONIC PATHOLOGY IN MODERNITY

The question to which we now turn is the extent to which Modernity is, in fact, a progressive and hopeful phase of an evolutionary trip which began with hunter gatherers, living on berries, nuts, and animals a million years ago; a trip that is now fulfilling the promises made over the past 200 years. Or is it in some degree a flawed and unbalanced way of life that may lead in the long run to one of the historical dead ends that Toynbee[6] discovered in his monumental study of the defunct civilizations of the past? Looking simply at current "facts" indicating the strengths and pathologies of the modern system, one finds a mixed picture. There are, of course, unparalleled technical advances in this way of life—in communication, transportation, biology and medicine. On a personal level, there is also greater personal freedom and increasing acceptance of religious, cultural and ideological diversity which comes with heightened respect for the individual. But there are also problems. Using statistics from Csikszentmihalyi's work up through the middle 1980s we find, for example, that:

> In the United States the per-capita frequency of violent crimes—murder, rape, robbery, assault—increased by well over 300 percent between 1960 and 1986.... In roughly the same period, the rate of divorce rose by about 400 percent.... The three- to four-fold increase in social pathology over the last generation holds true in an astonishing number of areas.[7]

Csikszentmihalyi then goes on to present rather dramatic evidence of pathology in the fields of mental illness, "paranoia" (money spent on "defense" budgets), children living in single parent families without broader communal support, number of children living below the poverty line, number of juveniles in prison, drug use, disappearance from home, pregnancies among unattached women and girls, teenage suicides, and general declines in educational achievement of youth.[8]

In our opinion, Modernity is comprised of many flawed cultural assumptions perpetuated generation after generation largely through the economic structure. For the sake of argument, let us consider the modern ideology of market capitalism, which is a product of Western Enlightenment science and the metaphysics of dualism. Enlightenment reality presumes a permanent division between mind and matter, and because humans, with their critical thinking neocortex can command the submission of matter, the rights, desires, and power of the individual are sacred. Although such an economic system is highly successful at meeting the needs of the individuals, a host of social and cultural pathologies flow from this concept of reality.

On the planet, there is a rapidly growing consumer/citizen base of six billion human beings, each of whom is theoretically seeking to maximize her/his personal self-interest. Where one lives, who one marries, how one is educated, where one works, who one's friends are, the car one drives, the food one eats, the style of life one lives are thus all matters of personal choice.

An example of questionable judgment by consumers within such a choice-centered society is our difficulty in regulating pollution-making technology and products. One can choose to live with noise, concrete and asphalt, and noxious gases if the tradeoff is having money to purchase consumer goods. If the consumer prefers to destroy rain forests or pave parking lots at the expense of biodiversity on the planet, that decision is to be made in the market place. So modern people gradually lose the capacity to discriminate between aspects of our world like the culture-sustaining capacities of active parenting as opposed to marginal custodial socialization and child care, or between the life-sustaining capacities of water and wetlands versus that offered by the comfort and convenience of asphalt and gasoline. The great masses of humans in the world now seem to see themselves (or their children) as destined to become entrepreneurs, marketers, producers, workers, and consumers within one or another versions of a highly competitive, mechanized, modern metropolitan world.

Humans are gradually seduced through advertising and propaganda into considering all value, including their own essential worth, as determined in large part by the price it will bring in the market place. What one is or what one will be "worth" is determined, not by some inner connectedness to the people one cares for, or the natural world that sustains one, or a transcendent reality that unites all being, but rather by the price a product or even one's own being can "command" in the market place.

The first standard for quality of life is the aggregate value of all goods and services exchanged—known variously as the "gross national product" or the "gross domestic product." This standard is commonly measured in some uniform currency of exchange (dollars, yen, pesos, etc.) It is thus possible to measure in quantitative terms the quality of life for a community/society/world. High quality of life comes from high aggregate values of goods and services.

Issues of justice or fairness (related to quality of life) can be inferred from equal/unequal distribution of goods and services. The equity issue may become serious when many people actually suffer physical or emotional trauma from lack of the necessities of life, while others consume what seem to be unnecessary luxuries. (Humans are commonly distressed by coming into direct visible contact with the suffering of other humans.) But aside from the fact that poor people may not be getting the necessities of life, modern people are loath to make judgments about the value of different goods and services in any absolute sense. If one chooses to spend one's wealth on 200 pairs of high fashion shoes while others choose to have an expensive car and still others choose to donate money to save an endangered species of wild life, it is seen as a matter of legitimate personal choice.

The market system does not discriminate between the value of activities and "products" essential for maintaining or renewing the culture and activities and products that might add only marginal pleasures or comforts to people's lives. For example, there is considerable evidence that parents will choose to work at jobs to earn money and pay surrogates to raise their children if it makes their lives more affluent and comfortable. (Their children, of course, then take on the same central values: affluence and comfort.) If both parents work for money and are able to hire inexpensive child care, this will presumably increase the aggregate wealth of the society. In the long run, however, such market-driven child care may seriously weaken family and communal institutions, although its consequences may not show up for one or two generations. Substantial time and energy for primary bonding among children and authentic parent figures may well be critical for positive cultural reproduction.

Whether by differences in temperament or ability or inherited privilege, in many nations economic development leads to increasing inequalities and exploitation of some humans by others in ways that diminish the humanity of both groups. In a modern society with a "welfare net," some basic services are provided to all citizens, normally in such areas as education, health, conflict resolution, police and fire protection, recreation. Services in excess of these basic needs are, however, bought and sold by private groups and individuals. While the ratio of private to public services is determined by voting and lobbying in the political process, the specific private goods and services are provided according to the way consumers spend money (vote) in the market place.

Within this "hidden hand" system, one's quality of life depends mainly on three considerations: 1)The quantity and quality of choices that are actually available in the market place; 2) The number of people who can afford to select these choices; and 3) How well the most vulnerable and needy—those most disadvantaged in the market place—are treated. In "hidden hand" economics it is assumed that poorer peoples, perhaps with a little help, will eventually make appropriate choices to improve their lot in life. But if the poor make poor choices (like having many children or little formal schooling), it is their own fault.

The problem of the rich and the poor brings into question two assumptions of the modern market society: first, the notion that eventually all people can be educated/prepared to act effectively in their own self-interest—to compete successfully either with the ballot or in the market place; and second, the notion that large scale human suffering associated with poverty can be countered by the charitable instincts of luckier or more affluent human beings. These assumptions seem, at best, problematic. And there is little doubt that conditions of wide scale gross poverty dehumanize both the rich and the poor.

The modern choice-centered market system is one of continuous growth in technology, in resources used, in worker time and jobs created, in products made, consumed, and trashed. When the economy slows down or stops growing, even for short periods of time, there is serious dislocation, suffering, fear. It is this fear of potential economic collapse that drives modern people to evade what is perhaps the most serious problem of all: the likely fact that the planet cannot provide the resources (air, water, fertile ground, ozone layer, stable climate, etc.) to support the continuous growth required of the modern system. If the system ever collapses, the only choice will be to accept coercive centralized political institutions. Those who have the military or police power to prevent massive violence and catastrophe will be required to control the distribution of finite resources in order to prevent class violence and ecological catastrophe.

When we describe the gravity of Modernity's problems, the common response given is that the system is essentially either a) self-correcting over some reasonable period of time—so one lives with the problems until the corrections take place, or b) governments can invoke direct action to regulate and correct problems that occur within faltering economic and social institutions. Both the hope for self-correction as well as the use of direct governmental action are based on faith in the pragmatic/technical problem-solving capacities inherent in the system — the same technical capacities that created the problems in the first place. So when industry creates dirty and congested cities, humans will invent ways to separate work places from living places (e.g., the suburbs). When natural resources are depleted, their prices will rise and new technology will create new resources to take their place. As poor nations of the world feel the weight of poverty compared with rich nations, production of goods will move to the poorer peoples who will work for cheaper wages; or people from poorer nations will emigrate to the more affluent nations to provide the cheap labor that affluent natives refuse to accept. As areas of the world become more violent and less safe, security forces will invent new and more effective ways to track down, destroy, imprison or otherwise control those who initiate this violence.

These corrective mechanisms are presumably based on a human capacity for making and carrying out rational decisions according to adequate technical calculations of costs and benefits to the system. This, of course, is the logic of the market place and the modern "rational" frame of mind. Speaking as a poet rather than a social scientist or historian, Walker Percy suggests that the flaws in the modern system cannot be corrected within the logic of the system itself. His evidence for this claim is the history of our current century. As he says:

> What theorists of the old modern age had to confront were the altogether unexpected disasters of the twentieth century: that after three hundred years of scientific revolution and the emergence of rational ethics in European Christendom, Western man in the twentieth century elected instead of an era of peace and freedom an orgy of wars, tortures, genocide, suicide, murder and rapine unparalleled in history.

The old modern age ended in 1914. In 1916 one million Frenchmen and Germans were killed in a single battle.

Future ages will look back on the attempts to account for man's perverse behavior in the twentieth century by the theory of the old modern age as one of the curiosities of the history of science.[9]

Like Percy, we feel that attempting to deal with the intractable problems of Modernity by looking ahead to the use of more sophisticated technology and relying essentially on the rationality and expertise of small groups of elite respected professionals and pragmatic policy makers will not yield particularly effective "solutions." We would note here Martin Janiche's analysis and critique of various efforts by environmental technicians and policy makers to "solve" fundamental ecological problems related to the modern industrial and economic system. Janiche distinguishes between what he calls "end-of-pipe policies" (trying to solve problems long after the fundamental structures that created the problems have been in place), versus the radical restructuring of obvious dysfunctional industrial and economic conditions.[10]

Janiche observes that currently the western world is moving mainly on a quick fix or "end of pipe" policy at a symptom-combating level. In general, we believe that the fundamental problems that we discussed earlier which extend beyond the environmental crisis to which Janiche refers are being worked at in a short term "end-of-pipe" way. Modern societies treat the rich-poor problem, for example, with welfare and food stamps. They treat the violence problem with prisons and the education problem with longer hours of schooling and examinations. And all of these solutions have little to do with fundamental conditions from which the problems emerge. As, for example, the excessive amounts of human trash and waste are left behind in a consumer driven society, modernity "treats" them at the end of the pipe by dumping them into streams or pits or transporting them to giant incinerators where they are burned and transformed into toxic exhausts.

It is our sense that most humans currently living on the planet have no clear vision of the profound changes foreshadowed in the future of modernity. Modern people have bound themselves into an uncritical belief that the human neocortex, the logic of the machine and the market, and the power of those who create, manage, and control it have the appropriate vision for the future progress of humankind in spite of the fact that humanity's deepest problems continue to fester and worsen. As Percy suggests, we seem to be losing our ability to dream beyond the limits of our own time.

RECONSIDERING THE POSITIVE CULTURAL QUALITIES OF ARCHAIC CULTURE AND WAYS OF LIFE

At this point we ask: What if we were to reevaluate the hypothesis of progressive biocultural human evolution and assume that local face-to-face cultures and civilizations of the present and past offer us powerful and significant lessons? Instead of thinking of ourselves as transcending the hunter-gatherer past, or the village past, or the archaic preindustrial urban-village past, suppose we were to seriously explore what qualities of these social systems have been left behind that might better have been carried forward. Or what if we were to explore some things carried forward that might better have been left behind? What if we were to begin again searching for a sense of our human past, not to celebrate our modern technical victories, but to identify critically important aspects of both earlier and contemporary primal cultures that can inform us of ways that humans might function more positively on the planet now? What are some of the things we might discover?

THE POSITIVE VALUE OF SEEING ONE'S SOCIETY AND CULTURE AS AN ORGANIC WHOLE

The ideological emphasis within Modernity prevents us from seeing life as a coherent whole, bound by communal rituals that celebrate a larger meaning system or cosmology. Life is more like an encyclopedia organized by an alphabet or a phone directory or cafeteria or the world-wide web, bound together by abstract verbal categories rather than by the contiguity afforded by place or narratives and relationships provided by old acquaintances and friends, or generational continuity provided by association with kin and elders and memories of the past.

As long ago as 1924 the linguist and anthropologist Edward Sapir identified this issue and used the term "genuine culture" to describe a coherent meaningful way of understanding reality as opposed to a more fragmented and abstract culture. He then related this sense of what he called "genuine culture" to simpler face-to-face societies.

It is easier, generally speaking, for a genuine culture to subsist on a lower level of civilization; the differentiation of individuals as regards their social and economic functions is so much less than in the higher levels that there is less danger of the reduction of the individual to an unintelligible fragment of the social organism.... We are far from having solved [the problem of increasing fragmentation and specialization] in America.... Yet the present world wide labor unrest has as one of its deepest roots some sort of perception of the cultural fallacy of the present form of industrialism.

It is perhaps the sensitive ethnologist who has studied an aboriginal civilization at first hand who is most impressed by the frequent vitality of culture in less sophisticated levels. He cannot but admire the well-rounded life of the average participant in the civilization of a typical American Indian tribe; the firmness with which every part of that life—economic, social, religious, and aesthetic—is bound together into a significant whole in respect to which he is far from a passive pawn; above all, the molding role, oftentimes definitely creative, that he plays in the mechanism of the culture.[11]

There is, of course, from our modern point of view, an ambiguity in Sapir's considering as positive such cultural characteristics as "firmness" and "bound togetherness." On the one hand, while a rich and highly integrated culture which connects artistic, religious, social and economic aspects of life may lead to a more vital experience, a shared reality, it may also be seen as leading to suffocating pressures toward individual conformity. It is, in fact, this tendency of cultures to become pathologically unbalanced in the direction of either the many splendered fragmented individual on the one hand, or the conformist communal individual on the other hand, to which much of this work is addressed. And the deeper issue we stress is that once balance is lost, encultured individuals of either stripe no longer experience the loss of balance. The unbalanced culture is then perceived as normal. This is precisely Sapir's reason for asking us to look at various "native" cultures with fresh eyes.

THE SENSE OF AN INTIMATE OR NURTURENT RELATIONSHIP WITH ONE'S IMMEDIATE SOCIAL AND NATURAL ENVIRONMENT

Stanley Diamond, a contemporary anthropologist has written extensively on the quality of life of peoples living in tribal systems. Diamond describes what he considers to be the critical features of primitive social

life, which he maintains lead to a different quality or mode of thinking
from that of their modern Western counterparts. As he states it, "primitive societies illuminate, by contrast, the dark side of a world civilization
which is in chronic crisis."[12] Some of these aspects of primitive life are
summarized below.

- Good nurturance. The extensive and intensive psychophysio-
  logical contact with a "mothering one."

- Many-sided, engaging personal relationships through all phases
  of the individual's life. This is a multilayered sense and actuality
  of self which cannot be understood in the one dimensional terms
  of "ego" psychology. This is the result of a hierarchy of experiences incorporated into an increasingly spiritualized being as
  maturation proceeds from birth through the multiple rebirths
  symbolized in the crisis rites, to the ancestry of others.

- Various forms of institutionalized deviancy which accommodate
  idiosyncratic individuals to the group while permitting unconventional behavior.

- The celebration and fusion of the sacred and the natural, the individual and society in ritual. Through ritual, life culminates in the
  form of drama.

- Direct engagement with nature and natural physiological functions, e.g., slaughtering animals and harvesting food.

- Active and manifold participation in culture (as opposed to simply being a spectator).

- Perceiving the natural environment in a continuous mode from
  the aesthetic to the practical as opposed to civilization which distinguishes between these two modes of reality. Artisanship is
  highly prized. Practicality, goodness, and beauty are not separated.

- Socioeconomic support as a natural inheritance.[13]

From Diamond's summary of anthropological evidence there appears to be a multilayered, more integrated and grounded sense of
knowing among primitive peoples than among moderns. In what Diamond calls "primitive personalism," for example, there is a profound
feeling for the "web of kinship," "organic community," and the "appre-
hension of consciousness throughout society and nature."[14] Diamond argues that modern societies must somehow incorporate this deeper

quality of experience to balance our modern impersonal and obsessive concern with abstract technical knowing. Maurice Stein makes a similar argument in an essay summarizing the contributions to our understanding of the positive qualities of life in "primitive" face-to-face societies relying on the observations of five distinguished anthropologists: Sapir, Benedict, Radin, Fortes, and Leach.[15]

CRITCHFIELD AND THE CONTEMPORARY VILLAGE

The works of Sapir, Diamond, and Stein refer mainly to tribal societies which have lived in relative isolation from the influences of contemporary modern life. Richard Critchfield has written two major books on contemporary life in villages all over the world. He is a student of the work of Robert Redfield and, like Redfield, has a sympathetic concern for the people with whom he has lived and whom he has studied. Redfield defined "the peasant view of the good life" as "an intense attachment to native soil; a reverent disposition toward habitat and ancestral ways; a restraint on individual self-seeking in favor of family and community; a certain suspicion, mixed with appreciation for town life; a sober earthy ethic."[16]

Critchfield then continues with a longer quotation from Redfield summarizing elements of the peasant/villager cosmology. As he says,

> Peasants find in life purpose and zest because accumulated experience has read into nature and suffering and joy and death significance that the peasant finds restated for him in his everyday work and play. There is a teaching, as much implicit as explicit, as to why it is that children come into the world and grow up to marry, labor, suffer, and die. There is an assurance that labor is not futile; that nature, or God, has some part of it.... [And] although peasants ... will quarrel and fear, gossip and hate, as do the rest of us, their very way of life, the persisting order and depth of their simple experiences, continue to make something humanly and intellectually acceptable of the world around them.[17]

While it is naive to celebrate uncritically the more primal existence of tribal peoples and villagers which was (is) often fraught with economic hardship and exploitation and atavistic attachments to painful and disfunctional rituals, it is also naive to ignore the positive elements in their lives: their involvement with place, land, family, and the sense of immanent connection with an unseen reality which broadened their understanding of the significance of life in the here and now. And even as some anthropologists describe these more "primitive people" as "concrete minded," (e.g., Oscar Lewis) there is another side to this quality of mind: the vivid feeling for color, texture, sound and smell that linked them to the actual stuff of the immediate world.

RECENT CONCERNS FOR RECLAIMING
THE PRIMAL AS THE "LOCAL"

Our pessimistic critique of Modernity given above is not meant to suggest a dogmatic retreat from our contemporary way of life. Nor do we recall the more positive aspects of the primal as described in the work of anthropologists like Sapir, Redfield, Diamond and Stein to suggest simply that we return to that past. The essential thrust of our thesis is to ask how we may reframe the problems of Modernity in a sufficiently compelling way so as to move it in the direction of creating a better balance between the primal and the modern elements of our biological and cultural potentialities. So while the normative location of our own work begins with the effort to reclaim elements of a primal heritage, social theorists who share our critique of Modernity often use or imply the term "local" or "communal" rather than our term "primal" or Sapir's term "genuine."[18] (Perhaps it is because the terms "primal" or "genuine" carry with them too much emotional baggage.)

The "local" form of human "association" is, for example, central to Mumford's positive analysis of the society he describes that emerged within the late Medieval chartered city, which we discuss later in this book. Likewise Robert Nisbet's influential study, *The Quest for Community*, provided a cogent counterweight to American scholars' and policy makers' post-war romance with "progressive global modernization." In the policy makers' vision, Modernity would transform the planet into technologically "developed" democratic nation-states populated by affluent individual citizens thriving under capitalist market-driven economies. After critiquing this vision, Nisbet concludes that "what we need above all else in this age is a new philosophy of laissez faire ... one that will begin not with the imaginary, abstract individual but with the personalities of human beings as they actually are in association ... [one that will] create conditions within which autonomous groups may prosper."[19]

In 1990 Stephen Toulmin developed a critique similar to that of Nisbet. He talks, for example, about "humanizing modernity" and sees the contemporary world as moving in this new direction in several fields, including medicine, technology, and modern science.

> So long as natural science developed within the Modern scaffolding and respected a hardline distinction between "rationality" of human thought and the "causality" of natural mechanisms, people in other fields modeled their ideas on the axiomatic pattern of Newton's mechanics.... As they [now] redirect science, technology, and medicine toward humanly relevant goals, they are humanizing their view of Modernity, too.[20]

He then describes the old "unreconstructed Modernity" as resting on the foundation of three principles: certainty, formal rationality, and the desire to begin with a clean slate, i.e., the rejection of any baggage left over from notions of human nature or historical myth. This foundation, he states, required a guarantee of stability and uniformity of both Science and the State (his terms). He suggests that what we now need is diversity and adaptability; a greater sense of context, a deeper feeling for the local and the particular, and a greater respect and concern for oral language and daily discourse. Somehow we need to add to the "intellectual grasp of theory" and "mastery of arts and techniques" the "wisdom needed to put techniques to work in concrete cases dealing with actual problems."[21]

Seeing the cosmos as predictable and universal, Toulmin maintains, is no longer feasible. We have to see and respect "idiosyncrasies of persons and cultures ... the decontextualizing of problems so typical of High Modernity is no longer a serious option." Echoing sentiments of Mumford some 50 years earlier, Toulmin sees us entering a "third" phase of Modernity which "obliges us to reappropriate values from Renaissance humanism that were lost in the heyday of Modernity."[22]

The joint work of policy analysts Peter Berger and Richard John Neuhaus echoes concerns similar to those of Toulmin. They propose that governments might well create policies which reemphasize and reclaim local institutions and provide a bridge between the nuclear family and larger corporate institutions. They call these local institutions "mediating structures" and refer more specifically to neighborhoods, the family, the church and voluntary associations. In their terms:

> Mediating structures are defined as those institutions standing between the individual in his private life and the large institutions of

public life. Modernization brings about an historically unprecedented dichotomy between public and private life. The most important large institution in the ordering of modern society is the modern state itself. In addition, there are large economic conglomerates of capitalist enterprise, big labor, and the growing bureaucracies that administer wide sectors of the society, such as in education and the organized professions. All of these we call the megastructures.

Then there is that modern phenomenon called private life. It is a curious kind of preserve left over by the large institutions and in which individuals carry on a bewildering variety of activities with only fragile institutional support.[23]

Berger and Neuhaus then propose that what they are calling "mediating institutions" such a neighborhoods, families, churches, and other local voluntary associations should be "more imaginatively recognized in public policy [so that] individuals would be more 'at home' in society, and the political order would be more 'meaningful.'"[24]

Arjun Appadurai, one of the more recent critics of the "megastructures" of Modernity, addresses the issue of maintaining some significant sense of the "local"—if for no other reason than it is the local place that is actually the core of that which most deeply encultures humans. As he says,

> The problems of cultural reproduction in a globalized world are only partly describable in terms of problems of race and class, gender and power, although these are surely crucially involved. An even more fundamental fact is that the production of locality—always ... a fragile and difficult achievement—is more than ever shot through with contradictions, destabilized by human motion, and displaced by the formation of new kinds of virtual neighborhoods.[25]

The "production of locality," as Appadurai calls it, depends ultimately on specific people doing specific things in specific places. Yet local places are under constant assault by powerful product-centered hierarchical corporations and the rapidly shifting contexts created by this form of transitory association. Thus the possibility of actually sustaining local places and the feelings or motivations required to keep them alive and vibrant are as "variable and incomplete" as the limited opportunities available for their initial constitution. Elaborating on this last point, he says:

> The many displaced, deterritorialized, and transient populations that constitute today's ethnoscapes are engaged in the construction of locality, as a structure of feeling, often in the face of erosion, dispersal, and implosion of neighborhoods as coherent social formations. This disjuncture between neighborhoods as social formations and locality as a property of social life is not without [historical] precedent.... What is new is the disjuncture between these processes and the mass-mediated discourses and practices (including those of economic liberalization, multiculturalism, human rights, and refugee claims) that now surround the nation state.[26]

In short, the institutions that are required to maintain the conditions for sustainable communities and the enculturation of healthy personalities who might live there, are persistently disrupted and rendered unstable. It is left to the nation-state as the only player willing and/or able to manage this instability and to provide some quality of civility and order within the larger political and economic scene.

While a major premise of our work is that any significant effort to ameliorate the pathologies and negative systemic trends of modernization requires that we sustain or reclaim more robust local/primal/mediating institutions, we realize that such efforts may be unrealistic and even futile. So before we invite readers to work through the claims and logic of this work, we should alert them, albeit briefly, to the historical difficulties encountered by earlier American critics of the modern system with words stronger and more eloquent than ours.

LASCH AND THE EARLY AMERICAN EXPERIENCE WITH MODERNIZATION

In his monumental study on "Progress and its Critics," Christopher Lasch examines the philosophical issue of significant and authentic work versus manufacturing and wage labor as he runs through a litany of 19th century American critics of modern "work."[27] Here one is struck by the shear amount and intensity of hostility expressed by industrial workers during the first hundred years of modernization in America as it was being "delocalized." (One wonders why Americans did not deal more realistically with the gravity of the impending destruction of local

institutions that might have made modern work or "labor" more humane.) Two examples from Lasch's work give a flavor of the pain and
alarm expressed by early figures in American history. He describes the
position of the early patriot, Thomas Paine, as favoring "a democracy of
small shopkeepers and artisans" which constituted the commercial
layer of society. It was, according to Lasch, these individuals "who kept
Paine's memory alive in the nineteenth century, idolizing him as the
champion of the 'producing classes' in their struggle against the 'para-
sites.'"[28] Lasch characterizes Paine's democracy of small property owners as having "little room for a permanent class of wage earners, much
less for a dependent class of paupers maintained at public expense"
(180).

Lasch discloses that nearly a half century later Orestes Brownson ech-
oed Paine's concern over a permanent laboring class which depended on
the capital and wealth of others to provide "jobs" to make a living.

> In 1841, still contending that the "mission of this country" was to
> "raise up the laboring classes, and make every man really free and
> independent," [Brownson] regretted the "division of society into
> working men and idlers, employees and operatives," a "learned
> class and an unlearned, a cultivated class and an uncultivated, a re-
> fined class and a vulgar." The only way to reverse this trend ... was
> to make every man a proprietor. This was the upshot of his famous
> essay of 1840, "The Laboring Classes." (191)

Toward the end of Lasch's extended discussion of angry 19th century
American intellectuals and reformers railing against the new factory and
wage-labor system, he confesses that

> by 1914, social democracy had already established itself ... as the
> principal alternative to a proprietary conception of opportunity.
> According to this way of thinking, a proper understanding of the
> "social question" had to begin with an acknowledgment of the irre-
> versibility of the industrial revolution. Huge corporations, the
> wage system, a more and more intricate subdivision of labor—
> these were the permanent features of modern society. (207)

Lasch concludes his summary of the struggle to retrieve the dignity of
meaningful and essential work in the American scene with the painful
admission that "American historical writing ... takes little account of the
possibility of tragedy—missed opportunities, fatal choices, conclusive

and irrevocable defeats. History has to have a happy ending" (221). Americans, Lasch suggests, are therefore forced to repress any reconsideration that the industrial revolution from a humane and a local perspective might actually have been a mistake, resulting in a persistent set of sociocultural and economic errors that could haunt their lives for generations to come. For many Americans, there was no "happy ending."

Throughout the last century (and into a new one) Americans have, in fact, often seen beyond the superficial optimism that attended the material affluence generated by "megastructures" and persisted in efforts to sustain the life of local or "middle level" places. For over the last century and a half, countless efforts have been made to reinforce old and invent new primal and mediating institutions running the gamut from common schools, settlement houses, summer camps, fraternal societies, churches, ethnic societies, intentional communities, utopian company towns, revitalized versions of rural community life, decentralized versions of urban life, pseudo-rural suburban/exurban "village" developments, and even electronically secure walled and gated pastoral "communities." The persistence in these varied efforts to "find" local community is, perhaps, evidence of profound feelings that there really is something wrong, that there is something out of balance, that modern people are still living through the consequences of a serious cultural error.

Our own response to Lasch's cynical comment that Americans are committed to the proposition that "history has to have a happy ending" is not blind acceptance of the limitations and errors of Modernity or the search for some new and hopeful approach to creating fringe communities on the edges of modern institutions. Rather, our response is an effort to refresh our imaginations and find some way to reframe and reconsider our recent history so as to keep the fundamental questions of both balance and progress alive. For if the history of the past 300 years has taught us anything, it is that no matter how settled circumstances may seem from time to time, the chronic pathologies of Modernity are unlikely to go away until the system transforms itself in some fundamental way. For us, the central question is whether or not significant local democratic community-centered places will be included in that transformation. The answer to that question depends, we think, on our ability to revisit and address the underlying errors of our current way of life rather than settle for the constant replay of short-term temporary technical fixes. We have no choice but to "live through" these errors—perhaps for several generations. Given this somewhat gloomy prospect, the issue then is how we can reframe our history and current predicament so as to make sense out of the drama involved in "living through." We confess at this point that we have no easy or quick answers to offer. We seek only to engage others in serious dialogue about how to reframe the problems of our day and reorient ourselves so that we may look in new directions and discuss more hopeful and genuine possibilities.

NOTES

1. Note exhibit below from Compton's Children's Encyclopedia, 1958.

2. For this generalization, the author credits Ralph Linton, *The Tree of Culture* (New York: Knopf, 1955), 278, chart.

3. R. R. Behrendt, "Socio-cultural Development Up to The Present Time And Our Place In It," in *Readings in Social Evolution and Development*, ed. S.N. Eisenstadt (Oxford: Pergamon Press, 1970), 279.

4. Ibid., 279-282.

5. Alex Inkeles and David H. Smith, *Becoming Modern* (Cambridge, MA: Harvard University Press, 1974), 9-24.

6. Arnold Toynbee, *A Study of History*, (New York and London: Oxford University, 1946).

7. Mihaly Csikszentmihalyi, *Flow*, (New York: Harper and Row, 1990).

8. Ibid., 14-16.

9. Walker Percy, *The Message in the Bottle* (New York: Farrar, Straus & Giroux, 1954), 25-27.

10. Janiche, M., *State Failure: The Impotence of Politics in Industrial Society* (Polity Press, 1990), 51-52.

11. Edward Sapir, *Selected Writings of Edward Sapir in Language, Culture, and Personality*, ed. David G. Mandelbaum (Berkeley and Los Angeles: University of California Press, 1949), 318.

12. Stanley Diamond, *In Search of the Primitive* (New Brunswick, NJ: Transaction Press, 1974), 169.

13. Ibid., 168-171.

14. Stanley Diamond, ed., *Primitive Views of the World* (New York: Columbia University Press, 1960), 173-174.

15. Maurice Stein, "Anthropological Perspectives on the Modern Community," in *Primitive Views of the World*, ed. Stanley Diamond (New York: Columbia University Press, 1960), 194-210.

16. Robert Redfield quoted in Richard Critchfield, *The Villagers* (New York: Anchor Books, Doubleday, 1994), 427.

17. Robert Redfield, *Peasant Society and Culture* (Chicago: University of Chicago Press, 1956), 74.

18. Edward Sapir, *Selected Writings of Edward Sapir in Language, Culture and Personality*, ed. David G. Mandelbaum (Berkeley: University of California Press, 1949).

19. Robert A. Nisbet, *The Quest for Community* (New York: Oxford, 1953), 278.

20. Stephen Toulmin, *Cosmopolis* (Chicago: University of Chicago Press, 1990), 183.

21. Ibid., 190.

22. Ibid., 200-201.

23. Peter L. Berger and Richard John Neuhaus, *To Empower People: The Role of Mediating Structures in Public Policy* (Washington, D.C.: American Enterprise Institute for Public Policy Research, 1977), 2-3.

24. Ibid., 200-201.

25. Appadurai, A., *Modernity at Large* (University of Minnesota Press, 1966),198

26. Ibid., 199.

27. Christopher Lasch, 1991, *The True and Only Heaven: Progress and Its Critics* (New York: Norton)

28. Ibid., 178.

CHAPTER TWO

Cultural Errors

In Chapter One we observed that Modernity has an abundance of positive qualities including the creation of increasingly sophisticated technology by which humans can control the physical properties of the planet and generate a vast supply of "products" and services to enrich their lives. It also enables an explosion in human knowledge, which provides a multitude of different ways of understanding and interpreting the world. But the downside is suggested by a rapid increase in the indicators of social pathology, e.g., increased numbers of fragile single adult families, child abuse and neglect, high crime rates and prison populations, suicide rates, increases in mental illness, and drug addiction.

Modern people have responded to these problems by creating a complex set of new and marginally effective institutions to remedy the situation, e.g., penitentiaries, mental hospitals, public school bureaucracies, reform schools, police forces, settlement houses, homeless shelters, welfare systems, foster homes, nursing homes, day care, and extended school programs. In general, these institutions, as indicated by their limited success over the past century, are more likely to treat the immediate symptoms of problems rather than their long term underlying causes. However effective the "cure" may be, we know the problems do not go away.

One underlying source of these problems is the attempt to eliminate an integrated, face-to-face, albeit less affluent, local world in exchange for an affluent, highly individualistic, consumer-centered, depersonalized corporate world. Instead of maintaining a balance between cultural patterns on the primal side of our nature (connections to kin, place, meaningful work, and qualities of the spirit) along with patterns on the modern side (individual choice, privacy, constant stimulation and excitement by novel technological devices and scientific discoveries, and increasing control over nature and people), modern people continue their one-way journey into a "progressive" future. This loss of cultural patterns and institutions which provide balance between the primal and the modern qualities of our nature we consider a persistent and serious cultural error.

We ended Chapter One with Lasch's somber conclusion that modern society, at least in America, has internalized the concept that we can solve our problems with a pragmatic technical orientation, one at a time. In Chapter Two, on the other hand, we introduce the argument that modern people cannot respond to basic errors of cultural imbalance or even begin to redress them without first reconsidering and reframing certain critical categories, metaphors, and assumptions which define the modern system itself.

THE IDEA OF CULTURAL ERRORS

While the term "cultural errors" may seem somewhat novel, our contention that humans have the capacity to construct cultures fraught with dysfunctional patterns or errors is certainly not a new insight. In 1959 Jules Henry made this point with compelling clarity.

> The lack of specificity of man's genetic mechanisms has placed him in the situation of constantly having to revise his social structures because of their frequent failure to guide interpersonal relations without tensions felt as burdensome even in the society in which they originate. Stated another way: because man's genetically determined mechanisms for governing interpersonal relations lack the specificity and predictability found in lower animals, man, in constructing society, frequently makes choices that create interpersonal situations heavily laden with stress....
>
> ... Thus, man has been presented with a unique evolutionary task: because his mechanisms for determining interpersonal relations lack specificity, he must attempt to maximize social adaptation through constant conscious and unconscious revision and experimentation, searching constantly for social structures, patterns of interpersonal relations, that will be more adaptive, as he feels them.... When he makes a "mistake," he tries to change.[1]

In an essay published some seven years after Henry's statement Walter Goldschmidt made a more general argument regarding the nature and consequences of cultural errors. He urged anthropologists to create cultural models in which they could compare examples of positive and negative institutions across societies. His objective was to better understand why some institutions or cultural patterns dealing with similar important human functions are adaptive and others are maladaptive or destructive. Goldschimdt's approach to the study of failures (errors) in cultural adaptation begins by probing assumptions about

> "the nature of man as a being, the character of the environment in which he operates, and the cultural appurtenances he is heir to; ... [taking] cognizance of the circumstances in which the society is operative and the consequences that can be shown to derive from the absence of [adequate] functional performance."[2]

The focus in Goldschmidt's approach was to study both positive adaptations and errors by first establishing the needs and requirements of human nature and then assessing the extent to which various societies have created particular cultural patterns or institutions to successfully meet these requirements. Goldschmidt works within a comprehensive, comparative framework to search out and describe possible relationships between the specific functions required and the effectiveness (or ineffectiveness) of institutions created by particular societies to perform these functions. In Goldschmidt's terms, we would consider a cultural "error" an instance of ineffective and/or destructive institutions within a society, or the lack of adequate institutions to provide for significant human needs.

Goldschmidt then implicitly differentiates between two types of potential cultural errors by giving two specific examples. His first example deals with the connection between family relationships and the economic sustainability of one's habitat.[3] Here he presents the problem of contradictory tendencies intrinsic to the human condition which lead to what we now understand as the "double-bind" problem. By way of illustration he presents the dilemma of how members of an older generation decide on a strategy for passing their land (or wealth) on to their children when resources are limited and the land will, in fact, support only one family. In this case children and parents alike are caught between the constraints of limited economic resources (how to keep the homestead as a single economic unit intact) and the desire to treat one's children with equal consideration. Here we might note a related dilemma: the problem of dealing with ambivalent feelings of love, jealousy, envy, and even anger toward one's siblings, spouses, children, in-laws, or others to whom one has become or once was deeply attached. This tendency often creates continuing tensions within families and communities which disrupt the normal cultural patterns required for cooperation and mutual aid.

Goldschmidt sees this kind of "double-bind" as part of those stressful but "normal" dilemmas we associate with simply being human. Beyond the "double-bind" error, he poses a second and more serious dilemma and potential error: using our considerable human intelligence and flexibility to construct and lock ourselves into what he calls "chain reaction" dysfunctional problems. He presents this error with a classic illustration.

After small groups of humans began the revolutionary change of leaving the nomadic hunter gatherer way of life and living in settled agricultural villages, they were faced with the problem of protecting their dwellings, animal herds, stored crops, and other property which accumulated there. To do this they presumably organized military cadres to protect and secure the village. Unfortunately, the new military groups began to take on a life of their own, to separate themselves from the villages, and ended up raiding and stealing the herds of the villagers—or demanding extortion for "protection." So the villagers' initial cultural invention resulted in a chain reaction of events which undercut the villagers' initial intentions to create a means of securing peace and the protection of their lands and wealth. The new military caste not only secured the villagers' animals and property but extended itself into a more complex institutionalized alternative society which kept the villagers in a state of continuing dependent exploitation.

In this example, Goldschmidt suggests that humans may enculture a "chain reaction" of serious errors from which societies cannot easily extricate themselves. Humans may be overwhelmed by "missing" or ineffective cultural patterns which may undercut their beneficent, natural tendencies (the need for protection). Humans may also fail to fully comprehend the long-range consequences that come from processes set in motion which result in destructive solutions that become institutionalized by enculturation. The military solution, once elaborated and established, then gradually replaces more cooperative and reciprocal cultural patterns for dealing with the problem of security. The problem is "solved" by a chain reaction of new cultural patterns which move from the use of military force to a stable hierarchy of military, economic, and social privilege—with the villagers on the bottom.

Goldschmidt's ominous "chain reaction" metaphor suggests a slippery slope ending up with destructive patterns which press societies beyond the reasonable limits of their normal adaptive capabilities. When this happens, societies may continue to function, albeit with difficulty and stress, until they meet a seemingly unsurpassable crisis which requires that they somehow reframe and reconstruct new adaptive patterns or simply die out. Of course, people rarely know whether they are living within a highly stressed or even terminally ill society that is living out dysfunctional stresses on the margin of human toleration or whether they are simply caught in less critical, double-bind dilemmas to which they can reasonably respond with rational pragmatic trial-and-error experiments. This analysis leads Goldschmidt to ask a set of fundamental questions:

> What is the nature of man? What are the limits of his adaptability to situations and his malleability to cultural demands? For surely we can no longer pretend to believe that he is anything, can be anything, or may be anything, under any circumstances.... While it may be true that it is possible, out of cultural motives, to make some individuals do almost anything and many individuals do some things, it is not true that culture can make all persons do anything.[4]

We would argue that Modernity does not easily accept the fundamental assumption that culture must adapt to and stay within the limits of human nature. Modern people are more likely to see cultural problems as puzzles, solvable within a very broad range of possibilities. So, for example, if modern parents must work outside the home in factories or mines or offices, one must figure out what to do with children. The answer: create similar institutions for children, i.e., schools. The rationale for these new institutions is that they prepare children for a rapidly changing and more complex work world. If poor children fail in this new institution, then create remedial institutions for "at risk" children or for those who have "cultural deficiencies." If this fails, set up standards, tests, and credentials administered objectively in both school and work so that some will succeed in school and work and others will live in poverty. When all else fails, let people wander the streets until they can be housed in shelters or warehoused in prisons. (At the turn of the twentieth century the United States was warehousing some 1.8 million people in prisons.)

If we accept the inevitability of this chain reaction, then maintaining full employment and finding adequate incentives or punishments so that all will, in fact, spend most of their time at work becomes a major objective for social policy reform. For instance, in the modern system a good deal of attention is paid to the distinction between "paid" work (which adds to the wealth of the community) and "unpaid" work, e.g., "mother work," which is done for one's own self interest or that of one's family. In this regard, there is little distinction made between necessary work, trivial work, destructive work (e.g., war), and constructive leisure. Given the priorities and structure of the market system, working to manufacture lethal weapons is not only more productive than caring for children, it is better compensated.

We would also stress the distinction between double-bind cultural errors which follow from Modernity's attempt to deal with dilemmas and contradictions in everyday life which may be "solved" by pragmatic thought and rational negotiation as opposed to chain reaction errors that tend to become locked into destructive institutionalized patterns after generations of struggle. Such patterns are changed, we feel, only after a society discovers a radical new way of reframing the problem itself which stands quite outside the society's normal habits. Long enduring feudal patterns changed in China, for example, only after the massive dislocations of a world war and a communist revolution. Deeply encultured dysfunctional cultural institutions, we are suggesting, do not yield to narrow pragmatic ways of reversing a long series of chain reactions. For as the metaphor implies, modern people are drawn into such a rapid and radical pace of social change that their common sense cannot keep up. By the time the momentum stops, people are uncritically encultured into both a new reality and a new set of problems which they understand only within the context of that new reality. If that new reality defines success as waging religious wars, they calculate how to win them and seek God's favor. If that new reality defines success in terms of the mass production of "products," they calculate how to produce such products more efficiently. The essential error is the narrow framework within which a presumed "successful" adaptation is defined.

Modern people are now encultured within this new modern cosmology and unable to respond creatively to its chronic pathologies (errors) except within its own terms. The critical issue is how to move out of this framework and see its problems within a broader philosophical, metaphysical, anthropological, societal, and historical framework. In order to break out of errors resulting from encultured chain reactions, we need to step back and reexamine Modernity from the ground up. From this point of view, we need to reconsider and reframe conditions that define the "genuine culture" or cultural "success" as one of a balance between the primal and modern aspects of human nature and culture, as one of a balance between grounded tradition and creative novelty.

MOVING TO NOVEL INSIGHTS THAT TRANSCEND EXISTING CULTURE

The question now becomes: How can we reframe patterns of action and belief that are already so deeply embedded in a culture which constantly urges us to become progressive and more modern? Our response is that while we assume most humans are embedded within a given culture, we also believe culture does not dictate the "all" of human thought and behavior. Some humans have the capacity to transcend culture and stay in touch with thoughts, actions, and impulses that come out of more balanced qualities of human nature as well as from their own idiosyncratic temperaments and personal inclinations. As Thoreau suggests, such people may follow the drum beat of their own deeper nature rather than the voice of mainstream culture. There is abundant evidence, moreover, that many modern people persist in yearning for more primal forms of association, living in local communities which foster traditional feelings for home. And while there are instances of happy and contented people living ultra-modern lifestyles that violate all kinds of primal human tendencies, we do not see this pattern as somehow the universal response leading to "the good life."

In short, our perspective on cultural change assumes that there are culturally resistant humans, not in a sociopathic sense but in a socially beneficial sense. It is in the nature of some (or many) humans to resist becoming encultured in ways that contradict their own deeper nature. Thus, we would suggest that humans apparently have the capacity in some instances to maintain a kind of "innocent" or intuitive "natural" common sense which compels them to expose some cultural practices as dysfunctional, as errors. Our history includes examples of humans who have fought against institutions which stretch our natural capacities near or beyond the limits of our nature—institutions such as slavery and concentration camps, penitentiaries, coal mining, factory assembly lines, sweat shops, etc.

SOURCES OF LEGITIMATE KNOWLEDGE FOR REFRAMING THE CULTURE OF MODERNITY

Looking at the problems and pathologies of Modernity in a fresh way is not easy. It requires that we change both the breadth of our vision and the standards of evidence common to the epistemology of normal science and technology. We have to ask not only: Does some technique "work" in achieving a particular objective? We have to bring into question assumptions regarding which cultural patterns are within the constructive limits of our human nature as well as within the great range of diverse temperaments that characterize individuals. It is clear that when we raise such questions, we run into serious conflicts with all manner of "normal" legitimating agencies.

More specifically we are required to confront the issue of what kinds of evidence or experiences are appropriate in our effort to frame or reframe any kind of "reality." We know there are multiple cultures with multiple cosmologies with different standards of proof. Who is to judge the validity of these standards? Within the disciplines of modern academic philosophy and anthropology, for example, we commonly operate from a "Western" or "scientific" set of premises. These premises presume that humans live in a naturalistic materialistic universe in which experience has a universal base available to all critical rational minds. It further assumes that so-called magical or mystical elements in a cosmology can either be discounted or reinterpreted in "scientific" or philosophical statements which simply make better sense to any critical, open-minded person. Furthermore, such statements must be supported by the near consensus of a jury of impartial reflective experts trained in appropriate disciplines. The fact that these criteria themselves come out of a limited and particular cultural tradition—Western law, philosophy, social science, etc.—is ordinarily not addressed by most academic scholars already embedded in these traditions.

A major exception is the work of Gordon Kaufman. Kaufman begins, as do we, by observing the tremendous diversity in the way humans construct societies and cultures, including the significant place that religious and metaphysical sensibilities play within culture. (He uses the term "religion" to designate the "underlying resources of meaning and ritual that inform and fund ongoing living and dying in a culture as a whole.")[5]

Like Goldschmidt, Kaufman argues that by actually looking at the human condition anthropologically and historically one can develop

> ... a normative conception of the human, in connection with which criteria and standards can be generated for identifying and addressing major problems. The concept of historicity ... enables us to understand to some extent the pernicious self-destructiveness and corruption into which human existence seems (always?) to fall: our historicity itself ... easily becomes corrupted, moving in convoluted spirals of self-destructiveness and evil from which women and men find it difficult to extricate themselves.[6]

Here Kaufman resonates with the main thesis of this work—that the human condition includes deep tragic elements (which we are here calling cultural "errors") that seem always to be with us; and it is this condition that requires us to develop a theory of imaginative reflection that will allow us to think and feel "realities" that extend beyond our conventional enculturation, language, and the canons of practical reason. For it is precisely our incredible human capacity for rationalization (which we commonly confuse with reason) that so often gets us into trouble with what Kaufman calls "convoluted spirals." As he says, when facing the deeper issues of reality, beyond the problems of everyday life, i.e., "whether life really has significant meaning or is just an absurd scene of pain and suffering," we need to move beyond the scientific empiricism of modernity. "Here the religious myths and practices of a society, drawing on and expressing its deepest symbolic resources, become especially important" (227).

As Kaufman then notes, "The deep and broad reserves of meaning which they [religio-metaphysical traditions and rituals] make available 'back up' the ongoing meaningfulness of everyday life and provide resources for times of profound personal and cultural tragedy." We confess to seeing the contemporary social system in which modern people live as a time of "profound personal and cultural tragedy."

At this point, the modern scientific critic might well reject this turn toward broader and less precise religious or metaphysical categories by suggesting that they are no more than emotional defense mechanisms designed to protect the tendency of superstitious humans from facing the stark reality of their condition on the planet. But the premise of this modernistic position is that there is some relatively certain empirical knowledge upon which to base our conceptions of the universal evolutionary cosmology, our own "progressive" history, our own logical and rational human nature.

Along with Kaufman, however, we believe "there is no strictly 'objective' way to address the ultimate metaphysical questions about the real and true nature of the universe and our place in that universe: we have only various imaginings to work with...." Therefore

> ... we are never in a position to choose our cosmic vision on the basis of careful examination of several alternatives, thus reaching the conclusion that one in particular is true (in the sense that it corresponds reasonably well to the "real universe"); rather, we carry on our lives within a particular cosmic vision (usually the one we have inherited) simply because it seems to make sense of life here on earth (254-256).

With Kaufman's argument above as introduction, we alert the reader that in this book we will consider broader and more speculative epistemological standards and sources of evidence than conventional Western science and philosophy. We shall include metaphysical perspectives from modern and perennial philosophy, insights from contemporary anthropology and social science, and accounts from scholars in a variety of other fields. We shall, however, attempt to make our arguments sensible or plausible to readers with a modern humanistic, naturalistic, or even scientific bent.

As Kaufman says, humans commonly begin with the cosmic vision they have inherited, and, even when they critique their own society, it is usually within the boundaries of that vision. Our own interpretation of the modern cosmic vision is that the material affluence and liberating choice-centered individualistic patterns which have evolved into what we are now calling Modernity must be balanced by the more primal or perennial qualities of culture (e.g., a rooted sense of place, secure connections with extended kin and community, a sense of honest or essential vocation, a feeling for the mystery of spirit). To be out of balance is to live in a cultural error.

RECONSIDERING AND REFRAMING HOW WE UNDERSTAND THE ERRORS OF MODERNITY

We want to make clear at this point that the objective of this work is to reconsider, to reconceptualize, and to reframe the errors of Modernity and place them within a broader philosophical/anthropological context. The focus is on finding constructive ways to think differently about the nature of modernity rather than giving in to the seductive impulse to rush in and find ways to "fix" it. With this more limited purpose in mind we propose to reconsider the fundamental error of primal-modern imbalance and a set of subordinate problems that go with it.

In Part Two we shall reconsider in some degree how modern people understand the nature of reality and compare this with an alternative process reality or cosmology that seems better suited for comprehending the multiple realities we encounter among the various peoples in the various multiple cultures of the planet.

In Part Three we critique and reconsider some of our modern notions of human nature, culture, and the potentialities of diversity.

In Part Four we deal with the limits within which modern humans are able to tolerate rapid technological and cultural change and the strategies they use to adapt to and maintain a significant sense of self. Here we also deal with a reconsideration of the idea of "place" and contrast the commercial corporate place with what we call the "living place."

In Part Five we present a comprehensive theory by which one might talk about the cultural requirements for a living place. We also develop more fully the idea of a vital center at three levels: in environmental, economic terms; in socio-cultural and political terms; and in meaning-making and experiential terms. Finally, we present an historical overview of the evolution of human places and provide a description of a more balanced place than most of us have experienced in the contemporary world.

In Part Six we reconsider the prospects for change in the modern system and focus especially on the extent to which middle level places and the commercial corporation can co-exist within a single social system.

Notes

1. Jules Henry, "Culture, Personality, and Evolution," *American Anthropologist* 61, no. 2 (April 1959): 221-222.

2. Walter Goldschmidt, *Comparative Functionalism* (Berkeley: University of California Press, 1966), 5-6.

3. Ibid., 119-120.

4. Ibid., 133-135.

5. Gordon D. Kaufman, *In Face of Mystery* (Cambridge and London: Harvard University Press, 1993), 227.

6. Ibid., 225-226.

PART TWO

Reconsidering Our Modern Way of Making Meaning

CHAPTER THREE

Reality, Being, And Becoming

Human cultures go down many and varied paths in the ways they understand their connection with the cosmos. These run the gamut from seeing humans as unique creatures caught between earth and heaven, part god and part animal, standing in both worlds, to seeing themselves as the only "intelligent" force in the universe which has the higher consciousness and technical power to guide the planet (and perhaps the universe) toward progress and perfection. Some cultures see nature as a neutral lifeless force consisting of matter and energy to be used for human pleasure and satisfaction while others see humans as fully "within" and part of nature, subject to the forces of a larger cosmos, including its physical, social, moral, and aesthetic laws.

In approaching such metaphysical issues one of the first questions we would ask is: Within how many layers of reality do humans exist? Our modern cosmology posits one dominant level of reality, the Natural Universe, consisting of various structures of matter and energy which have evolved into complex non-living and living forms along with a second "expressive" level, containing elements left over from a pre-modern consciousness which we interpret as personal or subjective concerns (e.g., religion, ritual, poetry, music, story). From this modern perspective, we distinguish between the primary reality of science and the secondary reality of particularistic humanly constructed "cultures."

If we begin as suggested in Chapter Two with Kaufman's more imaginative and speculative assumptions about reality, we observe that there is considerable variation among peoples all over the world in the number and significance of various levels or domains in the cosmos. Going back to an earlier period in American philosophy, Emerson developed

an explicit layered cosmology presented below in a commentary by
Brooks Atkinson.

"The Oversoul" may be regarded as the cornerstone of his faith. In
the notes to the complete work, Emerson's son has pointed out that
the first series of essays derive from a plan set down in the journals:

> There is one soul,
>
> It is related to the world.
>
> Art is its action thereon.
>
> Science finds its methods.
>
> Literature is its record.
>
> Religion is the emotion of reverence that it inspires.
>
> Ethics is the soul illustrated in the human life.
>
> Society is the finding of this soul by individuals in each
> other.
>
> Trades are the learning of the soul in nature by labor.
>
> Politics is the activity of the soul illustrated in power.
>
> Manners are the silent and mediate expression of soul.

Atkinson emphasizes Emerson's view that this layered set of realms (art,
science, literature, religion, etc.) is bound together for individuals by the
unity of the soul, and for the cosmos by an "oversoul." Quoting Emerson, he says, "We see the world piece by piece as the sun, the moon, the
animal, the tree, but the whole, of which these are the shining parts, is the
soul."[1]

Adding a more subtle point which presumably ties the layers together, Catherine Albanese, a contemporary scholar, describes Emerson's view of layered realities as moving in continuous dynamic
synchronized "corresponding motion" as each plane brings forth a common moment with each making its own particular contribution to human experience. Albanese summarizes Emerson's poetic rendition of
this dynamic "process" view of experience as follows:

> In "The Over-soul," Emerson's gospel of motion received perhaps
> its most distinctive expression. Immediately behind each person,
> the soul—clothed in the "web of events" as a "flowing robe"—was
> the empowering force. "When it breathes through his intellect, it is
> genius; when it breathes through his will, it is virtue; when it flows

through his affection, it is love." Yet the soul participated in a larger reality, and revelation granted "an influx of the Divine mind into our mind." An ebb of the individual rivulet before the flowing surges of the sea of life. In this all-encompassing sacredness, true communion with one another could be found: "By the same fire, vital, consecrating, celestial, which burns until it shall dissolve all things into waves and surges of an ocean of light, we see and know each other, and what spirit each is of" (49). "Circles," in turn, reiterated the thesis of continual motion which shaped the message of the "Over-soul."[2]

David Bidney, from a less poetic anthropological perspective, gives a more literal view of the multilayered cosmos that humans commonly apprehend and to which they have, in varying degrees, access.

> Man may be conceived as living in a five-dimensional world. First there is the world of nature, that which offers resistance to human efforts and whose powers and laws he must obey. Secondly, there is the conceptual or symbolic world, by which he interprets and envisages the natural world. Thirdly, there is the world of cultural reality, the man-made world of artifacts and sociofacts which is the creation of society. Fourthly, there is the ideal world of conceptual possibilities and values which transcend both the actual world of nature and the actual world of culture, the ideal world of utopias and the intelligible world of ideal forms. Fifthly, there is the private world, which the ego inhabits and which it does not share with others. Thus, in one sense, man may be said to discover the world in which he lives, and in another sense he may be thought of as constructing and creating or fashioning his world.[3]

In this chapter we argue that given the common tendency for cultures to experience reality in several layers, it is important that we revisit and reconsider our modern habit of folding all reality into only two dualistic levels called "objective nature" and "subjective personal experience." We begin by recognizing those peoples and cultures which embrace a fuller and more pluralistic feeling for the cosmos. In short, we claim that human nature is embedded in and allows one to apprehend and respond to several layers or domains of reality, although these different layers may well be understood with varying degrees of precision and clarity. We suggest therefore that humans have the faculties to penetrate in some significant degree at least the following domains of reality:

- We can imagine our own nature as a domain embedded within a larger natural universe consisting of matter, energy, and living forms of all kinds.

- We can see "nature" or the natural universe as connected to and flowing from a deeper source of creation commonly associated with religion or spirituality.

- Beneath the general qualities of our human nature we can see our unique human capacity for participating in or co-creating novel technologies and inventions in the world around us—a powerful generative capacity we associate with the ideas of imagination and culture.

- And within the regularities of the enormous diversity of human cultures we see the work of a great variety of individual human beings or souls, who often express a commonality of understanding and meaning that is less diverse than the cultures of which they are a part.

Within this pluralistic conception of reality, we assume that these various domains are related one to the others. Thus we speculate that our idiosyncratic Being is embedded in, connected to, and in part evolves from Culture; Culture is embedded in, connected to, and in part evolves from our Human Nature; Human Nature is embedded in, connected to, and in part evolves from elements of the Natural Universe; the Natural Universe is embedded in, connected to, and evolves in some significant degree from elements of a metaphysical source. In short, given a fuller reading of the historical and cultural evidence of humankind, it is more likely that the cosmos or universe is, at the same time, both one and many (or many-layered) rather than simply a materialistic "natural universe" and a subjective human mind.

In an alternative "process" interpretation of the cosmos discussed in Chapters Four and Five below we suggest that humans participate both in the emergence of the actuality in the world around them and in their experience of that world. Thus, they themselves create, in part, the world and their experience of the world, which, in some final sense, cannot be separated. So the essence of emergent reality and material actuality is a process of "becoming" in the movement from one domain to another. We are, as Emerson suggests, inextricably embedded in the process of creating the connections among these various levels of emergence as they happen. Both being and experience "happen" or come about from our participation in the flow of such connections. In this understanding of reality there is, ultimately, no "out there" which separates subjects from objects. There is only a flow of connections and dissolutions.

From this perspective, we argue that two serious modern metaphysical errors are: 1) to assume that there is but one dominant domain of reality, the natural universe, (coupled with other second-rate realities like God, spirituality, the arts, private feelings and sensibilities, viewed as matters of private or personal interest); and 2) to assume that our primary and most reliable awareness of reality comes from our viewing the natural universe from the outside as an objective spectator.

A related error is the assumption that the increased clarity and specificity with which one can describe the natural universe automatically increases the validity of one's observations. So, modern people conclude that their capacity for describing rocks with greater specificity than their capacity for describing souls or ghosts means that souls and ghosts are less likely to be real or actual. Our assumption here is that elusive observations are not necessarily illusory observations.

RECONSIDERING MODERN CULTURE'S IDEOLOGY OF DUALISM

Our hypothesis is that modern people experience the world as if they live in two separate domains: the world "out there" and the world "within." On the one hand they assume there is a shared public objective world "out there"—the universal world that is potentially knowable to all in so far as one has the sensibility and intelligence to know it. This includes the concrete world of happenings and things as well as the concepts and abstractions which delineate and frame these events in time and space. It is the world presented by careful observers and journalists; it is the world that jurors deliberate about in an effort to determine the facts of litigation; it is the world studied and described by scientists and engineers. It is a world constrained by natural lawful regularities which can be discovered and quantified through scientific research. It is a world viewed as potentially controllable through practical knowledge, science, technology, and engineering.

Then, there is the other world—the world of idiosyncratic private subjective experience. Although this world can be communicated and shared through story, poetry, fantasy, and the like, it is seen as a world of private speculation, intuition, and opinion. Our perceptions, feelings, and understandings in this personal world do not seem to require the kind of public specification, clarification and justification as do statements about the universal objective domain of the first world. We assume, for example, that anyone can write valid poetry.

Our misgivings about the modern dualistic cosmology begin with the observation that traditional peoples (including many non-western peoples) living within the close knit engagements and patterns of village life tend to see reality as a continuous flowing stream. In this view reality emerges from an unseen world of thoughts, spirits, and the unknown, and moves into the world of nature and the domain of routine human affairs. No sharp separation is made between the domain of public universal knowledge (which we call "nature" or "science") and two more speculative domains—the broader domain(s) of cosmic insight related to metaphysics, religion, and spirituality and the personal (yet socially conditioned) domain(s)of narrative, ritual, sport, or art. The meaning derived from all three domains is what constitutes one's overarching cosmology.

Given this competing tendency of other cultures to view reality as continuously "flowing" and emerging, "coming into being," similar to that described by Emerson, we wonder what has led modern people to consider science and technology as the universal exclusive way of understanding the cosmos. We would ask, just how applicable is this view of realty to the multitude of experiences which we humans apprehend? It may be that Newton's great discovery of a systematic basis by which one can describe and predict certain physical and astronomical events in mathematical time and space—arguably the genesis of the modern scientific revolution—applies to only a small segment of significant events in the "actual" world. The remainder of the vast cosmos within which we exist may well be open to constant multiple interpretations and even defy our human ability to untangle its web of meaning in any precise way. Much of our reality may consist of cultural constructions representing inconsistent or even contradictory understandings (within and across societies) of the degrees of orderliness and disorderliness in the myriad of occasions which we daily experience and in which we participate.

But despite our growing skepticism regarding the generality of scientific findings as potentially describing the "all" of the universe, there still remains the power and resiliency of this dualistic cosmology. The universe is filled with creative and unexplainable novelty, yet what modern people tend to see is a kind of presumed or explicit science-based regularity (or the potentiality for regularity) and the opportunity to construct more regularity with new research which will produce a still more predictable and "progressive" future. Faith in science and the technology it spawns is such that it seems perfectly reasonable, in a segmented kind of way, to exploit scientific knowledge to build atom bombs, teach all humans to master the reading and writing of abstract, complex, decontextualized language, and condition humans to develop steadfast habits of punctuality needed to leave their homes and get to work or the job on time.

So one must ask: Given the fact that humans really know so little about so much in the world around them in any precise scientific sense, how is it that so many modern people appear to live as though most of the great mysteries of the world have been made or are at the very least accessible to the "scientific method?" And given the plausibility of alternative cosmologies, how do we explain the resiliency of the scientific method and the dogmatic commitment of modern people to its cause? How is it that such a meaning system and set of institutions has been able to persuade the peoples of Europe, North America and now the entire planet over the past four hundred years to dismiss local spiritual sensibilities and rituals as mere superstition and entertainment? How is it that ancient societies seem to be in the process of exchanging ageless and honored practices we would associate with complex "genuine culture" in order to move into an era which celebrates an oversimplified materialism—the worship of trinkets as it were—which pollute the landscape with ugly sounds, sights, smells, feelings, and machines? How did it get started in the first place? Who planted the ideological seeds? We would speculate that one part of the answer may well be the influence of Lockean thought planted deep in our Anglo-American psyches some 200 years ago. This cosmology apparently became a major cultural force in the latter part of the eighteenth and nineteenth centuries in the heyday of the Enlightenment. It is to these questions that we now turn in somewhat greater detail.

MEANING-MAKING AND THE
REALITY OF MODERN CULTURE

Although the dualistic cosmology is commonly attributed to Descartes, the version we know best in America comes more directly from Locke and his influence on early American political thought.[4] A major problem posed by this view was the stark fact of human culture. Groups of humans living in close geographic proximity over long periods of time develop common language and deep common understandings about the nature of reality. In fields as diverse as science and religion our confidence in our sanity rests on the fact that others share our cosmology and our feeling for a particular order in the universe. But in the American experience we were caught up in a radical paradox: a dominant cultural/ethnic group (the founding "fathers" of the Enlightenment in both Europe and America) constructed a belief system that denied the legitimacy and significance of culture and the deep process of enculturation itself. It came to see each individual as (potentially) a rational spectator of an authentic world of mathematical/physical space and mechanical time.

Within this cultural system, humans were commonly liberated from their parochial cultures and superstitions, and guided by reason and intelligence to function with something called "natural" insight. Humans were taught, ironically, through the powerful instruments of sociocultural institutions, that they have no essential social nature. Instead, humans are blessed with a primary, rational quality which allows them to negotiate their lives with other humans through reciprocal covenants and contracts—just as they came to negotiate with the natural world through science and technology. And in fact a more open enlightened culture was created based on more reflective critical qualities of negotiation rather than rules and dogma handed down from prior generations.

This was the birth of the cultural ideology of radical individualism and our commentary on this phenomenon developed below is based largely on Northrop's treatment of its Lockean roots in his classic work, *The Meeting of East and West*, written some fifty years ago. It is worth reviewing in some detail for its contemporary relevance and insight.[5]

According to Northrop, our modern cosmology began with the brilliant work of two great geniuses in the history of western thought, Galileo and Newton, who came to understand "reality" as a three-termed relationship in which

> the public, colorless, odorless, material substances in mathematical space and time are one term, the aesthetic data in their sensed spatial and temporal relations are a second term, and the individual observer is the third term. It is because the mathematically defined space and time with their postulated, unobservable, atomic physical objects are independent of their relation to the observer that there is a public world the same for everybody, regardless of the differences in what different people immediately apprehend. It is because the immediately sensed factors are not intrinsic properties of the public physical objects in the public world but are dependent in part upon the latter and in part upon the observer that they are termed by Galileo and Newton "apparent" rather than "real" things. It is because of the dependence upon the observer also that it follows, as Galileo asserts, that were the observer removed sensed colors, sounds, and warmth would not exist.[6]

In sum, the world is divided into a hierarchy. First there is the "most" real world existing in mathematical-physical time and space made up of moving dead material atoms. Second, there is the "sensed" world of feelings, emotions, colors, and warmth happening in "sensed" time, which Northrop calls "aesthetic data." The great mystery in the character of these "aesthetic data" is that they are holistically and vividly sensed, felt, and heard rather than reflectively deduced as theoretical abstractions. They are at the interface of objective reality and human sensibility. In this Newtonian cosmology, human reality consists of three parts: the physical body made up of material atoms (in mathematical-physical time and space); the human's rational capacity to uncover, understand, interpret the abstract truly real mathematical-physical world—the first level world (which includes one's body); and finally the "mental substance" which allows the human to "sense" or apprehend the aesthetic world of color, sound, odor, pain, pleasure, etc. existing in subjectively sensed time and space. Since this sensed world has no existence independent of the organism that experiences it, it is considered as merely "subjective" or "second rate," as only the "appearance" of reality. The compelling (and erroneous) insight of Locke was to use Newton's model of how the mathematical-physical world worked to construct the world of politics, religion, economics, and human affairs which relied on a metaphysics based essentially on mathematics and physics.

The ancient view of human nature which had been passed down from the Greeks to the medieval Christians did not survive this modern epistemological shift. Humans soon began to move away from the beliefs that humanity is but one link in the network of grand continuous cosmic connections with the gods and nature. Northrop describes this earlier ancient and medieval view of cosmic networks and connections as follows:

> Political organization is of the nature of man and not something from which he can desist, or into which he may enter, according to the mere suggestion of his purely private, subjective opinion. Similarly, man, to fulfill his own individual nature, must participate in the hierarchical order not merely of society but of nature. Moreover, this hierarchical order is defined by an empirically determined law of nature existing quite independently of the opinion and social conventions of men (88).

So, according to Northrop, Aristotle's humans by their very nature are embedded in and required to participate in a chain of being from the cosmos to nature to culture to private soul. They cannot simply escape into their inner private human tendencies alone to seek beauty, love, and harmony, nor can they stand outside of nature and become external observers and manipulators of the cosmos. The inner private world is connected to the outer natural world within a larger order or cosmos much as Emerson envisioned. For Locke's enlightened person, however, one's inner subjective qualities, one's emotions, passions, and other aesthetic materials such as colors and sounds [were] given "... a second-rate and third-rate status," (91) and differentiated from the objective universe.

From the point of view of the founders of our modern Anglo-American culture, the more fragile sensibilities of our humanity are to be private and personal, and, as Northrop notes: "The really important things are either the material substances with which the businessman and the engineer 'with his feet on the ground' concerns himself during the six workdays of the week; or the blank, purely spiritual, intrinsically unemotional introspectively given mental substance with which, in meeting hall, preferably without colors or sounds to disturb him, he communes on the Sabbath "(92). In Northrop's terms, according to this

Lockean view of the world, "The relation between a person and other persons is equally clear. There is no specific relation at all. It remains to be negotiated. As we have noted, the relation between mental substances is difficult to conceive" (93).

In Locke's view, atomic physical substance is most real. The human body is such a substance, so it also is most real. Likewise, the property that one owns and protects is most real and science, technology, and business are the fields of human endeavor most associated with substance and property. (The term "real estate" comes to mind.) These are, moreover, the central universal elements of reality, not simply "things" to which a culture assigns its own labels and meanings.

Northrop's major critique of the Lockean cosmology relates essentially to these three central points: 1) the hyper-individualism implicit in the notion that each "mind" is a separate substance; 2) the isolation of humans from any social connection to a larger cosmic domain; and 3) the sharp separation of "first rate" science- or physics-based reality from "second rate" immediately sensed "aesthetic" experiences which are considered only as "appearances." Regarding the issue of a larger cosmic reality connected to a god or gods, Northrop comments wryly that there is no need in Lockean theory to posit such a domain. As he says:

> The Lockean scientific and philosophical assumptions of the modern world ...[locate] the sole basis for religion in the introspective or the spiritual nature of one's private mental substance ... It [thus] frees religion from any recourse to the traditional causal or cosmological arguments from nature to the existence of God. In fact, according to Newtonian science, nature is determined solely by the material substances, which behave according to mechanical causation. Consequently, in the modern world the traditional arguments from nature to the existence of God become untenable. Even the ontological argument [that one can move] from our idea of a perfect being to the existence of such a being, which Descartes as well as St. Anselm accepted, becomes untenable also (89).

Northrop's third central commentary on Lockean theory relates to its denigration of the human capacity for experiencing colors, passions, feelings and the like as only pseudo reality, as mere "appearances," since they require a human mind to make them happen.[7]

To summarize this discussion, the "modern" person believes him/herself to be living in two separate albeit connected worlds. The first is an objective world guided partly or mostly by a natural physical order, which humans can research, understand, manipulate, and control. The second is a subjective private world guided by local taste and desire which are fulfilled by acting on personal choices. The laws or rules which guide the natural objective world can be (potentially) experienced by all and are universally true for all beings in the universe. The laws or rules which order the subjective worlds are true for each separate being (or small groups of intimates), although there is often evidence which suggests that private worlds, in some degree, are accessible to larger publics. Finally, cosmologically, all experience takes place within a kind of uniform time/space/matter/energy "universe" which we apprehend exclusively through our senses and interpret within separate nervous systems.

This cosmology assumes that, at bottom, our world/universe is populated by substantial "things." To understand the world is to be able to identify and name "things." Once modern people accept the fact that the essential world is constituted of things, they can, with relative ease, answer a basic question regarding the nature of meaning: What does it mean to "know" something? From a modern point of view, the answer is clear and obvious: Modern people identify the multitude of things within the plenum, name them, and then proceed to describe or define their qualities or characteristics. The knowledgeable seer or scientist or scholar is one who can name and describe the "things" in his/her field of expertise—as they appear within the universe that we inhabit. The ornithologist, for example, can name birds, describe their habitats, their migration routes, their songs, their nesting and reproduction habits. The medical specialist can name various diseases, their symptoms and etiology, their course, and their possible treatments.

The next critical step in deriving *meaning* from within a dualistic cosmology, is to determine what caused the "thing" to "be" or to happen in this particular way, at this time, in this place. This is ordinarily a matter of describing a sequence of events in time. The sequence can be a simple before-after kind of analysis. (The American Revolution was caused by prior actions of the British Parliament.) It can suggest "unseen" actions or events as causative agents based on inference and speculation. (Mountains and earthquakes are caused by underground "plates" in the earth's crust converging on each other.) More sophisticated and more "scientific" explanations can reduce a set of complicated events to an "underlying" complex theory. (The particular species of plants/animals which inhabit this planet at any given time are the result of a set of inter-related factors: geological changes in the environment, genetic variation caused by mutations and sexual reproduction, and natural selection.)

Perhaps the most sophisticated validation for the modern meaning system came from the scientific discoveries which reveal evidence of an orderly "micro" world that explains the history or course of events in the macro world. Inhabitants of such micro-worlds include, for example, the spectrum of electromagnetic waves, the characteristics of chemicals revealed on the periodic table of basic chemical elements, DNA molecules and their connection to amino acids and living tissue, or the characteristics of such micro particles as atoms, electrons, muons, and the like.

The modern tendency is to ascribe meaning that has the weight of "truth" to qualities of reality that are reduced to earlier or underlying "basic" causes, especially causes that seem to dwell in a micro world—including the worlds of non-living particles or waves or the world of microscopic organelles. In medicine, for example, modern people distinguish between the visible "symptoms" of a disease and the "real" disease. Cholera is "really" the action of a particular microorganism on the digestive system; diarrhea, fever, and dehydration are only symptoms or consequences. The light streaming down from behind cloud banks is "really" only the visible part of the electromagnetic band of particles/waves interacting with nerve tissue within the eye.

To summarize, dualistic metaphysics is the basis of most modern cultures and some of its major characteristics may be listed as follows:

- There is a first-priority dominant objective reality that characterizes the actual world and a second-rate subjective reality that is our own private indulgence, both of which are identified by our senses.
- The objective world is best understood as inhabited by discrete "things" sitting or moving within a plenum defined by homogeneously organized time and space inferred from clocks and measuring devices.
- The nature of these "things" can best be discerned by searching for appropriate criteria or qualities by which to describe them.

- A thing is "caused" by prior circumstances outside the thing which somehow created it, and to "know" or understand something is, in some sense, to know how these outside forces cause the thing to be created, which, in turn, may give us the power to control and manipulate "things." In this theory, actual things are only imperfect examples of a class of things. Here we would note, for example, differences between *photographs* of events or things one sees in science and medical textbooks as opposed to their *schematic portrayal.* The schematic drawings are always so very clean, clear, and coherent compared to the more ambiguous and messy "actual" photographs. From the modern perspective, the world is thus populated by transitory and imperfect but actual examples of observed things which are better described and made "more real" by our capacity to state their generic names and to list their abstract characteristics, most powerfully in quantitative terms and/or through abstract algorithmic formulae.
- We, the observers, describers, interpreters, explainers stand outside the things observed and transform data into coherent and more real abstractions.

MEANING-MAKING AND THE
REALITY OF DIVERSE CULTURES

What happens when one assumes that this modern metaphysics does not "work" for everyone, i.e., is not grasped as universally true for all human beings? If moderns understand only two aspects of reality, what do they make of the fact that humans are highly social animals who live in groups which create a great variety of idiosyncratic context-specific meaning systems or cosmologies that include claims and assumptions about the world which are neither cross-culturally universal nor considered as simply one's own individualistic personal affair? Many of these local claims, values, rituals, myths, and cultural "facts," moreover, provide meaningful explanations for concerns as deep and problematic as issues related to the nature of being, the ultimate meaning of life and the fact of human mortality. What, for example, is the role of the human senses in experiencing the world? Are the dreams that we imagine and the stories we invent "real?" Does time flow only in one direction? Is there a cyclical time, an eternal time, a time standing still, a recoverable time? Do some/all beings have an inner quality of spirit or life or soul? Is the universe conscious, or are only living things conscious, or are only human living things conscious? Do different kinds of beings share a common consciousness with each other and/or with the universe? And so on. From Kaufman's earlier analysis of the role of history and imagination in our human interpretation of reality, the variety of answers to these question coming from a great multiplicity of cultures raises questions regarding the universal applicability of modern science to all domains in the universe.

When we look at how various humans in diverse cultures respond to these fundamental and awesome questions, we find that human experience does not fit within two (or even three) neatly separated realms—the universal/objective and the personal/subjective. The world is not populated exclusively by easily nameable things which can be understood and described by carefully selected qualities and quantities determined by science or by the market place. Nor is it always easy to dismiss this thing or event as only an imperfect "actual" example of a "real" universal concept. One has only to think of the Christian assumption that a singular historical fact—the birth and life of Jesus—permanently changed history and the universe for all time. And we can think likewise of the Big Bang as another singular event or the singularities of the presumed existence of black holes. For a great many humans Jesus cannot be construed simply as another example of a prophet, a guru, a messiah, a savior, or God's son. Nor is the Big Bang for planetary scientists just an example of another Big Bang which happens to start a new universe.

To some humans, the actualities of a given moment are often critically real, in fact more real than the universal abstractions of which they seem to be but examples. Moreover, many of the most powerful and lasting human experiences happen within unique families, small groups, and within small societies, and cannot be warranted as universal objective claims. And the moment we come into contact with humans raised among friends and kin in other strange or alien places, we realize that what is universal for us is not universal for everyone. Our human response to the world around us is contingent upon the unique prior experience of having been raised within a particular cohort of humans who share a common way of being and living, and these particular ways of being and living are often experienced equally as both immediate fact and universal insight.

More importantly, the many and diverse cultures modern people encounter often have not only varied constructions of what is authentic experience, but also methodologies and strategies (or rituals?) through
which one can enter the process of significant and valid experience. Humans are remarkably adept at constructing knowledge by defining contexts which presumably lead one toward experiences which may
enhance, distort, or limit what one comes to know or believe. In one culture, for example, humans enter the unseen world of spirits through
meditation or trance. In another culture, humans enter the unseen world
by looking under a microscope or by searching for shadow patterns
picked up on light sensitive photographic paper. In another culture humans take communion, drink wine and eat bread, and are transformed
in some deep spiritual way into the blood and flesh of the divine. And,
one may ask, how does one culture-bearer convince another that his/her
method/practice/ritual used to invoke authentic experience is more or
less valid than that used by the other?

So members of different cultures not only experience different realities, they systematically set up the conditions which make significant experience possible or likely—and conversely they often see no point in
entering settings which will yield only trivial or irrelevant experience. A
classic way of illustrating how different cultures understand and deal
with the unseen world is to ask how they understand the presence of
ghosts or spirits. For an individual convinced that there is no information available to humans from the realm of the afterlife, ghosts or spirits,
even when vividly observed, are likely to be considered as illusions or
hallucinations. For one who has been taught from early childhood that
the ghosts of one's forebears walk the earth and commonly visit their
children, shadows and rustling leaves may be experienced as a ghostly
presence. From the point of view of the skeptical scientific materialist, it
is probably useless to develop techniques of mediation and meditation
to experience such an occult world. From the point of view of one who
visits regularly with such spirits, it may seem foolish to develop scientific objective "tests" to check out whether or not one is "truly" feeling
the presence of these beings.

A modern person immersed in a set of assumptions about reality has
to face the issue of how he or she reacts to contact with other humans
who experience the world so differently. Do modern people assume that
their science and technology coupled with their commitment to private

personal choices is "the" appropriate universal cosmology that all cultures should embrace? Do they expect the great majority of the world's populations to convert to such a modern scientific commercial cosmology because it appears more authentic and effective in maximizing human happiness or survival?

Or should we ask the more difficult question: To what extent do modern people understand that our way of construing many aspects of "reality" applies to only one particular culture? How might our modern cosmology be reframed so as to give due credit or credibility to a broader way of experiencing the world which acknowledges that there may be "realities" which we often dismiss? For example, may there not be a "non-material" basis for some beings?

We are, in fact, now confronted with a situation in which the great majority of cultures in the world are being undermined and overwhelmed by modern people who seem to raise few questions about limitations in the way they construct and experience the world. Nor do they seem to have any sense of the profound loss involved in the cultural extinctions wrought by modern technology and economic institutions which carry such powerful residue of our modern epistemology. Modern people cannot seem to grasp the notion that their inability to move humbly and carefully across alien cultural terrain may well be a consequence, in part, of their denial that much of their own cosmology is culturally and ideologically based rather than dictated by some objective scheme inherent in "the natural universe" or in nature itself.

MULTIPLE REALITIES

Despite years of increasing domination of Western thought, there have been "fault-lines" within the modern cosmology, and these have taken a number of forms. The inner world of private consciousness, trivialized by Enlightenment scholars as matters of personal taste, has had its periodic romantic revolts. The tension between romanticism and objectivism has long been an internal feud for moderns. But deeper issues are now surfacing as new and powerful technologies, the job and consumer market system, the dogma of hyper-individualism, and the socio-economic domination of ways of being confront peoples and cultures across the entire planet.

We are increasingly required to deal with these fundamental aspects of reality because we are no longer challenged only by the tensions and problematics of our own modern cosmology; we are challenged by cosmologies of very old and deeply understood ways of understanding reality which now appear in our own back yard. Slogans that celebrate and automatically connect "science," "democracy," "education," "growth," "technology," and the "open market," with universal human "progress" are no longer enough. We have to begin looking and imagining how humans over the course of their history within the broader context of multiple places, cultures, and cosmologies, have experienced the world.

The great difficulty we often have communicating across cultures has less to do with the specific language that one or another ethnic group uses to identify and name things in the world/universe and much more to do with the broader cosmological context within which the process of experiencing is placed. Perhaps the greatest obstacle preventing modern people from developing a genuine facility in cross-cultural communication is the simplistic assumption that such communication is only a matter of engaging a well-trained translator to substitute a more abstract or complex "universal" language in place of the local vernacular. Once translated, we can know what the local culture bearer really means. As the anthropologist Richard Shweder puts it:

> This is the stance associated with the ... spirit of universalism and the Platonic quest for pure form. From [this] perspective, for example, ancestral spirit attack [which allegedly happens in some cultures] might be viewed as just a way of speaking about repressed childhood memories or fantasies about malevolent aspects of parents.... In other words, [to the extent that] we can make rational sense of [another ethnic group's] conception of things, then their conception of things is not that different from ours, for it must make sense in terms that are understandable to us.[8]

In Shweder's view, however, human cultures and the languages they invent are fundamentally "multiple from the start. Our indigenous conceptions are diverse, whether they are centered in our official texts or our underground newspapers, in our public discourse or our psychoanalytic soliloquies, in our customary practices or our idiosyncratic routines, our daytime task analysis or our nighttime fantasies."[9]

Modern "enlightened" people, who live embedded in a society that can manipulate the power of the atom and global markets seem to have great difficulty acknowledging the inherent capacity of humans to create cultural and cosmological worlds that are so profoundly "multiple from the start." They seem especially confused about why their expertise in predicting/controlling a limited range of events in narrow technical domains (e.g., leveling forests, dredging canals, flying jets, performing open heart surgery) should not provide an appropriate and adequate understanding for all domains of reality for all humans everywhere. For some strange reason, they have difficulty reminding themselves that they are not "universal" beings but rather cultural beings and, as any human ethnic, they create cultural "facts" which other subgroups or cultures, even within their own society, find alien. It is one thing for modern people to remind themselves occasionally that much of the fabric of their reality was inherited from an individualistic, work-centered, mercantile profit centered, success-oriented, past; it is quite something else to believe and act as though one is truly living out the implications of such a narrow and parochial culture.

To give an example of how significant is this process of enculturation, Shweder cites research on speech perception with infants of English-speaking parents listening to language-specific phonemic contrasts in Hindu and in a similarly difficult-to-pronounce American Indian language, Nthlakapmx.

The dramatic finding is that four-month-olds seem able to discriminate the phonemic distinctions peculiar to those disparate languages, a capacity that adult English speakers no longer possess. If this early capacity to detect a sound contrast is kept alive through even a small amount of initial second-language learning during the first two years of life, it is maintained into adulthood. Typically … it disappears by the end of the first year of life, with the onset of exclusive single language learning and can be recovered later in life only with difficulty.… It would seem that in the case of speech perception, knowledge … has its origins in experiences that are prior to the experience of this individual in this life. Yet it is this worldly experience, this time around, that sets the threshold for the accessibility or availability of that which is known. One wonders about the relevance of maintenance-loss models to other domains [of human experience], such as emotions.… Human infants come into the world possessing a complex emotional keyboard; yet as they become Eskimo, Balinese, or Oriya only some keys get played. Do the other keys get stuck because they are hardly played at all?[10]

An especially difficult insight for modern ethnics to accept is the notion that there are "tunes"or "harmonies" (or even whole systems for composing, playing, and hearing music) which one will never hear as coherent sound simply because "other" tunes or systems have preempted their neural space by being encultured at an earlier point in time. (Incoherent music is assumed to come from strange and incoherent people rather than from our own ignorance based on our earlier enculturation.)

Another contemporary anthropologist, Bradd Shore, discusses the issue of humans' inhabiting different metaphysical and biological realities with an emphasis on the latter. He asks: Do all humans have a sufficiently similar nervous system such that at some point shared experience and communication will allow us to transcend our multicultural Babel and understand a common objective world? The evidence suggests, he argues, much as does Shweder, that this is *not* the case. From a biological perspective, paradoxically, the problem is one of initial "soft" neurological similarity coupled with flexibility (at birth or conception) followed by degrees of relatively deep or even "hard-wired" developmental- and environmentally-based "programming" changes in the early years of life as the human nervous system matures and stabilizes. This results in profound cultural differences across societies when people have been raised under radically different environmental and social conditions. In Shores' words:

> ... Attention to the biological and evolutionary basis of cognition does not really support any significant notion of [universal human] psychic unity. Modern neurobiology does not paint an essentialist picture of the human nervous system. Our mental hardware [at birth] turns out not to be as "hard" as we had presumed. Many neurobiologists view the human nervous system as the biological basis of an "adaptive intelligence."[11] The nervous system is highly programmable within the limits of what Changeux terms its "genetic envelope."... The flexibility of the human brain, its openness to the world around it, is suggested by the fact that much of its development and all of the myelinization of the cortex take place outside the womb in the first five years of life.[12]

> It is thus clear that the active human psyche cannot be reduced to its common biological substrate, abstracted from the conditions of its development and the particular environment within which it is functioning at any given time.... In the face of the complex and

equivocal character of the human brain, the immediate question becomes why, for so many years, anthropologists have chosen largely to ignore the implications of culture for understanding the important degree of psychic diversity characteristic of the species.[13]

Shore answers this question by suggesting that his fellow anthropologists resisted dealing with the obvious *depth of cross cultural differences* in their understanding of the human condition because the "psychic unity doctrine became entangled in complex ways with the discredited ideas of racial character and 'progressive' cultural evolution."[14] The idea that psychic and cultural differences can be a permanent feature of the human condition also threatens and confuses the sharp modern (Lockean) distinction made between the subjective and the objective. This debate forces us to accept a human world inhabited by physiologically different "objective" human realities. We may all agree on a limited array of universal "physics-type" facts while conceding (or celebrating) the fact that our metaphysical, historical, social, and moral realities may, in fact, remain legitimately diverse.

Shore's observations reinforce Shweder's point that different cultures may "actually" live in different realities and that as such they are "different from the start." Shweder moves beyond this insight, however, and presents, after the work of D'Andrade, a radical theory of multiple cultural worlds. He suggests that different cultures may actually inhabit objectively different worlds. From this point of view, he argues, we can clarify the problem of communicating across cultural or ethnic boundaries by assuming that an adequate theory of experience or understanding is one in which "the scope and nature of the generalizations developed in any domain are appropriate to the kind of order found in that domain...."[15] That is to say—with some risk of distorting Shweder's (and D'Andrade's) argument—they are suggesting that different cultures might well embrace common physics-type "facts" but quite different historical and cultural "facts."

This is much the same conclusion reached by Shore. With this in mind, one can easily imagine two societies sharing common physical facts such as the temperature at which various liquids turn to solids, yet living in very different worlds regarding historical and cultural facts, for example, how one construes the "fact" of personal identity, self, or soul. For one culture the "self" may be "understood" as an entity that dies with the body; for another the "soul" may be understood as a permanent entity that exists beyond the life of the body. Assuming that cultures embracing such contradictory views of personal identity exist in the "same" world, one is compelled to ask: Who is right? But if one imagines that the two cultures are living in different "actual worlds," as Shweder suggests, the question is dramatically transformed. In Shweder's terms: "When you live in the same world all disagreements are matters of error, ignorance, or misunderstanding. When you live in different worlds, there is far more to disagreement than meets the eye."[16]

In short, from this point of view we may simply assume that while there is only one "physics-type" reality, there may well be a multiplicity of cultural and historical realities generated by the force of human intentionality, imagination, dreams, and action interacting with the larger cosmos. Within this framework, for example, we might speculate that some humans have permanent souls while others simply have temporary selves. Nor, according to Shweder, should this be particularly disturbing. As he says, "[cultural inconsistency] is not something we need to resolve; it is something we need to seek, so that through astonishment we may stay on the move between different worlds, and in that way become more complete."[17]

CONSIDERING A REALITY IN WHICH THE OBSERVER IS PARTICIPANT NOT SPECTATOR

In the various constructions of reality described above, including Shweder's tripartite worlds of physics, history, and culture, the theories retain the epistemological categories of "facticity" and "objectivity," and simply attempt to differentiate among different kinds of "fact." From this point of view, one can, for example, apprehend an objective world constituted of physical, historical, and cultural "facts" and understand that encultured beliefs are simply different ways of experiencing facts. And while this may lead us out of some sticky cross-cultural arguments attempting to determine what is superstition and what is science, there remains a second serious issue: the modern assumption that the observer remains separate from or outside the "facts" observed.

Even in contemporary science, it is no longer tenable to assume that one can apprehend objects or events in the world as separate from the organism doing the apprehending. We know the unit of reality is not simply the organism or the milieu within which the organism exists. The fundamental metaphysical error of the early modern way of viewing reality—beyond seeing the world primarily as "objects out there"—is to assume that that the observer stands separate from reality, observing and controlling actions in nature. In fact, the observer participates continually in the reality of which s/he is a part. The "spectator-viewing-an-object" understanding of experience may be a useful experiential unit for considering how we can come to know and cope with some kinds of practical events, but as a general theory of experience it violates our most profound common-sensical feelings which tell us that we are not really all that separate from the world in which we participate.

A more adequate understanding of reality coming out of both quantum physics and process theory is to assume that the cosmos is a set of flowing connections, as experience-and-reality-coming-into-being. This is Whitehead's ontological insight; Whitehead's unit of reality is a nexus. From this point of view, there is never an entirely separate world "out there" that is simply grasped as vibration, photon, image, concept, picture, sound, story, interpretation. There is, rather, the emergence of patterns which are momentarily created within the organism, and are constituted of both "internal" and "external" data emerging, initially, into a oneness. From this point of view we never apprehend the world, at least in the beginning, as a "thing" or an "object" (whether as physical, historical, or cultural objects or events), but rather as a pulsing process, participating in a "becoming," microsecond-by-microsecond, as data from the cosmos (at whatever level) interact and "come together" as a novel entity or occasion.

Humans are socially connected beings, connected both to other humans as well as to entities in the broader environment and cosmos. They do not function simply as a cohort of Lockean atomistic individuals, each using the economic and political system to maximize his/her own self-interest. We would argue that Modernity seriously underplays the importance of local and multiple realities in the broadest sense of the term by basing its ideology on the concept of the "autonomous and independent observer." In order to "feel" the deeper experiences of any culture, e.g., maintaining rituals for social bonding and mutual aid, small-group/family/community institutions we have earlier called the balanced or vital center must play a critical role in providing the social context.

One might note the simple fact that in most modern societies certain vocations which bring people into intimate contact with the raw physical needs of others, vocations such as mothering, caring for and teaching children, preparing food, and nursing the sick are considered to be of lower status than vocations in which one can keep people at an objective distance. Professionalized and technically trained physicians, professors, and mental health workers commonly embrace an ethos of impersonal objectivity. Professional helpers within this mode constantly strive to maintain an objective distance from both the problem and the "client." In short, the modern system understates the critical importance of engagement within communal places. The notion is that such engagement may interfere with the professional autonomy of the practitioner. Yet in so doing, it prevents the expression of intimate qualities of human bonding or connection essential for sharing a more profound reality. From this point of view the whole enterprise of modern science and its application to professions grounded in the findings of modern science are constructed on the problematic premise that observers exist and function, in considerable degree, excluded from the broader intimate social (and often silent and unseen) connections with the world they observe.

The cosmology of traditional peoples and/or local villagers does not commonly work this way. Local households and villagers are present and participate in the world they occupy—they rarely see themselves as being "alone." The unseen world of the private unconscious for the modern person is neither unseen nor private for traditional peoples. It is inhabited by the spirit-presence of friends, kin, and the souls of those close by and those who have gone before. One is always present, "included," woven into the fabric of an environment, a reality which defines and is defined by one's social presence. Before one "knows," one has to "be," and the source of being is a cosmos with vaguely felt but very real beginnings. From this perspective all reality emerges in the midst of "social" connections. One does not imagine any such thing as a private separate person outside the pale of a living spirit-filled world, observing physical or historical or cultural facts as totally independent separate objective events or entities.

SUMMARY

We began this critique of modernity by reframing the metaphysical assumptions upon which modern society is based. The modern assumption is that reality is defined primarily through the observations and measurements of an enlightenment science, the theories of which are based upon a Lockean/Newtonian foundation that separates the physical from the metaphysical. Northrup's analysis of dualism and the subsequent evolution of modern epistemology points out errors inherent in this ideology.

Northrop's critique of Lockean philosophy and its influence on the American experience concludes with the more general thesis that what he calls an "ideal society"—what Sapir has called "genuine" culture—must include a balance between the theoretical and narrowly empirical component of experience central to mechanistic science as well as the aesthetic component which is emphasized in more traditional cultures. Northrop discusses the need for reforming our Western-oriented culture so as to move toward this kind of balance. In his terms:

> ... the ideal society must return to the primitive intuition of the past with respect to its aesthetically grounded portion and advance to the sophisticated science of the present with respect to its theoretically based part. This has one very radical consequence for Westerners. It means that the traditional Western tendency to regard the primitive as inferior or evil must be rejected with respect to the aesthetic component of culture. A people leaves the primitive aesthetic intuitions of its past at its peril. It must move forward to the scientific theory of the future, taking along the primitive aesthetic intuition of the past.... Thus every society needs those who cultivate intuition and contemplation with respect to things in their naive aesthetic immediacy as well as those who pursue science to the philosophical articulation of the theoretically known factor in things.[18]

Northrop's vision of a revised Western cosmology which stresses a greater balance between the logical-empirical and more abstract or theoretical component of experience and the vivid holistic aesthetic component moves very much in the direction we advocate here. So as literal theoretical humans we would see the world as scientific spectators from the outside; as aesthetic humans we would engage in and participate in the reality that emerges from the unseen to the fullness of being. The challenge for humans is to construct cultures which creatively integrate these two central qualities of our humanity. Some very old societies which still exist, such as the Balinese and the Hopi, perhaps, represent such successful genuine cultures. We seem to be able to recognize such societies after the fact but are hard pressed to invent them or even move in that direction once the balance has tipped too far in the primal or the modern direction.

NOTES

1. *The Selected Writings of Ralph Waldo Emerson*, edited by Brooks Atkinson (New York: The Modern Library, 1940/1950), xxi-xxii.

2. Catherine L. Albanese, *Corresponding Motion* (Philadelphia: Temple University Press, 1977), 68-69.

3. David Bidney, *Theoretical Anthropology* (New York: Schoken Books, 1967), 18.

4. See, for example, John Locke, *Of Civil Government* (New York: Everyman's Library, Dutton)

5. F .S. C. Northrop, *The Meeting of East and West* (New York: Macmillan Company, 1946).

6. Ibid., 80.

7. "Passion, according to this Lockean Anglo-American theory, is merely an item in one's consciousness, purely phenomenal in character, quite independent of one's essential spiritual nature, which a man who is wise, in the modern Lockean sense of the word, will merely look at cooly and from a distance, as he would examine anything anything else which is an object other than himself, rather than an instinctive expression of his deepest and truest, most vital nature." (91)

8. Richard A. Shweder, *Thinking Through Culture: Expeditions in Cultural Psychology* (Cambridge, MA: Harvard University Press, 1991), 4-5.

9. Ibid., 6.

10. Ibid., 6-7.

11. See also Jean-Pierre Changeux, *Neuronal Man* (New York: Oxford University Press, 1986); Charles Laughlin, John McManus, and Eugene D'Aquili, *Brain, Symbol, and Experience* (New York: Columbia University Press, 1990); and Jean Piaget, J. Martenagro, and J. Billeter, *Biology and Knowledge* (Chicago: University of Chicago Press, 1971).

12. Bradd Shore, *Culture in Mind*, in reference to Changeux (1983) (New York: Oxford University Press, 1996), 16.

13. Ibid., 17.

14. Ibid.

15. Shweder, *Thinking through Cultures*, 19.

16. Ibid., 18.

17. Ibid., 19.

18. Northrup, *The Meeting of East and West*, 458-459.

CHAPTER FOUR

The Cosmos as Emerging Phases of Reality and Meaning

In an effort to escape from the subject-object dualism which celebrates a materialistic science, we will begin here to analyze issues of reality and meaning from the point of view of the basic metaphor of "organism." The philosopher who approaches "reality" from this perspective is Alfred North Whitehead. Whitehead, ironically, was one of the first modern scholars to reconsider the nature of matter and make use of the new quantum physics in his cosmology, shifting from the dominant physics metaphor of mass or substance to what he called a "philosophy of organism."

> … Organic theory represents directly what physics actually does assume respecting its ultimate entities. We also notice the complete futility of these entities if they are conceived as full concrete individuals. So far as [quantum] physics is concerned they are wholly occupied in moving each other about and they have no reality outside this function.[1]

Within Whitehead's process philosophy the core unit of reality moves from substantive objects or individuals to what he calls "actual occasions" or "actual entities." The name itself implies movement, a happening, a transformation not unlike concepts in quantum physics. The actual occasion is a dynamic process, an ever-changing pattern of relationships, not an item of mindless material; every final real thing is "alive" and in the process of becoming. And if the final realities are events that are constantly transformed, then we should see nothing static in the universe. And as Whitehead notes, that is just what we see.

From a process orientation, the essence of being is neither mind nor matter. This is the organic metaphor of emergence, flowing movement, growth, and decay suggesting a continuous transformative process that brings to the fore two central principles which the mechanistic clockwork universe ignores: self-transformation and novelty. Living things come out of the stuff and the form of that which has perished; yet they come forth as unique and novel entities. They are not "created" by others. In some mysterious way they create themselves.

UNDERSTANDING THE PROCESS OF EXPERIENCE AS EMERGING PHASES WITHIN DYNAMIC OCCASIONS

Viewing reality "objectively" suggests that humans see a world containing objects/ideas or "things out there" which can be described accurately—how and what things actually are and how they came to be that way. A person who "knows" something is able to place a particular entity or occasion into a generic category and then demonstrates the ability to recite the characteristics or criteria that describe or define the category. There is, of course, nothing intrinsically "erroneous" in this object-centered view of reality as long as humans see it simply as a useful and pragmatic way of coping with some of the immediate problems of functioning or surviving in the world. (Likewise maps are tremendously useful technical constructions so long as humans do not confuse them with the terrain.) Embracing an object-centered theory of knowing becomes an issue, however, when humans see it as the primary or essential way of understanding reality.

Our task, here, is to imagine qualities of reality and meaning which flow ontologically through perhaps several metaphysical domains (perhaps from a Source or Tao to a transitional Ground to the Natural Universe), transforming itself along the way through various modes or phases of experience (perhaps from vague emergent "feelings," to narrative story, to critical reflection, to ritual expression, and finally to a perishing and return to the Source or Tao). To make this shift of consciousness, we must apprehend a cosmos that is more inclusive than the materialistic natural universe, one in which we ourselves are participating, not simply looking at it. While we may choose to focus on one domain at a time (e.g., nature/the natural universe) or one experiential phase at a time (e.g., the emerging existential narrative) as a central quality of our knowing, we must also see these phases as related to one another, as a single ontological thread or throb of the "becoming," as an occasion of experience.

In Table 2 we speculate in the spirit of playful heuristics about the number and order of the various possible phases of experience within this ontological theory.

THE CREDIBILITY OF A
DYNAMIC PROCESS MODEL OF EXPERIENCE

This more complex view of experience requires that we include qualities of knowing that modern people commonly discount as fiction or superstition, e.g., the existence of a non-material Source of Tao, ritual enactment, poetic/mythic elements of a cosmology, eschatology, perishing, and the return of information to void/source. For instance, the process of experiencing can be thought of as similar to the process by which any entity or occasion comes into being, since experience is a kind of "entity." Plants, for example, are notorious for tropic responses (growing toward the sun or wilting for lack of water).

One might say that these occasions happen because the plant "knows" or "remembers" that it needs more or less light/water; it "experiences" an overabundance or a deficiency. In this sense, we see the plant and its responses as a set of actualities. We can also see the plant as "knowing something." Or we might take the example of a spider responding to vibrating patterns coming in from a moving web. The web, the vibrations, and the spider's neural responses are "things" as well as information and experience. Knowing and being can be construed as emerging from and/or reflecting a similar ontological process.

Once we assume that diverse qualities of "experience/being" participate, at least potentially, in a phase-like unitary process of "becoming," one must ask: How can we speculate about this process in a plausible way? Does it emerge, as a Platonist might suggest, from a non-material world of form or information which gives shape to and guides the creation of micro material "things" when they are just coming into being? And if this is the case, what is the process by which information and micro-particles are transformed into more substantial or material "things" that appear on the world scene to humans or other organisms as a neurological or physical presence? And what is the nature of the process by which "informed" micro-particles are transformed into significant information for organic beings, information in the nature of subtle feelings or more focused patterns of image and sound?

Table 2. Speculative Phases in a Theory of Organic Experience
Feeling of creative emergence from an undifferentiated source or oneness
Construction within our unconscious being of an imaginative world of multiple potentialities which move us to begin considering what the reality of this moment will become
Emergence of a dualistic narrative world which includes both our internal consciousness of self for the moment that is observing an occasion coming into being as well as the particular figures of the story coming to life in the moment outside of us
Critical reflection on the new story or narrative leading to an interpretation of this story that has emerged, leading us to ask whether or not the story is novel, singularly unique and/or significant or whether it has "natural" lawful predictable properties and can be treated as a repeatable story—as having the characteristics of a "stable" or scientifically understandable phenomenon within a generalizable theory
Fitting the story (or in more scientific terms "data") into a larger mythic holistic cosmology within which various interpretations are woven into grander stories to explain how things "came to be this way" for a particular people, e.g., the creation story of the Bible or the Darwinian evolution story
Transforming significant stories for mythic or metaphorical inclusion into an imaginative dramatic world of ritual wherein one can enact and renew the stories and myths that are deeply embedded within a people's cosmology, e.g., the Last Supper or the awarding of Nobel prizes for significant scientific discoveries
Creation of powerful rituals and beliefs which lead one back to the "Source" of emergent reality, e.g., funerals
And finally the sense that the novel information spawned from occasions of experience in nature can return to and renew or add information to the Source—to the "Tao" within the domain of non-material potentiality. For example, human discoveries of natural events, once having taken place for the first time, seem to be "remembered" by the Source[2]

A major objective here involves reframing the limits of our modern understanding of reality, in order to interpret cross-cultural experience. The cross-cultural issue then must account not only for the universalistic claims of modern science about what constitutes "reality;" it requires that we also account for the experience of sophisticated "educated" people in the way they seek to honor the richness and connectedness of a fuller process of coming to know—the Shweders of the world, as it were. As Shweder suggests, we must entertain the possibility of being seriously astonished and not simply dismissing cultural constructions of peoples which seem strange or alien to us.

If one is not willing to speculate about what constitutes a "fuller process of coming to know," then the cross-cultural conversation simply breaks down. In short, we are suggesting that in order for members of different cultures to talk across fundamentally different frames or theories of experience, we need a broad and inclusive set of overarching categories which respect assumptions of reality that both traditional and modern observers (among others) are likely to see as plausible. Such categories must, in fact, give accounts of how different individuals or members of different cultures may actually experience the fullness of an occasion, not simply as narrow, albeit, reliable facts, or complex abstract theories. Moreover it must respect the possibility that a similar set of circumstances may be experienced in different ways by two different individuals or cultures, and that the different experiences may be both authentic and "real." We need a theory of experience that allows people from radically different cultures to "imagine" how alternative understandings of a common historical or cultural "fact" or occasion can be believed.

CONSIDERING THE COSMOLOGY OF GENUINE CULTURE

Assuming that this kind of metaphysical speculation does not pass beyond the boundary of "common sense" for moderns, we shall now elaborate the nature of our cosmology which, hypothetically, includes three domains of reality: 1) a Source or Void or Tao which includes a unity of all elements of being, yet includes or implies the manyness that emerges into the natural or "actual" world; 2) a Ground as the transitional generative process which connects elements of the non-material patterned schema in the Void with the material manyness of Nature; and

3) Nature or the natural universe which includes the complex, dynamic, interrelated, partially ordered and partially chaotic "actuality" of "things" in ordinary every day life with which we are most familiar. The initial phase of experience or "coming into being,"(which we have called "emergence") would indicate the emergence of information from Void into the Ground of becoming after which it enters into and shapes the material manyness or "things" in Nature. Below we elaborate these three "domains," which should be distinguished from phases, which we discuss later.

DOMAIN ONE: VOID

We would posit that Void/Source/Tao is constituted of an undifferentiated fullness or potential for everything that we (and all other entities) can experience or "be" in the world. The Void "contains" and is potentially the source of everything and nothing or No-"Thing." The flow of novel "things" into Nature presumably draws from a non-sense-based domain of information, (at least for humans) the data which Whitehead refers to as "eternal objects."

Void is, of course, one of the central tenants of Taoism. In the words of the Taoist scholar, Max Kaltenmark, "The Void remains one of the great themes of Taoist thought.... In the Tao Te Ching it is the space between Heaven and Earth ... like a bellows. It is empty, but gives a supply that never falls; when it is in motion, it never stops producing."[7]

In some mysterious way elements of this undifferentiated "all" or fullness are "drawn forth," grasped or prehended and become available within an emergent Ground of becoming, which is the transitional state between the no-thing of Void and the materially based "things" of the natural world.

DOMAIN TWO: GROUND

Following Whitehead, we would speculate that novel actuality (things in the natural material world) of which experience is one form, emerge and draw from both conceptual schema that originate in the Void as well as from physical schema that have entered and are "present" in and/or inherited from previously existing physical material events within the immediate environment. In the latter case, "substantial beings" are similar recurring dynamic patterns or schema which somehow "remember" what they are supposed to be. They thus present us with the illusion of a static "thing" having a sustained existence when in fact they are really similar recurring events that know how to reproduce themselves. (Molecules and droplets of water "know" how to create themselves within a given environment, because the schema are already immediate there. The water in the ocean always seems the same, although it is constantly being transformed and recreating itself.)

DOMAIN THREE:
NATURE OR THE NATURAL UNIVERSE

Once we enter the material domain of Nature, we assume there is a world of constant becoming, of flow and throb, constituted of micro-elements which "thicken" into macro-elements of greater size and complexity. This is, moreover, a relational/conditional world in which everything—in greater or lesser degrees—is related to everything else. It is also—in varying ways for varying forms of being—a "living world" and even a "conscious" world in which the quality of life and consciousness quickens all being, since everything participates in the process of its own creation. (This is metaphorically related to the Gaia metaphor which suggests that we inhabit a living planet, all aspects of which are "alive.")[4]

It is a world of occasion and action as well as a world of beings and entities and the distinction between being and happening is never clear. In sum, the world of Nature may be envisioned, felt, or understood as a great network of Nodes and Connections. The Nodes are more like things; the Connections are more relational. From this point of view, one is not surprised to find that physicists puzzle over the fact that "elementary matter" appears in two forms—particles and waves.

As a point of clarification we would add that our use of the term "Nature" is roughly consistent with its common sensical meaning for the average inhabitant of the modern world, although somewhat broader than that used by some classical physical scientists who embrace the modernistic Enlightenment cosmology. Our use of the terms void or source is a speculative construct, used partly because of its presence in much philosophical/religious literature, and partly to explain phenomena that seem to stand outside the exclusively materialistic domain most modern people associate with the idea of nature. The term "ground" is used to suggest a transitional domain of *becoming* (comparable, perhaps, to the activities of a Platonic demiurgos) which transforms information from the non-material, undifferentiated domain of void to the actualized material domain of nature. When one watches living cells divide in the remarkable process called mitosis, it is clear what we would mean if we were to speak of a "demiurgos in action."

AN ELABORATION OF SIX PHASES
WITHIN OCCASIONS OF EXPERIENCE

In order to further explore our multi-domain theory of reality which includes source, ground, and nature, we would suggest a sequence of phases within which a "being" of information emerges from the void and begins the process of "becoming" in the world. Within this framework occasions might be seen to evolve through six phases.

A Throb of Process Experience presumably begins with fragments of meaning which are amplified and synthesized as they emerge from primary (unconscious) prehension and perception into conscious figuration and narrative. In this early phase, experience is immersed in vague and significant feeling. Both the feeling and the meaning emerge from the preconscious into consciousness and self-consciousness. Cultures, in fact, honor dreams and invent and construct deep rituals which probe the unconscious in order to reclaim fuller feelings and forgotten "visions" or images from the prehensive world of the unseen as well as forgotten elements from significant and archetypical narratives. What modern people often call "being objective" is their attempt to find social consensus regarding the objects and stories that emerge from this "unseen world," as well as ways of interpreting these stories such that they will make sense across cultures and within within their larger theories and cosmology.

A fundamental difference between process experience and modern experience suggested by this interpretation takes us back to the roots in the Cartesian model. Modern people tend to give priority to those elements of meaning and reality that are the clearest, the most tangible, and reliable and least ambiguous over that which is more vague and tacit. Given this restriction to a limited range of objects, stories and interpretations which satisfy their narrow warrants of proof, modern people are suspicious of or tend to ignore the more tacit elements in the unseen world and appeals to insights gained from enacted ritualist expression.

In Table 2 we speculated on the number and order of various possible phases that might be found within our hypothetical theory of experience. Table 3 below is a summary of these phases.

Table 3. Summary of the Six Phases
Phase One: Emergence (Prehension)   • External data enters and is prehended by organism   • Emergence of patterns within the organism is transformed into tropes and metaphors   • Using tropes organism organizes alternative realities and moves toward an interpretation of an occasion
Phase Two: Story Making
Phase Three: Critical Observation, Experimentation and Interpretation
Phase Four: Mythic Holistic Cosmology
Phase Five: Ritual Enactment of Mythic Qualities of Cosmos
Phase Six: Ritualistic Return to the Source of Emergent Reality

Similar phases have been identified and described in various ways by other process philosophers. However, since they form the basis of our particular theory of reality and meaning, we shall here present a somewhat elaborated interpretation. Of course, phases do not necessarily move through this cycle in an orderly and consistent fashion within the model. They can get "stuck;" or they can oscillate back and forth between two phases rather than move on; they can abort; etc. What is often described as the "scientific method," for example, involves the movement between observed data (stories) and efforts to organize and interpret stories within broader theory. Grand theories (e.g., the "big bang") might be considered as elements of larger myth-based cosmologies.

In presenting this very broad and inclusive theory of reality, we emphasize that the identity and quantity of these phases of being/experience are speculations and are presented to illustrate only the rough outlines as well as some particulars in the project of cosmology-making. Our schema are intended not as revelations or mystical insights, but rather as an appeal to imagination and common sense. In short, this theory of domains and phases of experience is an effort to name and describe shifts in the meaning of what it means to "understand" or "know" or "warrant" a belief as multi-level human beings move from one level of understanding to another within occasions in the world. Furthermore, we assume that the appropriateness or "correctness" of the particular language and the construction of these ideas is a highly tentative, flexible matter depending on the creative insights available to specific people in particular societies and cultures.

PHASE ONE: EMERGENCE

Human experience begins with a phase we would characterize as an inner-outer synapse or connection between the larger reality of void—an undifferentiated domain containing the potential for all being—and the world of the particular organism. This initial aspect of experience includes an interaction between elements in nature and consciousness in which focused energy and data from "outside" initially interacts with an organism and both come to share a common moment or spirit (anima/mana).

A new occasion is born and endowed with spirit. This common spirit becomes part of the organism and energizes the self, our soul. It may include conceptual data from the non-material world (void)—an "ether" domain as it were. It may include physical-material data from outside or from inside the body of the organism. This is obviously a highly speculative moment and poorly understood by Western minds. Tribal and archaic societies as well as Eastern cultures, however, have often given rich descriptions of what is happening during this process. Because this phase is, at least for modern people, largely preconscious, preverbal, and unacknowledged, we characterize it here as the "unseen world." But tribal and village cultures commonly develop rituals and/or trance-inducing conditions to activate a later memory so that the experience may not be lost.

Emergence is the phase in which elements of meaning connect with and position themselves within the organism. These elements include selection from the genetic memory of the organism—instinctual and archetypical connections with the internal and "external" environment. They also include elements from the personal memory of the organism. The organism selects those elements within the prehensive phase which are necessary for its survival and continuing adaptation. We are guessing that this initial prehensive phase has roughly three parts: the subtle connection with an ethereal domain (Tao or void); the grounding or emergence of patterns in the body; and the beginning of some kind of transformation of "felt" reality into symbols, signs, syntax, and complex language.

At some point in this emergent phase new information is "felt" and in some degree apprehended by the subject and organized into meaningful "possibilities." This process of considering alternative realities converging into a single "becoming" of experience is reminiscent of the quantum physicist's "alternative particles." These possibilities (commonly below the level of awareness) begin to present some coherent schema or pictures upon which the subject not only can experience but can act in the world.

Of fundamental importance to human beings at this point is their ability to imagine a variety of possible or plausible realities (scenarios) for the next micro-second of action. The human capacity to imagine multiple realities, we would guess, is spontaneous (not under our control), and conditioned partly by past experience. That is, to imagine a variety of possibilities the individual must have prior experiences that suggest which possibilities are plausible and which are "unrealistic." Finally, emergence includes the dramatic ability to act out in one's quasi-conscious dreaming or day-dreaming a variety of possible coherent stories that will make sense of the concrescing events of the moment.

PHASE TWO:
THE NARRATIVE WORLD OF OBJECTS AND STORIES

Figuration/Objectification. The organism becomes aware of an array of meaningful objects "out there"—the "ten thousand" things of which the Tao speaks. Depending on one's early tropic history, the organism is conscious of either participating in a world of many things and/or of observing objects "from the outside."

In process-oriented village cultures such as the Hopi Native Americans in the Southwest, it is often difficult for individuals to imagine being "outside" the world one is observing. Early cultural conditioning creates embodied metaphors in the form of spirits or images or sounds which constantly "draw" one into an inner unseen world of emergence. For modern people, however, the "unseen world" is often considered a world of illusion, dreams, or images which exist only in the neural structure of the brain or in fantasies. And while it may distort or block out the "objective" world beyond oneself, one deals with it as a private matter, not as a micro or quantum beginning of authentic reality.

Story-Making. Contiguous figures or objects become related in a coherent narrative or story. As indicated above, at some moment in time the prehensive emergent meaning of the immediate existential occasion "breaks" into conscious experience and we are observers of a differentiated objectified world outside ourselves. The world is suddenly filled with separate objects, related to each other and to us. They are often connected to us through a history of spatial contiguity and through human social or natural relationships. These relationships are expressed in the form of story, scraps of narrative, sounds and images, as, for example, our dreaming (after waking), our day-dreaming, and the stream of consciousness to which we suddenly pay attention. These often seem more in the order of imagined rather than as full-blown narrative. But as objects and figures enter the foreground of our experience, we tend to order them as a story, a story of the moment, which, when recounted, tells the world that we "know what is happening in the here and now."

PHASE THREE:
CRITICAL OBSERVATION, EXPERIMENTATION, INTERPRETATION, AND GENERALIZATION

Critical observation, experimentation, interpretation and generalization are included in the self-conscious reflective world of truth testing—checking out the authenticity and verifiability of specific stories (which scientists often call and/or reduce to "data"), and generating general propositions that describe regularities or natural laws of the current cosmos. This is the phase of experience of most concern to professionals such as scientists, lawyers, and engineers because it leads toward the explanation and control of the natural world.

At a deeper level, however, stories are systematically and compulsively reflected upon because they are connected to the mythic or metaphorical truthfulness of the larger cosmology that gives significance to the specific facts, theories, and sacred history in which a particular culture is commonly embedded.

In our modern cosmology we associate interpretation with academic disciplines and practical professions, so we seek to generate stories (or data) to which we can apply our research constructs in fields like history, geology, astronomy, physics, law, medicine, etc. This is a world of consciously manipulated abstract propositions and the systematic warranting of "stories" as facts or data to support the more general propositions. It is a world of concern for the logic, coherence, completeness, and provability of more abstract theories set within the framework of universal knowledge which can be applied to human cultures and societies in all places at all times.

In sum, Phase Three denotes the significance of specific stories and the attempt to place a story within some broader theoretical or historical context to give it richer meaning and/or predictive power. One of the ironies of interpretation is that, in the end, it tends to elevate the importance of interpretive categories (which often have the compelling power of abstract logical relatedness) and diminishes the particular stories which are reduced to mere "data" or "facts" used simply to give more general categories or abstractions significance and credibility.

Within academic disciplines and practical professional fields, stories are commonly reduced to "instances," either as case studies, as "research studies," or simply as numbers where they lose their richness, texture, and vivid metaphorical power. We rarely learn, for example, many of the rich details of Darwin's observations on the Beagle or of Einstein's ride through space on a photon. We learn only of the significant scientific discoveries and abstract principles that followed. The story or stories are, in fact, a primary source of fuller statements of actuality in which are embedded potentially powerful principles and insights. Turning the common meaning of interpretation upside down, one can look to see the extent to which primary data "make sense" given the primary, fully contextualized stories present in our common experience rather than the extent to which data confirm the validity of our stories.

PHASE FOUR:
CREATING A FULL AND AUTHENTIC COSMOLOGY

Phase four involves the transformation of both particular stories and their abstract interpretive theories into a broad and comprehensive cosmology. A cosmology is imbued with mythic significance and rich meaning which then yields deep understandings, stories, and theories—moral theories, empirical theories, aesthetic theories, or spiritual theories. Thus, stories generalize to theories and theories generalize to deeper cosmological sensibilities which result in moral and predictive assumptions about the way the natural universe works and how it connects to a larger cosmic reality.

Traditional societies work back and forth between significant stories and myth/cosmology more often than do modern people, who tend to stay within the boundaries of middle level empirical theories and disciplines, i.e., within the "factual" interpretive realm. We might note, however, Brian Swimme's work and his effort to construct a comprehensive story (an evolutionary cosmology) from the various findings of modern scientific disciplines.[5]

PHASE FIVE: RITUAL ENACTMENT—INTEGRATING AND REVITALIZING THE WHOLE

This is an effort to recapture and integrate the major qualities of experience suggested above including the unseen world, the narrative world, the interpretive world, and the mythic/cosmological world through compressed bodily feeling, symbols and the expressive arts. Through bodily enactment, movement, drama, sport, and music we may recall and recapture the integrated feeling and meaning of several phases of experience. The occasions selected for such enactment are usually those dramatic events most closely related to fundamental "occasions of survival" for the society, e.g., predation and eating, courting and sex, social bonding necessary for collective coping, controversy and conflict, illness and death, and dealing with crucial requirements for survival in the natural universe. In sport, for example, humans may recapture the excitement of the hunt by physically stalking each other and "bringing each other to the ground" as happens in the act of tackling in football. Dance allows humans to dramatize occasions of courtship, sexual acts, friendship, and related forms of bonding. We would also note commonplace comparisons in ritual behavior between animals and humans. Many animals act out complex rituals related to behavior connected to courtship, predation, or play. (Play, for example, often reveals patterns of dominance and deference related to cooperative behavior as well as preparation for predation.)

This kind of wired or presumably instinctive behavior may be considered a form of "adaptation" rather than simply "ritual," since it seems directly related to the requirements for the organism's survival rather than an effort to recall or renew the whole of an experiential moment. Of course recalling and renewing a culture's sense of the whole may well be regarded, in the long run, as necessary for the maintenance of a society's capacity for cooperation and cohesion — which are very necessary for survival.

PHASE SIX: RETURN TO THE SOURCE

It is assumed in this theory of reality that the universe and beyond the universe the "all" is constantly increasing in manyness and complexity. This means that there has to be some kind of memory. Of course in the material world of nature there is memory in the lawful relationships within the natural world. Water "remembers" to run down hill and freeze at a somewhat constant temperature. And as novel molecules and organisms are created many "remember" how to create themselves. But we assume that they continue on in a non-material reality in the form of schematic potential within the Void. In this phase, the organism "lets go" of the occasion and experiences the perishing of the moment. Novel elements generated in this pulse then return to the Void or Tao or the All. They are then available as "data" or information at the prehensive "unseen world" phase in the creation of new future occasions of experience.

SUMMARY

We have here described an overview of a process theory of reality and meaning to suggest a more pluralistic and complex way of understanding culture diversity. The issue of cultural diversity is central to our argument for primal-modern balance as a normative criterion for what we have called a genuine culture—that is a culture that is adaptive within the authentic or reasonable limits of our human nature.

The chapter began with a reference to Whitehead's philosophy of organism in which the core unit of reality is reframed as "actual occasions." This concept implies a dynamic process of transformation in which reality is an ever-flowing experience of information coming into being, growing and decaying. The organic metaphor is no longer rooted primarily in the mechanistic scientific regularities which allow us to classify and predict the behavior of objects, but are rather in the creative self-creation of entities or occasions as they attempt to fulfill a novel potential.

This theory of reality and being assumes as its primary cosmology a metaphysical existence consisting of three domains—source, a transitional state called ground, and the natural universe. The organism which experiences and participates in this reality does so in a series of phases beginning in a pre-emergent state called void moving to a state of consciousness which gives rise to stories and rituals that reenact the experience of emergence.

Finally, we have described the "becoming of experience" in which metaphors, symbols, and images are transformed into our awareness of objects (outside of ourselves) in nature which become embedded in coherent stories. These stories are then often abstracted into data, interpretations, and theory which we know as science, myth, and, more broadly, as cosmology. In an effort to understand the connection among these various aspects of reality and meaning, humans commonly create rituals which integrate reality and meaning into a single moment of insight. An example of such a ritual is the Christian rite of communion or the Holy Eucharist.

For now we will name the cosmology that assumes something like our three domains of reality and these phases of experience as "Nature in an Open Universe," or simply "NOUS."

We remind the reader that our effort to present this fuller organic metaphysical vision is intimately related to our discussions of the structure and meaning of life in local places where we see some form of process metaphysics as significantly more appropriate for understanding how and why people may and do construct a deep culture—a culture that is considerably more consistent with the inherent limits, tensions, and potentialities of our nature than one based on either subject-object dualism, pure materialism, or pure spirit. The following chapter is an elaboration and commentary on the subject-object view of experience compared with our own theory of Nature in an Open Universe.

NOTES

1. Alfred North Whitehead, *Science and the Modern World* (New York: Macmillan, 1925), 155.

2. For evidence of information passing through a "non-material natural world," see the work of Rupert Sheldrake, *The Presence of the Past*, (New York: Times Book, 1988).

3. Max Kaltenmark, *Lao Tsu and Taoism*, Translated from the French by Roger Greaves. (Stanford, CA: Stanford University Press, 1968), 43.

4. The Gaia metaphor referring to a "living earth" is developed in the work of James Lovelock, *Gaia: A New Look at Life on Earth* (New York: Oxford University Press, 1979).

5. See for example, Brian Swimme, *The Universe is a Green Dragon* (Santa Fe: Bear and Co., 1985).

CHAPTER FIVE

Comparing NOUS with The Subject-Object View of Experience

As we stated in Chapter Three, in order for members of different cultures to engage one another across fundamentally different frames or theories of experience, we need a common set of assumptions about "reality" that both traditional and modern peoples consider plausible. The NOUS cosmology which postulates multiple phases of experience among several domains of reality is an attempt to undertake this cross-cultural metaphysical project. In this chapter we make a further attempt to clarify the contrasts between subject-object dualism and our process, or NOUS theory, of reality.

A significant point of ambiguity for modern people is the connection between pragmatic science, technology, and culture. Modern people intuitively assume that technology is based on the universal "facts" of science and therefore transcends the seeming relativity of cultural "facts." (A steam engine would seem to be a universal fact. It functions in a predictable way based on established principles of physics in whatever cultural milieu it finds itself.) Yet how people construct, organize, and use both "science" (i.e., pragmatic science) and technology happens within the framework of an existing set of encultured beliefs.

A key issue here is a rather stubborn inability by modern people to honor the power and significance of constructed cultural "facts," and it is perhaps for this reason that science and technology seem to "compel" them, for example, to solve transportation problems by building more cars and highways rather than simply accepting the constraint of living closer to their work or relying on mass transit.

It does not occur to many that attitudes toward geographic mobility, for example, (modern people commonly move about in search of economic opportunities and novel lifestyles rather than maintain a loyalty to their native home) or attitudes toward private and public space (modern people often refuse to give up the use of their private cars even in the face of traffic congestion, pollution, and global warming) are based on deeply encultured predispositions in favor of a highly individualistic culture which determines the "reality" within which they live, what technology they construct, and how much they value and use it. From the point of view of our process theory of experience, the technologies we "invent" and develop have already been prefigured in the unseen inner world of our private cosmic and cultural imagination. The seeds of their use are already in the cultural and social institutions of the people who created them long before they "happened" to appear in the "objective" world.

A major purpose of this chapter, then, is to return to a central theme of modern cosmology—the subject-object view of reality—and compare it with basic aspects of NOUS (Nature in an Open Universe).

THE SPECTATOR ROLE OF EXPERIENCE

The first major difference between the two theories is in the role of the spectator. In process theory the "soul" or "self" is actually *in* the occasion that is coming into being, rather than standing outside of it, watching it happen. In a process-centered culture we feel ourselves engaged "in" the universe. Our observation is that for those raised in more primal cultures, there is a tendency to apprehend and participate subconsciously in an "unseen world," biologically and culturally, often through intense rituals. It is only later in more modern cultures that we assume the "occasion coming into being" is the result of individual intention in which individuals engage in and negotiate culture within an objective world. Our hypothesis is that for all humans, however, it is the *tropic images, metaphors, voices, sounds, and patterns of thought embedded unconsciously within our bodies* which initially connect us to our environment, our language, and our social relationships.

Much of what we are calling the emergent or "unseen" world is repressed and ignored or considered as "simply" a private or personal matter—in the realm of religion, imagination, or fiction. Our sense is that we grossly *underestimate* the extent to which subtle subconscious temperamental or cultural symbols and metaphors influence how we interpret our conscious and self-conscious "objective" world. From our point of view our unique human capacities for critical, "scientific" and philosophical interpretations of fact and the warranting and justification of fact sit on a host of underlying modes of being which are hidden in the shadow of an earlier phase of unseen and perhaps unfelt experience. Our range of doubt and skepticism regarding this assumption is limited by the fullness or narrowness of our metaphysics.

ORGANISMS PARTICIPATE WITH THE WORLD AS IT EMERGES

The second important aspect of the process model of experience is its assumption that various qualities of knowing emerge and grow and perish; they do not suddenly present themselves as objective story or knowledge or "thing" to be observed and recorded by an observer or spectator from the outside. From the process point of view, emergence happens within dynamic pulses or "occasions." Occasions, in this sense, are nested within one another. They initially consist of micro-second pulses later nested within stories nested within histories nested within cosmologies connected to ritual experience. We are never standing outside of our stories or our histories or our cosmologies. We are ever present within micro-occasions that have just passed as they relate to our stories, our theories, our rituals, and our sense of continuity and renewal. So that which we experience in the "unseen world" is a critical preconscious prelude to that which we more commonly call "experience"—from stream of consciousness to conscious reflective knowing to ritual expression.

We are also hypothesizing that an early phase of experience (the symbolic/metaphorical/imaginative phase) is heavily preconditioned by our genetic potentialities which constantly connect us in some subtle way to the requirements for our survival. But this subtle preconditioning may require significant cultural experiences to become activated. To use Shweder's metaphor, it is as if the organism were a piano with 88 keys and has the possibility of playing a great variety of tunes and harmonies. But unless these keys are played early in life through cultural practice, their potential is lost. Epigenetic potentials are latent; culture activates these possibilities and actualizes patterns of life.

We might take the example of dreams. It is quite possible that dreaming gives us powerful connections with an otherwise "unseen" world, but unless one is taught early in life to recall or relive dreams, to see them as more than fantasy, to connect them to "signs" within the story and interpretive world, then much of the potential for a fuller experience is lost. Modern culture, for example, tends to end up with only a thin but practical mechanical understanding of only those things in the world that engineers can and like to control.

THE CRITICAL ROLE OF IMAGINATION

A third major difference between process and subject-object theories of experience relates to the function of imagination. In our view of process theory, imagination is understood as the tacit connecting link between the emergent or "unseen world" which happens spontaneously and unconsciously and the conscious "story making" narrative world. In the modern subject-object view of experience, however, imagination is often presented as a skill which can be educated and made part of an explicit, controlled problem solving process. (We would note, for example, courses or programs to develop "creativity.") While this latter conception of imagination may be pragmatically useful, it ignores the more primal sense of the term and reinforces our modern notion that all experience can be transformed into a conscious self-conscious process of knowing.

Process theory suggests that the culture of modernity might do well to reconnect the conscious interpretive mode of experience which stresses objective forms of public communication and reflection with the more subtle unconscious processes through which private experience emerges and begins to come into being. It is within the unseen embryological stage of intuitive aesthetic sensibility, as Northrop suggests, that the oneness of the universe is most compelling and obvious, and it is here that feeling and facticity, imagination and imaging, literal speech and metaphor, dreams and focused consciousness initially come to us in a reality of oneness, seemingly out of their own volition and out of our control.

In the theory of experience developed by the process philosopher Robert Neville, the central link between what we are calling emergence/

prehension and story/interpretation resides in the inherently ambiguous and subtle function of imagination. As he says,

> ... imagination is a fundamental synthesis by which any conditions for thinking, particularly physical conditions, are transformed into the stuff of experience. Images are forms of synthesis. Imagination involves the creation of a self that engages reality, where otherwise there would be just one more thing reacting to other things in brute causal fashion.[1]

The imaginative function described here by Neville is a preconscious (presumably preverbal) spontaneous naturalistic process by which schema and/or images (sound, touch, smell, etc., as well as sight) are first formed and begin to cohere in some consciously (however vague) distinguishable form. But imagination is also the term we give for the self-conscious, partially controlled creative process by which we attempt to engage the world in a novel way e.g., in the process of "brainstorming." Imagination in this sense provides us with various hypothetical constructions of possible stories and allows for multiple interpretations of the world. The former view of imagination is as an unconscious autonomous perceptual process; the latter is part of the deliberate reflective problem-solving process which was so central to the work of Dewey, emphasizing deliberate constructivist practical thought and problem-solving. An adequate theory of reality (and genuine culture) must deal with the tremendous gap between the seemingly "irrational" out-of-control imaginative process of early preconscious perception and the hyper-rational process of deliberate brainstorming and disciplined scientific truth-testing.

This ambiguity in our understanding of imagination relates directly to the contrast between the spectator view of reality presented as formed knowledge versus seeing knowing, at least in its initial phases, as an emerging process. To embrace the notion of perception as a neural process *corresponding* to what is simply out there in the world is, as Neville suggests, no longer tenable:

> The model, common in Western modernity, of reality "out there" to be mirrored "in the mind" is no longer taken seriously. There simply is no way to compare the two, and this has been known since Hume, Kant, and Hegel, despite its appeal to our naively realistic scientific attitudes.[2]

Neville goes on to argue that for our experience to connect with the "outside world" requires the transformation from imagination to story and interpretation. And this involves seeing imagination both as a primal reality and later as a self-conscious constructed reality. "On the one hand, imagination is a synthetic human activity that constitutes the forms of experience such that we have a world." That is, it is a critical element of preconscious perception. But, as he says, it can also be part of conscious engagement in the creation of stories and interpretations. It is only in its initial primal phase as a natural causal process that it allows for the "plausible connection between the reality of oneself and everything else."[3] This is, of course, a radical metaphysical position when one considers the full meaning of the term "everything else."[4]

Perhaps the most dramatic error of our modern theory of experience is its cultural suppression of the unseen emergent or unconscious aspect of meaning-making, which includes the central role of imagination as a culturally conditioned but natural causal process. Thus, modern people live with the illusion that somehow the "self actualizing ego" can make rational determinations of fact and conscious choices and judgments about what is true, natural, beautiful, or real in a world projected beyond the self. From a process point of view, much that exists in the "natural" world beyond us is already unconsciously given. In Neville's words:

> In the modern period, imagination has been identified with the individual ego, despite the fact that it is a social phenomenon such that individuals are token bearers of images. When the ego is construed as subject, over against reality as object, imagination seems to be the individual's projection of personally created forms on a screen that remains subjective. Our culture thus rests on an ambiguous situation. On the one hand truth depends on [self-conscious rational deliberate] interpretation, which in turn depends on imagination functioning as a genuine mediator of other things to ourselves. In a naturalistic theory, imagination is precisely this. [And in a naturalistic culture, imagination functions in precisely this way.]
>
> On the other hand, the modern scientific culture has said that imagination is subjective. If so, then mediation becomes mysterious and the world is reduced to a reference to our [private subjective] imaginative representations. What do the imaginative representations

then represent? The real world? How could we know? Are creative imaginations [only subjective] projections?[5]

Neville's questions point up the fundamental error in modern thought in which it "solves" the problem of the "unseen world" or the "unconscious" by construing imagination as related to a subjective world of fantasy. Its failure to connect the unconscious and the conscious realms of meaning in any credible way results in what Neville calls the potential "terror of imagination." If, in fact, Neville's world of primary causal imagination and Jung's "second" world of unconscious dreams are actual prefigurations of later states of conscious reality, the result is likely to be a nervous and even paranoid and pathological culture. For the unseen and the unconscious second realities lurk just below the surface in every moment of our lives.

Imagination thus provides people living in a genuine culture with a real connection to an actual social environment, not a private egocentric fantasy. And we make this assumption because we associate genuine culture with a high level of face-to-face direct and full communication that results from long-term close association between people and people, between people and the natural world, and between the natural universe and sensibilities relating to the larger cosmos.

We would note here the use of imagination in modern psychotherapy. Early on psychotherapists used such therapeutic tools as dream analysis, free association, and "fantasy" stories based on ink blots and ambiguous pictures to reveal neurotic burdens of the mentally disturbed. Irrational and destructive fantasies, presumably generated in the "primary processes" of the unconscious were thus revealed. From the point of view of our modern dualistic cosmology, a major goal of mental activity is self-control and the control of the world around us. Having a semi-autonomous unconscious world of imagination "out of control" is therefore considered a condition of mental or moral deviance. For psychotherapy, out of control "primary processes" are often construed, not as part of one's normal capacity for meaning-making similar to one's autonomic nervous system, but rather as unconscious images one conjures up from previously repressed or forgotten experience associated with personal or cultural pathology, e.g., sexual or aggressive fantasies directed at one's parents.

Such an understanding of imagination is certainly grounds for modernity to expose and thus control the potential "terror" embedded deep within the emergent information coming from an "unseen world." This loss of control is associated with the early preconscious phase of human experience, and suggests a return to a set of atavistic feelings/images/ actions unbecoming to the fully rational, "civilized" modern human psyche. Whereas, in a process culture, imagination acts as a release from the often rigid and inauthentic constraints of destructive cultural conditioning (as a way of balancing the rational controlling world with the deeper intuitive world). Within modernity, the tacit and subtle images of our preverbal "prehensions" tend to evoke only the possible presence of ominous and illusory demons connected with ill-fortune.

THE ROLE OF NARRATIVE IN PROCESS EXPERIENCE

Modern people tend to be much concerned with cause and effect, control, and the prediction of the requirements for success and progress. With their focus on control and progress, they are then concerned that good "progressive" stories be repeated and bad stories be corrected and/or abolished. (Imaginative and fictional stories are considered mainly as entertainment.) Modern people thus tend to quickly translate "true" stories (i.e., scientific data) into predictive abstractions leading to pragmatic possibilities. They ask: How can the data of the story be used to create the circumstances for improving the world? They commonly make a significant distinction between "cultural stories" that provide journalistic entertainment or meaning to enrich one's understanding of the contemporary world or the past (i.e., history) and the transformation of "true" stories into data which may be useful for creating new science/ technology which may lead to greater economic control of the environment. Pragmatic science then constructs theories based on inferences from stories (transformed into data), experimental or statistical analysis, and the testing of such inferences, and seeks to predict regular lawful relationships from its analysis. Thus our modern impulse is to avoid using history or philosophy to probe the deeper meaning of the human condition, including tragic or erroneous cultural turns, unless such tragedies or errors appear saleable as commodities in mass media (e.g., as film or magazine or book) or unless they have commercial value as progressive policy programs fundable within the framework of science and technology. One obvious example of this issue of probing deeply the dark side of stories is what we now know as the "war on drugs." Countless movies and documentaries have been made on this topic and billions of dollars spent all the way from defoliating the fields which provide the source of drugs to the mounting of massive advertising campaigns to frighten people who might use them. But currently there is little change in the rate of drug use, at least in the United States.

So for modern people, "subjective" and journalistic stories tend to be seen as either fictional or incidental history useful in providing casual insight and/or entertainment, while story transformed into data becomes part of the corpus of applied science used to improve the world. And, of course, with the move toward systematic research and development, modern people no longer wait for stories to come into their world on a casual basis; they invent and control reality in the laboratory and construct (develop) technology which generates new and magnificent stories, e.g., factories, airports, malls.

Perhaps, the most significant difference between modern narrative and process narrative is that modern narrative is fragmented; it comes in bits and pieces "from the "outside" while process narrative is connected with an unseen emergent world on the one hand and with broader forms of interpretation which we associate with theory, myth, and cosmology.

PROBLEM SOLVING AND SCIENTIFIC REDUCTIONISM

Balanced or genuine cultures, we would argue, tend to move within a circle of meaning from the emergent becoming of reality, to story, to interpretation, to cosmology, to ritual, and returns to the sense of a larger source or cosmos. All of these elements of experience and meaning are connected. So as life unfolds, the explanation of "why" things happen is very complex. For instance, in the face of a large disaster people might ask: Were humans insensitive to elements in the emergent ontological process or becoming of the world? Did people think "bad" thoughts? Was the significance of an important story misinterpreted? Was it explained wrong? Did the interpretation of a story make sense within the meaning of the larger myth or cosmology? Is there some error in our larger myth or cosmology? Did one find or use an inappropriate prayer or ritual or scientific discovery to deal with a story? And so on.

The modern person tends to function from a pragmatic adaptive posture largely within the limits of the material data presented by stories and by theories which predict how to respond to and control specific short-term future stories. This tends to lead modern people toward technical modifications of their circumstance rather than raising basic questions about the fabric of their larger cosmology. Problems are most likely to be reduced to technical manipulation of the material events that presumably "caused" the problem. Modern people treat the issue of violence, for example, by arming police and soldiers to threaten or do counter violence or imprison those who might commit acts of violence. They treat the uglification or destruction of the natural environment with economic incentives within the existing market system. And since there is no clear sense of a larger cosmos or larger order which limits the ways humans might appropriately adapt to the universe, there can be no appeal beyond the norms and techniques of existing science and technology. Living within one dominant materialistic domain reduces all reality to one level of understanding.

ONE DOMAIN OF SCIENTIFIC MATERIALISM: A QUESTIONABLE ALTERNATIVE TO NOUS

Philosopher Myra Schectman presents us with an opportunity to explore whether or not it is possible to integrate the two realities of scientific dualism—subjective/mind/meaning and objective/body/matter—and create a one-domain model of reality to which modern people might subscribe more easily than to process theory. Schectman's paper entitled, "The Story of the Mind: Psychological and Biological Explanations of Human Behavior," deals with a proposal to integrate the material physiological basis of experience (brains, hormones, etc.) with the psychology or "meaning" of experience. The issue is set within a psychotherapeutic context. It is important, perhaps, to note that the paper was presented at a conference attended by scientists, philosophers, and religious scholars around the topic: "Knowledge Most Worth Having in the Decade of the Brain."

Schectman begins by summarizing what she calls "the metaphysical controversy" with which she (and we) are dealing:

> The central challenge facing philosophers of mind is to understand the nature of mind and its relation to body. Human beings have a curious dual nature. On the one hand, they are psychological subjects, who act from reasons and passions in accord with their beliefs, values and desires. On the other hand, they are physical presences—objects composed of essentially the same elements as

all physical objects and moved by essentially the same forces. The question is how to reconcile these two aspects.... Human beings, then, are creatures to whom two different explanatory schemes can be applied, and some account is required of how we are to understand this fact....[6]

Schectman then briefly states the Cartesian position: Humans are made up of two kinds of substance—an immaterial mind and a physical body. Modern humans understand that the mind and the body relate through a process of psychophysical interaction, but the interaction is between two very different forms of being. The major difficulty with the Cartesian theory is, she asserts, its inability to work through in some clear way how an "immaterial" mental substance can relate to a material substance and cause it to act in specific ways. Largely because of this difficulty, she notes that, "In the contemporary philosophical discussion, substance dualism generally is considered to be more or less thoroughly repudiated, and some form of scientific materialism usually is assumed as a starting point."[7] Therefore, she maintains, contemporary science now assumes that the universe is composed exclusively of matter. She continues:

Scientific materialism avoids the difficulties of substance dualism by holding that there is only one type of substance—material substance—the kind that is defined and described by the physical sciences. In this view, persons do not have minds that are separate entities; they have only bodies, which are entirely subject to physical laws. This approach certainly avoids the problems raised by assuming a causal interaction between different kinds of substance, but the scientific materialist is left with the challenge of explaining the way in which a body alone can have the psychological aspect that is definitive of human life.[8]

Schectman then explains that there are two philosophical strategies for dealing with the psychological vs. biological aspects of a materialistic world. One is reductionism in which one assumes that all linguistic, symbolic, or feeling content can be reduced to physiological explanations with no information left over.

The second position, what she calls the anti-reductionist approach, maintains that there is an irreducible mental or psychological aspect to human life such that experience cannot be boiled down to biology without loss of information. Here she introduces a computer analogy:

The mind ... is like software running on the hardware of the brain. The level of software, although constrained by the hardware on which it will run, is distinct from it. Fortunately, one can learn a great deal about how to use a particular computer program while knowing little or nothing about the physical events in the computer on which it is running. A software problem is not a hardware problem and requires a different kind of attention. (601)

She then continues, noting that the anti-reductionist is uncomfortable with the assumption that all meaning and mental "stuff" can be reduced to "precise physical explanations." With the computer analogy, the anti-reductionist can assume that "the physical and psychological aspects of persons coexist happily side by side as different levels of explanation" much as software exists as a level of reality and meaning separate from but dependent on hardware (601).

Schectman concludes her philosophical discussion by asserting that, "Neither of the two major proposed views of mind is, in the end, entirely satisfying" and moves on to what she calls "the clinical debate," which provides a specific context or arena for dealing with the issue (602). Using obsessive-compulsive mental disorder as a benchmark case, she discusses two clinical approaches toward its explanation. The first is the familiar Freudian position, which maintains that there is an unconscious psychological life that, when understood, provides an adequate understanding for the seemingly irrational or bizarre behavior characteristic of obsessive/compulsive behavior. On the other hand, there is a biological-medical approach which construes mental disorders as caused not by unconscious drives or desires, but rather by problems in the neurochemical activity of the brain.

Again, Schectman is not satisfied with this either/or construction of the issue, i.e., explanations as either psychological or biological. She maintains that in the work of Peter Kramer (described in his book *Listening to Prozak*) there are the germs of a third and more integrative approach to the problem of mind-body dualism.

Schectman's interpretation of Kramer's work indicates that symptoms are not simply the result of psychological trauma translated into psychobiological terms that affect the brain. It is rather the psychological meaning of traumatic and/or repeated experiences, such as grief or fear or rejection that actually alters the brain. As she says, "The words 'I guess that's the last time I'll be seeing you' have one meaning when uttered by the doctor giving a clear bill of health after a course of treatment for a terrifying ailment and quite another when uttered by a spouse leaving after a failed attempt at reconciliation (610-611).

She distinguishes her position from standard Cartesian dualism by maintaining that the connection between mind and body is not to be left in some fuzzy no-man's land, but rather requires that there be careful research specifying the precise empirical connection between meaning and its biological counterpart. This empirical precision is possible now that we understand that there is really only one substance in nature—matter; as she says, beliefs, desires, and feelings have material existence just as do neurons, synapses, and serotonin (613).

Perhaps the most interesting aspect of Schectman's position is that there really is no radical shift in this new view of dualism. We have simply switched from mind-idea vs. matter-body dualism to two different kinds of matter—"meaning-idea" matter and "physical-body" matter. So one has to ask: Where does this take us? What is the point of staying within the single realm of nature/matter? Schectman's answer is that this allows us to continue to understand and deal with the world as normal science, even in the most subtle field of personal human meaning. As long as modern people know that meanings, ideas, and feelings are material "things" of some sort or other, like neurons and serotonin, they can assume, as does the scientist, that they conform to the objective methodologies that characterize all modern science. As Schectman herself suggests, the major advantage of her clarification and reconceptualization of the dualism problem is that it does not presuppose "a realm outside of [materialistic] science." She then adds that the reason modern people need a one-realm reality is that it is the only position consistent with science, and that "the progress of science itself … leads to the conclusion that psychological and biological factors must be interwoven to give the best account of both human behavior and brain functioning" (612-613).

In short, Schectman's "best account" of reality apparently *requires* that she remain within the narrow empirical constructs and methodologies of current science. Our speculation is that there is an unstated cultural motivation for sticking with this one-level materialistic commitment, and it is related to the necessity felt by scientists that they "control" the materials and methodologies connected to the problems with which they are confronted. The deeper dualism that does not disappear in

Schectman's work is the separation between subject and object in which subject is the observing/controlling scientist and the objects are the things or products that s/he manipulates to get results (including the client or patient or research subject). The one-matter exclusively materialistic world allows modernity to keep the meaning-making scientist in control, for it is s/he who interprets what the patient "really" means; it is s/he who controls the methods of treatment and remediation. So modernity must keep the consciousness of the scientist "on the outside" of material reality where s/he can develop techniques for studying "scientifically" the interaction between psychologically based meaning-type matter and physiologically based matter-type matter.

One can imagine, of course, a different kind of "science" in which the scientist seeks to enter the personal or cultural world of others, to understand meaning "from the inside." Interestingly enough, traditional peoples are notorious for living *within* both meaning and matter. They commonly see experience as a continuous stream moving across and through vague feelings about the presence of spirits on to dreams, songs, words, and the relationships of the aforementioned experiences to public narratives and actions. From this more primal perspective obsessive/compulsive impulses may be related to vaguely felt sensibilities coming from a non-material or simply "another" realm of reality, and the responsibility for these feelings may well be grounded in a pathology associated with the shared transpersonal culture of several people in one's native place rather than simply being "in" the individual.

When we begin to think in this way, we can imagine a radically different kind of "science," one in which the scientist would be required to enter both the personal and cultural world of the "subject" and actually surrender, in some degree, one's concern for "objective" external observation.

SUMMARY

Throughout this discussion of modern metaphysics, we have tried to step beyond the Lockean and Cartesian cosmologies and the reality commonly embraced by those who do research in engineering-related science. (We understand that some scientists, especially those in the fields of theoretical quantum physics have gone beyond what we have called the modern cosmology.) Our attempt at this reconstruction of a more adequate metaphysics has been built on a variation of process theory of experience related to that initially envisioned by Whitehead and developed further by Neville. The assumption within this theoretical framework begins with the proposition that organisms participate continuously in the coming into being of the particular reality in which they "live." Living organisms are not detached external spectators capable of consciously constructing meaning and controlling the world "out there" for their self-interest. Rather they exist within a context of creative connections to their environment and, in the last analysis, to the cosmos.

Our multiphase model illustrates a circular flow of experience beginning with a nascent occasion which has within it epigenetic physical and cultural preconditioned potentialities. Such occasions pulse from source to unconscious image and metaphor to the imaginative construction of alternative possibilities and then into consciousness. And therein begins the process of connecting the unseen world with narrative and the more abstract worlds of history, science, philosophy. Modern cosmology tends to dismiss, deny, or keep in the shadow of inattention this entire tacit unseen process which goes mostly unnoticed within the "common sense" world of contemporary humans. It focuses rather on the more obvious clear "actual" stories and stuff and the interpretation of these after they have emerged into the dualistic reality of subject/observers and external/objects.

Finally, we have discussed the critical issue of imagination. A process theory of experience assumes that imagination is far more than simply something like unconscious dreaming or semi-conscious daydreaming or stream of consciousness. Rather, it is the process by which organisms construct preconscious "real" multiple interpretations of the world. In this sense, imagination is a "real" causal aspect of the world just as the idea of preparing a meal is a real causal phase in the process of "eating dinner." Conceivably the most significant error of a modern theory of experience is the suppression of the prehensive aspect of meaning-making which includes the role of imagination as part of a causal process in culture-making. More specifically, we believe that in balanced or genuine cultures imagination connects preconscious emergent experience with everyday life in the form of tropic images such as metaphor and irony. In modern cultures, however, the celebration of the unconscious imagination, for example, in dreams, (when not considered fantasy or fiction) borders on mental or moral deviance and must either be suppressed or brought under conscious control by various therapeutic techniques.

Children soon learn, when attending a modern school, that one is not to daydream. It is wasting time.

This understanding of imagination is further illustrated by Schectman's proposal to integrate the *material* physiological basis of experience with the psychological *meaning* of experience. Despite her attempt to solve the dualism problem with a more precise, explicit operational definition of meaning-making, Schectman's one-realm matter-based reality places her as a particular outside meaning-making professional observing and controlling the inner experience of her patients (her objects of study). We wonder how such a professional would deal with a patient who sought to interconnect the meanings of the inner lives of both therapist and patient so that both could see the reality of one's life as background to the other. Thus both become spectators and both become observers in the midst of a common occasion. In such a case what would it mean to be a "professional" and what would it mean to be a "patient?" Perhaps the reality of such a situation would then better be described as a unity of connections rather than as material meanings and material objects "out there."

NOTES

1. Robert Cummings Neville, *Recovery of the Measure.* (Albany: State University of New York Press, 1989), 4-5.

2. Ibid., 19.

3. Ibid.

4. This assumption of an "unseen" alternative reality seated in an unconscious self that connects more directly to the larger cosmos than our conscious self is, of course, a central assumption of the great corpus of work carried on by Jung over a lifetime. Jung sought to demonstrate by careful scientific introspection what Whitehead and Neville tried to work through by philosophical speculation.

5. Ibid., 19-20.

6. Myra Schectman, "The Story of the Mind: Psychological and Biological Explanations of Human Behavior," *Zygon* 31, no. 4 (December, 1996) 598.

7. Ibid., 599.

8. Ibid., 599-600.

PART THREE

Reconsidering Our Modern Understanding Of Human Nature, Culture, and Diversity

CHAPTER SIX

Human Nature
And Culture

THE INTEGRATED QUALITY OF HUMAN NATURE:
REVISITING LOCKE

The modern concept of human nature suggests that pragmatic reason is a separate and dominant aspect of our nature and can act as a constant progressive force in changing culture to make it more efficient and adaptive. The deep primal cultural patterns that humans develop are then often considered as either impediments to or unrelated to progress. (Actions such as bonding with a mate, playing with children, or eating a meal with friends are not generally characterized as "progress," while constructing a new airport or highway is.) The modern person, we suggest, has difficulty comprehending the fact that the rational pragmatic potentialities of the human psyche are integrated within the primal aspects of human nature; nor do many humans understand the extent to which these "non-rational" potentialities have been adapted to serve modern ends. One might say, for example, that humans engage in war for the most "primal" of reasons yet use the most sophisticated and "progressive" weapons in this process. War is not commonly seen as progress while the invention and use of jet fighter aircraft or atomic weapons is.

Roger Masters, a political scientist, has written extensively on this issue and argues that the erroneous understanding of the role of reason or "reflection" in our human nature goes back to the Lockean model which states that the mind is essentially a blank slate. Locke's legacy has been to glorify the cognitive function of the human brain because of its capacity to interpret and shape meaning and presumably overrule or eliminate the tendency toward emotive or sensory distortions in human experience. The mind registers information on a sensory blank slate and reflection gives the data meaning. Masters (1993) speaks directly to the ethical implications of modern brain research on the Lockean model:

> In the *Essays Concerning Human Understanding*, Locke describes 'sensation' and 'reflection' as the two 'fountains' of knowledge, from whence all the ideas we have, or can have, naturally have come. He describes sensation and the senses in themselves as passive: they record 'qualities' of 'external objects,' not those objects themselves. We have no direct access by sense perception to what Kant would call the 'thing-in-itself' but only can sense external stimuli or 'phenomena.' To this 'passive capacity,' Locke projects a second active source or 'fountain' of information called 'reflection.'[1]

Quoting Locke, Masters states that, "the ideas ... [reflection] affords being such only as the mind gets by reflecting on its own operations within itself." Thus, Locke is claiming that:

> this active reflection is the source of the categories or ideas of our conscious perception and reasoning about the world. Since natural sensation is merely the material on which the mind operates, such concepts as color and taste are conventions or customs produced by *reflection*.[2]

Masters then argues that the findings of modern neuroscience, in fact, contradict Locke's theory and challenge assumptions regarding the source and flexibility of human experience. As he says, our current understanding of the human nervous system suggests that sensory input is "processed in a hierarchical manner such that the first processes, at least in the visual and auditory pathways, are highly abstract cues (e.g., straight versus curved lines or movement at each point in the sensory field)...." Then at higher cortical levels these primary abstract cues are "reconstituted" such that they yield information that we "intuitively associate with reality"—such as color, texture, shape, movement, etc. This is, according to Masters, a parallel system of discrimination in which the separate primary and secondary processes are "integrated before we become conscious of a perception." Returning to Locke's mistaken view of the human mind, he says:

> Whereas Locke thought that abstractions such as 'straight' versus 'curved' were higher-order phenomena resulting from 'reflection'

on the primary facts of sensory experience, these abstractions are *innate*; what Locke took as primary 'facts' of sensation seem to be the result of the brain's activity integrating multiple sensory processes.[3]

Masters then gives the example of taste discrimination between bitter and sweet which are based on specialized cells, not on some kind of learned or conventional reflection. He concludes that "[T]he brain is thus not at all a 'blank slate' but rather a highly structured and hierarchically organized system for perceiving and interpreting the world (12). Humans—and, indeed, mammals generally—have what Locke called 'innate ideas' about things as well as about other members of the species."[4] Conditions in one's life history, both the experiential and the "biological," interact with initial genetic conditions and then wire in new integrative information. Repeating an example similar to one given earlier by Shweder, he notes that although the human capacity for language generally is genetically wired, by forty-eight hours the newborn shows a preference for the language spoken in the social environment to which it has been exposed, and by puberty the brain may have largely lost its capacity to discriminate sounds never encountered. Thus:

> The neuronal structure of the brain is the product of an interaction between natural potentiality and individual experiences that are shaped by culture and society but not entirely reducible to them.... The unity of an individual's thoughts reflects a complex integration of many factors, some inherited and others acquired, some conscious and others automatic.

> As has been shown experimentally, much of this integrative process occurs without our being conscious of it and hence cannot be attributed to what Locke calls active or conscious 'reflection.' The gulf between nature and nurture, on which moderns following Locke elaborated the fact-value dichotomy, has dissolved in the light of contemporary scientific research. Not only are there innate ideas, but ... some of these innate ideas directly concern social behavior, forming the basis of our judgment of the feelings, traits, and leadership of others.[5]

Here Masters stresses the point that while there are biologically based innate ideas, one cannot separate nature from nurture or biology from cultural/environmental factors in the extent to which these ideas or behaviors are expressed. He refutes, as did Shore's work, the oft stated modernist position which has claimed that for behavior to be considered "innate" or "instinctive" within the human species it must be universally and similarly expressed by all people everywhere.

Biologists are now telling us that there is a "natural" or physiological substrate for many kinds of behavior, but this is modified biologically by the deep influences of culture/environment such that the final manifestation of behavioral patterns is the result of nature/culture acting together. As Goldschmidt suggested some sixty years ago, human nature may set the outside limits of our potentiality for individuals as well as the species, but nature interacting with culture/environment does not yield a uniform result for all humans or all cultures. Thus the linking of human nature with the presumption that it will be expressed in a common universal way is a serious misconception of fact and logic.

Of special interest is Masters' additional point that our more "primitive drives emotions, and complex cognition" are related to the triune structure of our mammalian brain which evolved over millions of years and includes the older limbic system and the more recent neocortex. The more primitive limbic system and the modern cortex are intimately connected and integrated so that more primitive emotions cannot be disconnected from more complex language and cognition.[6] Moreover, he points out that "[c]ognitive neuroscience challenges the conventional view of mind-body dualism and human consciousness. It is no longer possible to assume that all cognitive processes are under conscious control; rather, preconscious information processing occurs in parallel as different sensory modalities and feature detectors respond to the environment."[7]

Here we emphasize the distinction between physiologically-based tendencies interacting with unconscious enculturation on the one hand and practical reason on the other, but not as oppositional forces in our human makeup. The fact is that humans most commonly construct culture unconsciously so that it will square with fundamental genetic or "natural tendencies"—otherwise most societies would be doomed. Moreover, this may be done with the unconscious or implicit assistance of practical reason to support basic tendencies toward the comfort and survival of the individual and/or community. Reason sits on and is connected to deeper unconscious processes of adaptation. And of course, as adaptive patterns are constructed and institutionalized, whether consciously or not, they are in some loose sense wired into the nervous system in various degrees of depth and reversibility. As Masters notes, our "understanding" of both individual and cultural differences are often deeply learned, i.e., learned in a way that such patterns of behavior and meaning are not under conscious human control.

The final point we would emphasize in Masters' argument for rethinking the link between deep culture, pragmatic reason, and their place in human nature is the degree to which cognition and practical reason somehow constitute an independent universal human instrument (in the Lockean sense) to be applied directly to human adaptation versus the extent to which they are influenced by profoundly unconscious qualities of human experience related to our more primal limbic system that evolved earlier in our history.

The Lockean notion that "objective" data appear on the screen of our blank mind and are then processed, interpreted, and given meaning by some "independent" internal reflective capacity seems absurd given what we know about our central nervous system. The Lockean model, moreover, carries on the pernicious Enlightenment myth that there are universal objective domains of "things" out there that are to be understood and described by a set of universal, rational, scientific disciplines inside the mind. But for reason or for "science" to be the platinum rod measuring universal nature would require that humans rid themselves of the deep personal and cultural linguistic constructs which have been encultured in the "mind" of the scientist before s/he is even conscious of their significance in his/her understanding of reality. (It is, in fact, our "deep culture," including the language that communicates much of it, that defines our humanity, including our science, in the first place.)

Thus, to see reason as an independent higher quality that is biologically separable from our more primal forms of communication and bonding is not only implausible, it is factually incorrect. This thing called reason that mysteriously emerges from the human neocortex sits on top of the more primal limbic system and the two operate in tandem. Thus to establish—in a paradoxical sense—deep traditions of rapid constant progressive change based on rational technological considerations of power, efficacy, and efficiency that then undermine existing primal tendencies which connect humans to place, to kin and friends runs the risk of enculturing a stressful, unbalanced and flawed society. In the long run, we would argue, such cultures do not "take" and eventually decline and are rejected as alien viruses. We simply cannot assume that reason is an objective monitor which will guide humans into the circumstances required for genuine culture. It rather serves an instrumental function in tandem with a set of more primal adaptive resources which support a complex layered set of dimensions of which humans are not aware or which they only dimly apprehend.

RECONSIDERING THE IMPORTANCE OF THE PRIMAL LEVEL OF HUMAN NATURE

A more plausible interpretation of our human nature is that humans have a multiple (but still limited) array of options by which to express their "instinctive" or their latent tropic or what E. O. Wilson calls our "epigenetic tendencies." These options require that humans function within place and cultures that balance the Lockean emphasis on their reflective capacities with the more primal physical and bonding capacities they share with many of our mammalian and primate relatives. We would suggest that when our multilayered nature gets out of balance, our deep "natural feelings" for our potentialities remain and continue to make compelling demands on our tendencies toward building more balanced cultures.

In the case of male-female bonding, for example, it is the drive toward sex, procreation, and the nurturing of the young that likely provides the "instinctive" imperative for building cultural patterns to fulfill these drives. So humans construct various patterns, taboos, and ways of controlling this instinct to keep it within the specific cultural boundaries required for adaptive "family life." But such patterns have a finite set of variations. Humans have, in fact, tried out a broad range of "rational" or "efficient" ways to "arrange" family life, but the more experimental ones seem to drop away as if they violated something in their underlying nature they cannot comfortably tolerate (e.g., group marriage in hippie communes, attempts to do away with spousal bonding altogether in Marxist communities, or the separation of young children from parents in sleeping arrangements in kibbutzim). The human experience also suggests, however, that the institution of long term monogamous bonding between sexual partners is a somewhat weak "natural tendency" that must compete with other natural tendencies, e.g., the tendency toward sexual experimentation and the desire for compatible interpersonal relationships.

Herein sits perhaps the most difficult problem for the human species—that is, having the insight to adequately foresee, comprehend, and act upon the complex process required to envision, construct, and institutionalize patterns of adaptive culture, which include:

- Imagining and constructing cultural patterns, either unconsciously or through deliberative pragmatic problem-solving or in the dimly felt process of simply making life work
- Apprehending in some vague way the radical shift in understanding and feeling after such patterns have become regularized and unconsciously accepted ("wired") to the point where they seem "natural" and not as arbitrary or stress ridden choices that should be challenged, altered or rejected, and
- Dealing with the tensions that come when older, anachronistic or flawed encultured patterns interfere or distort efforts to create new and more adaptive cultural patterns.

Thus, patterns of culture are "invented" through an integrated and mixed process involving practical intelligence and memory, a less mindful experiential process of trial and error, and/or pure chance, and then transformed over time into stable social institutions. From our point of view, it is preferable to distinguish clearly between a fully encultured institutional pattern (naming it just that) and the underlying vaguely felt feeling of a biological drive or imperative that is the epigenetic basis for inventing the pattern in the first place. The persistent ambiguity of the long-term monogamous marriage rule in Anglo-Saxon western societies mentioned above is, perhaps, an enculturation problem worth reflecting upon. The modern conditions of physical mobility, the economic independence of individuals who commonly work away from home and away from marriage partners, the opportunities for private communication in cars and through electronics all invite sexual and social experimentation outside of marriage. But how to change and legitimate the marriage rule which does tend to provide for the nurturing of children?

A fundamental irony of the human condition is that while humans are seemingly "free" to choose, cast aside, ignore, or repress some of their deep epigenetic "instinctive" tendencies, at least in the short run, or to dogmatically "over-express" some at the expense of others, they also tend to suffer tensions and pathologies. Humans live for periods in the uncertain state of not knowing whether there is something fundamentally flawed in the larger culture itself or whether it is a contradiction built into the human condition which one simply tolerates. In short, humans have the tendency to deny some elements of their nature in what may be the immoderate and/or impulsive pursuit of others. And since cultures are constructed in considerable degree by chance, inventions of human imagination and historical happenstance, they can easily and unknowingly get "out of balance." In short, humans, despite the cleverness provided by their very large neocortex, often lack the "rational" control and foresight to construct long-term full and balanced cultures. That is, for humans "reason" or "rational behavior" is always "understood" within the context of one's existing culture and the deeper logic of that culture—which is less accessible since it commonly extends well beyond one's short-term surface consciousness.

Modern Efforts to Confront the Human Potential for Cultural Error

Only recently have some of us begun to recognize this very ancient aspect of the human condition and realize that to sustain a genuine culture we must maintain a precarious balance among the various layered qualities of our nature. A major example of "getting out of balance" is the conflict for humans who live primarily in organic local villages, towns or native cities confronting societies which are organized around individuals in large product-centered corporate organizations run by centralized elites. As an adaptive mechanism, the draw of human nature toward sustaining local, face-to-face communities (or "bands") is apparently powerful but not determinative.

The evolutionary source of this fateful ambivalence in our nature, i.e., the inability to distinguish the required balance between hyper-primal or hyper-modern patterns, may well be explained partly by Stephen J. Gould's "spandrel" theory. Gould speculates that our species (as other species) may well have undergone particular genetic mutations which provided the biological basis for significant positive adaptations, but these adaptations were accompanied by neutral or even dysfunctional genetic tendencies simply because the latter were biologically hooked to the initial highly adaptive genetic changes.[8] It is not difficult to imagine that the evolution of the human neocortex brought with it powerful capacities for language and problem solving attended by the dysfunctional arrogant illusion that this potentiality would eventually yield the solution to all of our primal "limitations," limitations such as the constraints of time, space, and even mortality. So for millennia before Darwin and well before more sophisticated contemporary evolutionary theories like that of Gould were proposed, humans have from time to time understood the species as possessing an almost unlimited potential for intellectual, technological, spiritual, and aesthetic development approaching perfection.

At this point it is important to remind ourselves that the two dominant meaning systems or cosmologies in modern western societies, Judeo-Christianity and Enlightenment Science, both assume there are in fact basic flaws or errors in the human condition that require correction. At some deep level we are aware of "the problem." For the Judeo-Christian the solution is to reconnect and communicate with some form of deity (through faith, good works, or obedience to holy prescriptions, etc.) and to follow an appropriate path toward redemption. From the point of view of Enlightenment Science, the solution is to embrace strategies of systematic investigation and empirical testing and translate the results into pragmatic technological strategies to correct and overcome various of our human flaws and frailties.

So, in this latter strategy, pain and illness are conquered by medicines, surgery, and finally by reprogramming our DNA. Time is conquered by jet travel and electronic communication. Emotional distress is conquered with therapy, chemicals, and support groups. War and conflict are controlled by rule of law, and techniques for negotiation, governing, and decision-making. Intellectual, artistic, and moral shortcomings are remedied by reconstructing the human psyche through education, systematic training, chemicals, and communication with computers.

At any rate, over the past four hundred years modern humans have become increasingly wedded to the idea that they can and will solve problems that have nettled human intelligence and culture for uncounted millennia. They bathe in a cosmology of hope and progress that leaves them unprepared for the "bad news" that humans, rather than simply being uniquely clever are also uniquely burdened with inadequate tendencies toward sustaining a balance between the primal and modern potentialities of the species.

In a chapter on "Evolutionary Ethnology" written some 50 years ago, David Bidney gives an account of 19th century Anglo-American anthropology including the writings of E.B. Tylor and Edmund Morgan promoting this doctrine of the inevitable progressive evolution of the species, especially the Western "civilized" version of the species. In Bidney's words:

> In general it may be said that Morgan shares Tylor's thesis of the development, or evolution, of civilization from a primitive state of savagery, through a middle state of barbarism to modern civilization. It is similarly presupposed that progress is linear and is measured by setting up nineteenth-century civilization of Europe and America as the norm. By both writers the stages in the evolution of civilization are reckoned by reference to technological achievement.[9]

Thus Tylor and Morgan reckon progress in terms of the modern characteristics of technology and complexity rather than in terms of primal-to-modern balance (or any form of balance).

As indicated above, we think this connection between human nature and progress comes from our modern assumption that science and practical intelligence automatically lead to a higher form of culture. One source of this misunderstanding is, perhaps, the historically conditioned Darwinian premise that practical intelligence in the interest of survival (and adaptation generally) is a metacultural element in human nature designed to critique both existing lower forms of culture and to provide the instrumental resources for humans to invent "higher" conditions of civilized taste and satisfaction. This is, of course, the Lockean misconception. So, modern people imagine that pragmatic science/technology and economics, the premier fields of reasoned knowledge generated by practical intelligence, transcend "culture." Practical intelligence is the "special gift" (along with, perhaps, the connection to a Judeo-Christian God) that generates the reflective knowledge and skills required for survival, comfort, and civilized conduct.

It should also be noted that this issue is seriously confounded by the fact that a number of highly respected and philosophically oriented scientists still embrace modern science and technology as the premier gift of human nature and envisage a time when the findings of science will begin to explain and go beyond the deepest and most perennial of human insights. Thus, according to the speculations of Edward O. Wilson, for example, there will come a time when the lure and lore of any or all of the great religious traditions will be explained and integrated into a scientific corpus of knowledge that transcends the narrower fragmented meanings of culture and tradition. In the words of Wilson:

> ... make no mistake about the power of scientific materialism. It presents the human mind with an alternative mythology that until now has always ... defeated traditional religion. Its narrative form is the epic: the evolution of the universe from the big bang ... to the beginnings of life on earth.... Every part of existence is considered to be obedient to physical laws requiring no external control. The scientist's devotion to parsimony in explanation excludes the divine spirit and other extraneous agents. Most importantly, we have come to the crucial stage in the history of biology when religion itself is subject to the explanations of the natural sciences. As I have tried to show, sociobiology can account for the very origin of mythology by the principle of natural selection acting on the genetically evolving material structure of the human brain.

> If this interpretation is correct, the final decisive edge enjoyed by scientific naturalism will come from its capacity to explain traditional religion [and presumably all phenomena that provide humans with substantial and significant meaning] ... as a wholly material phenomenon.[10]

Contrary to Wilson's optimistic view of the future of the Enlightenment project, we assume that science and practical intelligence are embedded within unconscious non-rational cultural habits and, as Sahlins argues, deep culture very likely guides both our practical actions and our less "rational" customary practices.[11] Despite substantial scientific evidence that our planet and human life may undergo massive disruptions because of global warming caused by the use of automobiles, for example, we are so seduced (encultured) by the use of automobiles in our everyday life that we appear unwilling to act "rationally."

RECENT SHIFTS IN OUR UNDERSTANDING OF HUMAN NATURE IN THE SOCIAL SCIENCES

We should caution the reader that the idea of arguing that there are limits, even somewhat flexible limits, to the rational potentialities of human nature or limits to the ability of humans to overcome their dark atavistic primal tendencies is an intellectually risky business. To utter words like "hard wiring" or to talk about epi "genetic" tendencies in human nature or to say that humans have a "biocultural" nature evokes memories of intolerance and racism even when no mention is made of class, race, gender, or any other subcategory of humanity. Until early in the last century there were indeed sharp battles over speculations in the extent to which biology influenced human behavior, e.g., the Aryan debacle. As indicated above, anthropological and educational schools of thought built theories suggesting that there was a pyramid of progress from savages to modern technological civilization which claimed, at least implicitly, that this "progressive" evolution was to some degree biologically or genetically based.

Between 1900 and 1950, this issue turned decisively against biology and in favor of an ideology which argued for highly malleable and flexible qualities underpinning various cultural conceptions of reality. Degler summarizes the historical mood during this period:

> In [Leslie] White's view there was no longer any point in talking about human nature. "The fallacy or illusion here is, of course," he wrote in 1949, making a play on words, "that what one takes for 'human nature' is not natural at all but cultural.... Five years later, the well-known anthropologist Ashley Montagu echoed White's cultural determinism when he wrote that man "has no instincts, because everything he is and has become he has learned, acquired, from his culture, from the man-made part of the environment, from other human beings."
>
> ... [Robert Ferris, president of the American Sociological Association reported to the association in 1961] "Barriers in many fields of knowledge are falling before the new optimism which is that anybody can learn anything." As a result, he concluded, "we have turned away from the concept of human ability as something fixed in the physiological structure, to that of a flexible and versatile mechanism subject to great improvement." Limits to performance, he admitted, "may eventually be shown to exist, but it seems certain that these are seldom if ever reached in any person, and in most of the population the levels of performance actually reached have virtually no relation to innate capacities."[12]

From Ferris' point of view, Degler reports, "Progress ... was almost unlimited, if only sociologists and other social scientists would devote their minds to the task."[13]

Recently, however, according to Degler there has been a resurgence of interest among social scientists in a more interactive and complex view of the connection between nature and culture.[14] One of the first major studies to which he refers is Harlow's experimental work on rhesus monkeys. Harlow showed that monkeys were attracted more to dummies constructed in the image of a female monkey when they were covered with soft cloth than when they were constructed with wire, even when the latter had a device which provided them with milk. The experiment suggested that the instinctive holistic response of clinging to the mother was more important than the behavioristically conditioned response of being rewarded with food, and it was not difficult to extrapolate this finding to humans.[15]

Degler then notes that there was much controversy over the interpretation of Harlow's work. The "culturalists" adamantly resisted the assumption that "mothering" could be anything other than a socially learned role. The "instinctualists," on the other hand, were much impressed with Harlow's demonstration of the potential role of instinct in primate mothering. Degler then discusses the shift in mood over the next ten years in the attitude of social scientists toward biology as an important part of our explanation for human behavior. He refers to the work in 1961 of two psychologists, Keller and Marian Breland, who had trained six thousand animals from thirty eight different species over several years with standard conditioning techniques. Then, for some strange reason, a large proportion of them began to experience breakdowns in their conditioned behavior. They, in fact, began to revert to the more primal food-seeking activities characteristic of their species. They concluded that "more needed to be known about an animal." Its "instinctive patterns, evolutionary history, and ecological niche" were essential information if it were to be understood.[16]

In another example, Degler notes that in 1972 Mazur and Robertson, a sociologist and psychologist, co-authored a book supporting the significance of ethology to inquiry into human behavior.[17] Degler reemphasizes this shifting mood among social scientists beginning in the 1950s by referring to the work of the highly respected European ethologists, Nikolaus Tinbergin and Konrad Lorenz. As he says:

> By 1971, University of Washington psychologist Robert Lockard was convinced of the merits of Lorenz's finding. "The old concept of an animal as having some degree of intelligence and thus able to

learn nearly anything in accord with its endowment," he observed, "is giving way to the view that natural selection has probably produced rather specific learning mechanisms that correspond to ecological demands."[18]

Degler then quoting Lockard:

But for humans, we would argue, the situation is considerably more complicated because of the critical role that enculturation plays in the adaptation of our species. Because the human nervous system continues to develop rapidly after birth, we, more than most species, are subject to "taking on" an integrated mix of deeply imprinted physiologically- and environmentally-based patterns of adaptation in the early years of life and, with sufficient trauma, throughout life.

These findings have immense importance for our understanding of human consciousness, not to mention their implications for epistemology and moral philosophy.... Because nonverbal expressions of emotion that communicate meaning are processed by ... structures in the brain, such notions as happiness or anger can properly be described as innate ideas.[19]

It is interesting to note how closely Lockard's observations published in 1971 fit with those of Masters published twenty two-years later, yet the tone of Masters' work at the later point in time is one of impatient frustration that the academic community is so slow to catch up on the complicated post-Lockean relationship between human nature and enculturation!

RETURNING TO ERRORS IN HUMAN CULTURE

At this point many modern people are inclined to believe that the idea of unlimited human progress is more self-deception than reality. In support of this loss of faith in progress one has only to take note of such stark historical events as:

- Unexplainably brutal and mindless wars: the American Civil War, World War I, the Viet Nam War
- Genocidal events in the U.S., Turkey, Germany, Bosnia, Africa, etc.
- Mass degradation of the natural environment in search of material abundance and an easier way of life—and full employment

- The inability to reconcile maintaining our deeper artistic and spiritual sensibilities in the face of market forces which measure all value in terms of physical power and material affluence
- The tendency to "fix" human problems through imposed rational management by specialized professionals who are constantly in the process of reforming the system but never seem to get it done
- The grasping at shallow religious slogans and simplistic interpretations of spirituality and soul in an attempt to dull the feelings of emptiness that comes from the dulling of unconscious connections to the larger historical and cosmological context within which we are inevitably imbedded
- The mass murder of over three thousand civilians in the terror attacks on New York City and Washington, D.C. on September 11, 2001, radically transforming the conventional rules of war.

What has seemed to stand in the way of a more realistic recognition of the dangers of misreading human nature and the consequent tendency toward cultural imbalance (whether it be based on biology or deep enculturation) is the fear that "dark" forces of intolerance will somehow use such information to effect oppressive social constraints on vulnerable populations. The history of this concern is related to, among other things, assumptions and practices dealing with social class, racial, ethnic, and gender exploitation and oppression. It tends to thrust humans into the dangerous naturalistic fallacy with a vengeance: If local folk people, for example, seem less complicated than cosmopolitan people, then they are biologically inferior and should be treated as inferiors. If dark people seem inferior to light people, then they should be treated as inferior. If social stratification and hierarchy based on age and gender are common among primates, then humans have little choice but to create and maintain practices consistent with their primate "nature."

We believe, however, that working from a complex human nature/culture view of the human condition is more liberating and less likely to lead to oppression than the inflated modern faith in the flexibility of human nature and the presumed power of formal education and reason to solve all problems of inequity or injustice. The belief that human behavior comes out of the subtle interaction between biology and cultural/social learning carries two messages that the optimistic social engineer does not want to hear. First, the fact that human enculturation is rooted in the interaction between biology and culture leads to the conclusion that such learning may well be sustained over long periods of time, comparable in some sense to "instinct." This then leads to a second conclusion: that the capacity of humans to unlearn or relearn early cultural patterns may be limited for these same biological/cultural reasons and thus resist conscious intentional programatic efforts to move beyond these limits.

This suggests that rapid technological changes invented and implemented by an aggressive, creative, and powerful elite (and the disruptions that accompany such changes) may well lead to negative cultural byproducts which will last as long as these processes of change remain in place. For example, the disruptive and destructive effects of early industrialization and the radical change from personal to impersonal modes of commercial transaction within legal/contractual institutions may undermine the morale of local, more traditional peoples for generations. That is, they may see themselves as always living in an im-personal and un-natural constantly changing world which can never really be trusted. And perhaps without some sense of tradition and continuity—and trust—there can never be a sane society.

One need only look, for example, at the invention of modern schooling. School environments which celebrate the importance of learning verbal/mathematical abstractions and foreign languages may be valued by academics, professionals and managers in order to prepare children for the abstract commercial environments in elite occupations in commerce, business, and the professions. Yet, what if this kind of education leads only to an elite and privileged status for some, and there is no alternative for children with other gifts and ambitions or from other cultures or subcultures except to consign them to office complexes filing information into computers or to work in factories, mines, and warehouses when they fail at school. Their failures are construed by the privileged elite as personal deficiencies rather than failures brought on by a new and alien social system.

The profound differences between professional elite cultures and local native or working class and rural cultures clearly relate to one's ability to succeed in school—that is, in schools fashioned and controlled by an intellectual and commercial elite. It is this ideological scenario that modern elites do not want to face. Hence they deceive themselves into believing that deep cultural learning, such as the traumatic effects of experiencing failure in doing schoolwork, can be unlearned or fixed, or that all humans can learn (or be taught) almost anything at almost any time if teachers will but exert the effort and use appropriate pedagogical methods.[20]

Along with Goldschmidt, we believe there are serious limitations in the capacity of humans to unlearn or relearn culture. When these limitations are reached, humans respond with various pathologies (drug addiction, crime, depression, or the disruption of the immune system) which are both biologically and environmentally based. Children who do not "make it" into elite professional fields of privilege and status seldom get second or third chances when they fail to learn the lessons of the academy or the market place, to say nothing of the farm or the factory.

What happens when specialization and fragmentation overtake a society to the point that only verbally complicated and clever people can function and adapt well to the pace of novelty and change generated by innovative engineers? And what happens to the more primal qualities of life for everyone under these circumstances? Although humans have an incredible capacity to plan, to organize, to create meaning in their social and technical world, there is a point at which human social structures and meanings become fragmented beyond most people's ability to cope. The more humans stand apart from their social and natural environment and ponder its meaning, whether in think tanks, retreats, universities or simply in street corner bull sessions, the more they are haunted by a sense that they are separated from the texture of their immediate reality and cast into a tangled set of incoherent abstractions.

SUMMARY

Currently there seems to be a glimmer of cautious realism emerging in many quarters by those of us who see amelioration of the human condition as unlikely to come from self-help projects, or an all-or-nothing redemption from sin, or as a straightforward educational project by pragmatic science, social science, and technology to complete the Enlightenment vision of progress and perfection. The way toward cultural balance may require that humans give up trying to "progress" toward more enlightened solutions (upward and onward, as it were) and reflect and act more on the larger cultural errors in which we have become mired. Rather we need a longer time perspective and a more forgiving and patient feeling toward the human condition. For there is no "solution" or scientific formula which will tell us how to modify and construct cultural institutions that maintain the delicate balance among competing potentialities of "human nature."

The most hopeful antidote for these false promises, perhaps, requires that we pay attention to both contemporary as well as anthropolgical/ archeological and historical records which describe various more or less successful cultural patterns humans have created and destroyed over the past centuries. For it is likely that it is this study of multiple and comparative ways of human life and culture which may provide rich, relevant, and powerful sources of insight into the limits of our human nature/culture and the possibilities for what we have referred to as "genuine culture." But it will help to begin from what are hopefully somewhat plausible premises in how we understand human nature.

NOTES

1. Roger Masters, *Beyond Relativism* (Hanover, NH: University Press of New England, 1993), 119.

2. Ibid., 118-119.

3. Ibid., 119-120.

4. Ibid., 12.

5. Ibid., 121-122.

6. Ibid., 142.

7. Ibid.

8. Stephen J. Gould, "The Pleasures of Pluralism," *The New York Review of Books*, XLIV, (11), June 26, 1997, 47.

9. Bidney, *Theoretical Anthropology*, 209-210.

10. E. O. Wilson, *On Human Nature* (Cambridge, MA: Harvard University Press, 1978), 192.

11. Marshall Sahlins, *Culture and Practical Reason* (Chicago: University of Chicago Press, 1976), 205-217.

12. Carl N. Degler, *In Search of Human Nature* (New York: Oxford University Press, 1991), 209-210.

13. Ibid., 210.

14. The "nature-nature" controversy over the interpretation of which should be given priority as a major determinant of human behavior has and still is very much alive , although currently the interaction theory now seems most compelling. Beneath whatever empirical evidence is generated on either side, however, there always appears to be deeply felt ideological assumptions that put their spin on the findings of social science. Liberals fear that "instinctivism" will be used to justify stratifying and oppressing members of a society who may be iden-

tified as "inferior" by such factors as race, ethnicity, test scores, etc. Those who favor genetic explations tend to down grade the power of social and cultural institutions to stratify or equalize individuals and accept the inevitable and permanent biological inequality of humans in any society.

15. Ibid., 222.

16. Ibid., 224, fn. 12.

17. Allan Mazur & Leon S. Robertson, *Biology and Social Behavior* (New York: Free Press, 1972).

18. Degler, 228 (for Lockard see 370, n 20).

19. Ibid., 143.

20. Note Bruner's oft quoted pronouncement to this effect in *The Process of Education*, and the later work of Lee Shulman with its assumptions about the inflated potential of clever pedagogy and teacher knowledge to teach almost anything.

CHAPTER SEVEN

Individual, Group, and Cultural Diversity

While humans give the appearance of sharing a common overall potentiality in their nature, apparently having the same deep structures in their various languages and symbols and similar capacities for enculturation and socialization, the specific cultural patterns actualized across societies are markedly different. Just as significant as these cultural differences is the fact that we observe substantially different patterns of behavior and meaning among separate subgroups and individuals within a single society—differences related to such factors as age, gender, temperament, talent, ethnicity, and social status. Of course, this works two ways. Two individuals from very different cultures, for example, may appear more alike because of shared gender, age, and temperament. And likewise, two individuals within the same culture may be strikingly different because of variations in gender, temperament, and subgroup enculturation. So it is apparent that human societies have the capacity to enculture individuals and groups within a society in very different ways.

Each society is, in fact, made up of diverse individuals or subgroups sharing *some* overall cultural patterns at a general level but differing substantially at more specific levels. We know that individuals and subgroups may speak different dialects or even different languages, have different and varied conceptions of family life, friendship, the meaning of success and the relative importance of vocations which, in some degree, represent such success.

Among modern cosmopolitan people, for example, the separate individual is commonly encultured as the significant social or moral unit. Family, group, and corporate social forms tend to be seen as temporary pragmatic arrangements used to achieve certain goals. This separate individual is seen as having (or working to have) certain universal human characteristics, e.g., a sense of independence, rationality, a dualistic self-other world view of reality, etc. Modern people are inclined to see this individualistic way of looking at the world as appropriate not only for "modern" societies and cultures, but as perhaps essential and even universal—as the appropriate moral unit for all societies.

Some close local societies or groups , on the other hand, often understand and experience the unit of human society as grounded in the life of the family or group or community.[1] In *The Lonely Crowd* Riesman considers this issue historically and suggests that the European Middle Ages was a period in which most people would be characterized as "tradition directed." As he says, "the term tradition directed refers to a common element, not only among the people of precapitalist Europe but also among such enormously different types of people as Hindus and Hopi Indians, Zulus and Chinese, North Africans Arabs and Balinese." Riesman feels secure in this analysis since, as he says, so many writers have found a similar unity amid diversity, a unity they express in such terms as "folk society" (as against "civilization"), a "status society" (as against a "contract society"), a"Gemeinschaft" as against "Gesellschaft" and so on.[2]

This distinction between what might be called the moral unit of social reality, we would argue, revolves around phenomena related to 1) social bonding, 2) the socio-cultural structures or "places" available for such bonding, e.g., families, villages, cities, and 3) the deep constructions of meaning and reality that come out of these circumstances. In this chapter we discuss sources of both individual and group diversity and the connection between the two. We explore, for example, the issue of whether or not "natural" sources of individual difference such as age, gender, temperament and talent, etc. are understood and treated differently within local communal societies as opposed to modern contract societies.

PRIMAL PATTERNS OF
SOCIAL STRUCTURE AND BONDING

We assume that human societies enculture or "fix" (favor or suppress) various kinds of individual behaviors related to such characteristics as age, gender, temperament, physical strength, and talent. Groups and societies then construct coherent socio-cultural patterns and roles to accommodate this diversity. We assume that societies construct social roles within forms such as spousal units, restricted and extended families, clans, mutual aid societies, villages, native towns and cities, and corporate-commercial cities an, thus, must enculture and socialize humans to fill the variety of roles required to make these varied social forms function. In short, we are arguing that diversity within society is useful, necessary, and adaptive so long as the cultural patterns required of societies, groups, or individuals are more or less consistent with and complement our natural temperamental resources. When individual natural tendencies are ignored and individuals or groups are enculatured only for the pragmatic convenience of dominant groups within society or out of blind respect for an existing tradition, the result may well be stress and systematic oppression of those who are coerced and "used" in this way.

Yet, for diversity to be found "useful" it must somehow fit into sources of bonding and the pragmatic requirements of a society. This point is illustrated in Elman Service's speculative account of the early development of families in human groups:

> We cannot know, nor even make a guess, about the size of the proto-human hordes or troops. It is reasonable, however, to assume that they included several females and their offspring and more than one male simply because all primate groups which forage in ecological circumstances similar to those of the Australopithecenes are of that sort.... The human nuclear family ... was formed when the total group created the reciprocal marriage rule, making such marriages not occasional ... but regular between themselves and one or more other groups. The family then crystallized as a relatively stable heterosexual pairing of adults in some consistent association with each other and their offspring.... The total exogamous group now became a part-society, inasmuch as some of its former members—its married females—were living in the other group or groups and forms of friendship, alliance, and cooperation now existed among these groups. Within the exogamous groups, a nucleus of cooperating males ("brothers") hunted and defended the camp.[3]

From Service's description it seems likely that early peoples commonly shared a self-in-community consciousness. Then, as new capacities for bonding evolved in the human nervous system, potentialities were created for both a variety and complexity of individual personalities. For example, in order to evolve a species pattern for the more complex practice of exogamous or outgroup marriage, men and women would have to be willing to leave a local place in which they had grown up and begin a spousal and family relationship with a group of relative strangers in an unfamiliar place. Presumably this "willingness" to relocate and bond in a spousal unit with quasi-strangers came about with the development of the restriction on sexual bonding between relatives and close friends that we now know as the incest taboo.

This requires a sorting out process in which social units will fit the "natural" diverse tendencies of individual people available to the species or a subset of the species. This leads us to explore, for example, the process that channeled the risk-taking temperaments of young males into institutionalized war, which required that they be willing to die in the process of killing other humans; or the process that encouraged some humans to express their "natural" potential toward sadism making possible the institution of slavery such that some people dominated and even brutalized others to control them. In these more extreme examples, one never knows, even today, whether or not individuals or groups are following the bent of their temperamental inclination or whether they are being coerced into "unnatural" actions they would rather avoid.

This enculturation of temperamentally diverse individuals to function in specialized roles within a society results in what Fromm and Riesman see as differential "social character types." Social character types are produced through a combination of forces within human nature, including the constitutional diversity inherent in the species, the early enculturation and socialization process of small children which further fixes and refines constitutional diversity, and finally the social and pragmatic pressures within the actions of everyday life. Following the work of Fromm, Riesman lays out the following line of reasoning for the use of the term "social character structure or type:"

> Let us begin by defining *character structure* as the more or less permanent, socially and historically conditioned organization of an individual's drives and satisfactions. The term as thus defined is *less inclusive* than "personality," the word which in current usage denotes the total self, with its inherited temperament and talents, its biological as well as psychological component, its evanescent as well as more or less permanent attributes.[4] My reason for selecting from this complex the abstraction called "character" is that ... I propose to deal with those components of personality that also play the

principal role in *the maintenance of social forms*—those that are *learned* in the lifelong process of socialization.

Riesman then goes on to note that once we begin to speak of character types as permanent attributes of a society, there is the inevitable connection to groups or subgroups within society which may enculture and institutionalize common types of character. As he says, when we speak of social character this allows us also to "speak elliptically but meaningfully of the character of classes, groups, regions, and nations."[5]

One may ask, of course, why humans might evolve in the direction of creating diverse social character types? Why didn't nature (or God or fate or natural selection) create humans as relatively constant and homogeneous beings so that there would be less potential for misunderstanding and conflict in the ways they experience their shared social lives? Fromm responds to this question directly:

> In order that any society may function well, its members must acquire the kind of character that makes them *want* to act in the way they *have* to act as members of the society or of a special class within it. They have to *desire* what objectively is *necessary* for them to do. *Outer force* is replaced by *inner compulsion*, and by the particular kind of human energy which is channeled into character traits.[6]

But while this "inner compulsion" is capable of preparing people for specialized roles which they more willingly undertake, as Riesman notes, it "serves not only to limit choice but also to channel action by foreclosing some of the otherwise limitless behavior choices of human beings."[7] He then adds a serious reservation regarding social character as a positive form of human adaptation.... "Character and culture can overreach themselves and thus swallow up all of life in enterprises whose only virtue is that they are shared."[8]

Along with Riesman's general caution that enculturation can lead to dysfunctional or suffocating conformity for whole cultures as well as for subgroups and individuals, there is the issue of the extent to which some individuals and subgroups within a single society can unknowingly or deliberately socialize others in selfish, exploitative, and destructive ways—ways that ignore natural humane considerations for the temperamental tendencies of the other.

Fromm and Maccoby use this concept of "social character" in a study reviewed later in this chapter as theoretical grounding for this understanding of the process of exploitative social class stratification. For him, the central elements of social character evolve from a person's initial endowment, the deep enculturation of early childhood experience, and the later pressures of social and economic coping. In his words:

> By constitution (or endowment) we mean more than just temperament in the classic sense. Rather, we refer to the basic structure of personality. Relationships in the family either help bring out this structure to its best fruition, or they tend to distort it. Just as a pear seed cannot produce an apple tree, but only better or worse pear trees, depending on the conditions of the soil, climate, so a child can only develop his given potential structure in the most harmonious vital form or in a negative form. For instance, a highly sensitive and unaggressive child may become, under favorable influences, an introspective, artistic, and spiritual-minded person. Under the influence of cold and authoritarian parents, the same child is likely to become intimidated, frightened, and resentful, with the result that he wastes most of his energy by not being able to be what he potentially is.... To be sure, one can condition a child by rewards and punishments, by manipulating his anxiety, to become what he is not, but the result will be inner conflict, waste of energy, lack of joy, in many cases neurosis, and sometimes psychosis.[9]

The idea of "social character" thus suggests that there are both constructive and destructive variations in the way individuals with different inherent temperaments respond to various forms of child rearing and later socio-economic and occupational socialization. As they say, "A serf, a free peasant, an industrial worker in the 19th century, and one in an automated society, an independent entrepreneur of the 19th century, and an industrial manager of the 20th century have different functions to fulfill."[10] Modern industrial workers have to be disciplined and punctual; the 19th century bourgeoisie have to be parsimonious, individualistic, and self-reliant. The point is that the demands of specific social roles can be consistent or inconsistent with the social character of people required to meet these demands.

The human potentiality for diverse social character types is important to our evolving theory of genuine culture since we assume that a balanced or holistic society is one that supports a wide variety of social character types and provides an equally extensive array of roles and places in which diverse humans can express their potential. Thus, the society which maintains a balanced number of small family farms, local neighborhood businesses and schools, along with small corporations is likely to accommodate a great diversity of people with various aptitudes and personalities. By ignoring the balance across primal to modern dimensions, a culture may press toward conformity to only two or three social types, e.g., the exploiters and the exploited, resulting in the development of inhumane and destructive social relationships.

One example of the dominance of modern progressive ideology over other more communal variations is the common school, which stresses rigorous academic settings and gives little leeway for differential temperaments and talents among children. All children, regardless of talent or inclination are required to spend the better part of the day for ten to twelve years attempting to master the finely honed skills of reading abstract academic literature, writing complex expository prose, and learning algebra, geometry and calculus within a competitive educational environment. Coal mining is another related example. In the interest of efficiency and reliability of energy production, mills and factories which once ran on direct water power changed to steam, which uses massive amounts of coal. Thereafter, we coerced or socialized large numbers of workers to seek fulfillment and affirmation in a life which required them to work for one third of their lives in dark caverns under the earth.

Fromm and Maccoby assume that humans are basically productive life-affirming creatures capable of transforming their surroundings into the materials, relationships, and ideas required to sustain and savor human life. As they say, "What matters in the productive attitude is not its particular object, which may be people, nature, or things, but rather the whole approach. The productive orientation is rooted in the love of life."[11] Following this optimistic goal for humans Fromm and Maccoby list three specific types of social character which may be expressed in both positive and negative ways, as well as being expressed in multiple combinations: a) the receptive character orientation, b) the exploitative character orientation, and c) the hoarding character orientation.[12] (See Table 4 below for a summary of these types described in both positive and negative terms.)

Table 4. Fromm's Theory of Character Orientations[13]	
Receptive Orientation (Accepting)	
Positive Aspect	Negative Aspect
accepting	passive, without initiative
responsive	opinionless, characterless
devoted	submissive
modest	without pride
charming	parasitical
adaptable	unprincipled
socially adjusted	servile, without self-confidence
idealistic	unrealistic
sensitive	cowardly
polite	spineless
optimistic	wishful thinking
trusting	gullible
tender	sentimental
Exploitative Orientation (Taking)	
Positive Aspect	Negative Aspect
active	exploitative
able to take initiative	aggressive
able to make claims	egocentric
proud	conceited
impulsive	rash
self- confident	arrogant
captivating	seducing

Table 4. Fromm's Theory of Character Orientations, Continued	
Hoarding Orientation (Preserving)	
Positive Aspect	Negative Aspect
practical	unimaginative
economical	stingy
careful	suspicious
reserved	cold
patient	lethargic
cautious	anxious
steadfast, tenacious	stubborn
imperturbable	indolent
composed under stress	inert
orderly	pedantic
methodical	obsessional
loyal	possessive

SOCIAL CHARACTER TYPES
WITHIN TWO VILLAGE SOCIETIES

In summary, we see an important connection between the recognition of social character as a central aspect of human diversity and what we have called genuine culture, i.e., a culture which functions within the reasonable capabilities of our human nature. From this point of view, one aspect of genuine culture is the extent to which the natural range of diverse endowments related to age, gender, temperament, etc., can be encultured as positive social character types so that the various qualities of our humanity can be expressed in positive and adaptive ways. This living out of adaptive roles, we argue, also requires an adequate array of primal-to-middle familial and local places in the balanced center (what we will later describe as the "vital center") as well as modern corporate places. It also relates directly to the adequacy and availability of vocations, multiple forms of bonding, and multiple forms of meaning which we discuss later in Chapter Eleven as criteria for genuine culture. Our theory suggests that a sufficiently complex or "full" set of roles, places and cultural patterns are required to accommodate the diverse kinds of humans we find in any complex society.

Below we review two studies which illustrate ways of dealing with diversity within society. Herbert Gans' study in the Old West End of Boston describes a working class Italian urban community in which the dominant form of bonding is what he calls a "person centered orientation," which is what we have described as "self-in-community." This community is quite different from the cosmopolitan environment that surrounds it. Although the cultural norm is more "village-like" and yields a relatively adaptive form of life for its inhabitants, the Old West End of Boston is seen by the dominant modern upper middle class people around it as "poor" and "slum-like." And while its people do not see themselves as living in poverty or deeply stressed, it is portrayed by its more affluent neighbors as somehow *not* a "good" place to live.

In the second study, Fromm and Maccoby focus on the quality of life in a once traditional agricultural Mexican village in transition toward becoming a "modern" center of commercial agriculture. They elaborate the relationship between social character types as an explanation of social class position and mobility, and the differences in quality of life various members of the community experience. Much of their initial theory has already been introduced above.

GANS' STUDY OF URBAN VILLAGERS AND THE PERSON-CENTERED CHARACTER ORIENTATION

The radically different experiential quality of consciousness that goes with the distinction between the "self-in-community" and the "individual-in-society" orientations is dramatically illustrated in Gans' study of urban villagers carried out in the early 1950s.[14] Gans discovered that the Italian immigrants who lived in the Old West End neighborhood of Boston tended to have highly sociable inward-looking lives in which they related to friends and small peer groups. Membership within the peer group was based primarily on kinship—brothers, sisters, cousins, spouses and in-laws, as well as godparents and long-term friends. The peer groups met regularly in one another's kitchens and living rooms or apartments to discuss events at work, sports, and, for women, housekeeping, child care, and topics relevant to home care. Only occasionally were politics or controversial issues a topic of conversation. The conversations were long, extending for hours, where the primary goal was to keep the conversation going, and often involved stories and anecdotes about their lives.

Group members were almost never alone. As Gans notes, "for most West Enders, people have been trained from childhood to function solely within the group, being alone brings discomfort and ultimately fear."[15] Housewives would get through their work quickly so they could visit. One boy expressed fear of going to prison mainly because he would be separated from friends and family.

Gans then clarifies the particular kind of "individuality" characteristic of these West Enders, lest we think that they were totally submerged within the peer group. As he says:

> Although the peer group is the most important entity in the West Ender's life, he is not merely a robot whose actions are determined by the group or the cultural tradition. In fact, peer group life in many ways is just the opposite of the cohesive and tightly-knit group that has served as a model for descriptions of primary relations in other societies. It is a spirited competition of individuals 'jockeying' for respect, power, and status.... Peer group members act as if they were held together by ties of rubber, which they alternately stretch and relax, but rarely break.[16]

Gans notes that social relationships within the peer group follow a narrow path between individualistic display and strictly enforced social control. "The group is set up to provide its members with an opportunity for displaying, expressing, and acting out their individuality, as long as this does not become too extreme" (88).

In his subsequent analysis Gans compares the group-individual relationship of West Enders with the cosmopolitan upper middle class— people we would describe as modern. Here he makes a distinction between what he calls an object-oriented versus a person-oriented culture. As he says, the distinction is best understood in terms of differences in aspirations. The object-oriented (modern) person is able to conceptualize in a self-conscious and deliberate manner various and diverse aspirations.

Object-oriented individualism involves striving toward the achievement of an "object." This may be a moral object, for exam-

> ple, a principle; an ideological object, such as "understanding;" a material object, such as a level of income; a cultural object, such as a style of life; or a social object, such as a career or status position. Although people strive after a variety of objects, they tend to verbalize ideological and moral ones more than material or social ones. (89)

West Enders have difficulty understanding object-oriented behavior. They have difficulty imagining people organizing group activities which have some common overall goal that transcends the continuity or integrity of their familistic peer group. They have difficulty understanding the nature of "administrative procedure and the rules of bureaucratic government" (95). These can be explained "only by concepts based on individual motivation and morality, for example, by honesty, selfishness, and greed." Life is personalized so that often the outside world is seen as "people against people," the latter being the West Enders who feel exploited (which they often were). This also makes it difficult for them to enter into "secondary relationships" with professional people, business people, or government officials. They live in a peer-oriented primary and middle-level group world in which human bonding is almost always communal and familistic (95).

As Gans adds, "[I]n order to participate in [a relatively purposeful impersonal group as modern people do] the individual must develop some detachment and self-consciousness about his activities and about himself, which leads to the creation of [an outer] self-image.... [This allows] the individual to confront new kinds of people and new experiences without too much difficulty or feeling of threat" (98). That is, one learns to deal with the outer world by presenting a controlled outer self-image which allows him or her to protect the inner-ego, which remains private.

In a summary statement, Gans compares the modern "object-oriented" middle class person with the first and second generation Italian-American "person-oriented" old West Ender:

> ... The modern middle class object-oriented individual can be described as having a dualistic self, which allows him to be sensitive to the actions of others as they become part of himself. He is able to be self-conscious and develops a self-image or sense of identity. When the communication process between "I" and "me" is disturbed, he becomes self-centered. The person-oriented type, on the

other hand, develops a monistic self, which makes it difficult for the individual to differentiate between his own and others' view of him. The lack of a clear self-image encourages and requires display. Thus the communication process between the "I" and other people is limited as much as possible to routine behavior among intimately known people....

In describing the West Ender as lacking a self-image or sense of identity, I do not mean to suggest that he feels himself to be impaired, for he moves in a society in which self-consciousness is not so urgent. He is at a disadvantage only if and when social conditions force him to become a full participant in the outside world, and he can protect himself from it by suspicion and rejection, as well as by the support he can get from the peer group society.

Conversely, from a different value position, an object-oriented person could be described as impaired, because he lacks such abilities as belonging totally to a group, retaining childhood friends, and expressing individuality among such people. He would also find it difficult to exist in a peer group society, since it pursues so few activities aimed at object-goals. Needless to say, he is not asked to do so. (100-102)

From this analysis, Gans is able to extrapolate his findings to the character types of social classes in America of the 1950s. He describes the "lower class" or "underclass" as being faced with such an enormous economic press that human survival itself seems at stake. This results in a high degree of individuated self-interest, except for the primary mother-child bond which may still be maintained. The idea of stable, organized work involving individual action and responsibility seems remote since it is rarely available. The family is under attack, on the verge of disintegration, or has already fallen apart.

In the "working class" (the socio-economic location of Gans' urban villagers), the family plays a dominant role; major life satisfaction is gained through social life with relatives and friends. Local personalistic relationships are central to the meaning of life. The larger society "outside" (representing universalistic institutions such as the school, police, landlords, merchants, social workers, professionals) is viewed with fear and suspicion. Stable work is sought as a means of survival, as a necessary evil, not as intrinsically meaningful.

In the striving middle class the family is also central and dominant, but is seen as a vehicle for mobility into higher strata of society. Work is seen as a series of stepping stones to improve family life and encourage the mobility aspirations for children. Education or work may or may not be intrinsically satisfying, but they are significant so long as they are materially rewarding.

In the upper-middle classes, especially the professional classes, work and education are seen as integral to meaningful personal development and a fully actualized life. The family is construed as only one, albeit the first, context within which this development is to occur. Life is seen as intensely progressive and one moves forward from family to education on the rungs of educational and vocational ladders leading one to significant material and professional or business "success."

SOCIAL CHARACTER TYPES AND SOCIAL CLASS WITHIN A MODERNIZING MEXICAN VILLAGE

The various ideologies and qualities of experience presented in Gans' social class characterizations above are born out in Fromm and Maccoby's study of Mexican villagers undergoing the transition from peasantry to commercial farming. Fromm and Maccoby, like Gans, discover that there are fundamental differences in how individuals from different socio-economic strata experience the social world. As described above, these differences are framed in Fromm's theory of "social character types"—the receptive type, the exploitative type, and the hoarding type.[17]

When Fromm and Maccoby apply systematic assessments of these social character types to villagers, they discover significant relationships between social character and socio-economic and cultural variables. In a summary of findings, they discover that "each main character type is molded by and adaptive to distinctive socioeconomic conditions." More specifically, a) the receptive character has been formed in the conditions of the hacienda or plantation-type farm worked mainly by poor laborers; b) the productive-hoarding characters have adapted themselves to traditional forms of small-scale agriculture; and c) the productive-exploitative character has adapted to the new commercial industrializing society and to capitalism.

The values, the ideology of the receptive villager are fatalistic and submissive with the tendency to idealize both authority and the

mother. These values supported the hacienda system. The productive-hoarding peasant values independence, responsibility, traditional relations of respect, and patriarchy, all of which support the
social organization of the free village. The productive-exploitative
villagers have the values of progress through schools and new
technology and social mobility, which support the new industrial
system. (124-125)

They conclude with a rather striking observation which, although not
directly related to their character analysis, bears more generally on our
thesis. They note that there is something about this Mexican village
which contrasts sharply with earlier medieval peasant villages. Referring to the historical accounts of Sombert, Tawney, and Weber, they
note that "the society of the medieval peasant was much more life centered than the material centered [Mexican] village society, which is
mainly oriented to monetary gain" (120).

In the medieval peasant society at its best, economic motives were
suspect, unlike the [modern Mexican] village society, where these
[economic] values determine the allocation of priorities and over-
shadow values of charity and personal salvation. Both in medieval
society and among Mayan peasants described by Redfield, work is
meant to be spiritually satisfying. In the [modern Mexican] village,
work is seen by all but the most productive individuals as a necessary evil and as a means for [personal] gain. (120)

We would here note the similarity of Fromm and Maccoby's Mexican villagers' view of the significance of work with that of Gans' description of
the American working class: Both see work only as a necessary evil,
which is fundamentally different from the view of upper middle class
thoroughly modern people.

Our interpretation is that the social character of these various
socio-economic groups or cohorts in Fromm and Maccoby's Mexican village are profoundly affected by the transition to modernity which has
transformed their consciousness from one of self-in-community within a
larger spiritual framework to one of individual-in-corporate society
within a secular materialistic framework. The transition is represented
in the four societal forms or types of place that dominate the society: the
traditional family, the hacienda, the free village, and the corporate market. Clearly the feudalistic hacienda and the corporate market tend to
yield significant benefits to a relatively small number of people with ex-

ploitative character types as opposed to those with more conservative and cautious, receptive and hoarding orientations. These societal places, with their stress on hierarchy and individualism, as opposed to communal collaboration, then tend to press people with non-exploitative orientations into conditions of stress and poverty.[18]

RECONSIDERING MODERN ASSUMPTIONS ABOUT THE DEPTH AND SIGNIFICANCE OF DIVERSITY

Conceivably Gans' application of the more communal person-oriented character type described in the Old West End Italian neighborhood to issues of ethnicity and social class and Fromm and Maccoby's application of three social character types to social class mobility and exploitation in the Mexican Village would also apply to characteristics related to race, ethnicity, and religion. Our hunch is that people we might roughly characterize as belonging to a cosmopolitan elite (e.g., upper level professionals) might well label such group characteristics as reflecting relatively "thin" or minor cultural differences. As indicated by Gans' study, social service professionals commonly assumed that when differences are related to income status and low exposure to high-culture experiences (e.g., books, museums, music, etc.) these "shortcomings" can and should be changed, and that such change is not all that difficult or profound. The social institutions associated with media, formal education, contact with social workers, job training, etc. will do the trick. But as Gans observes, when cosmopolitan outsiders such as teachers, psychologists, guidance counselors, and ministers intervene in the lives of children whose early family experience socialized them into fiercely local self-in-community orientations, the outside care givers often wonder at the difficulty of changing their "dysfunctional non-progressive or parochial ways." It is, moreover, as Gans notes, also risky for members of communities like the Old West End of Boston to trust the alien, more affluent outsider. In this instance, for example, the mistrust was born out by the fact that it was the "do gooder" elite professionals and bureaucrats who finally managed to have the old "slum" neighborhood bulldozed, the locals displaced, moved out, and the buildings replaced by high rise luxury apartments.

We understand that the research of Gans and Fromm and Maccoby is at best only suggestive. It is, nonetheless, especially interesting because it reveals a much more complicated (and perhaps realistic) cultural state-

ment of the deep connection between communal identity and consciousness, and the loss of diverse roles consistent with this consciousness when
modernization comes. The new high rise apartments in the Old West End
that replaced the old frame triple deckers housed very private small family units and destroyed the diverse communal social fabric of this part of
the city. The reason for framing the meaning of "genuine" or "balanced"
culture so as to take into account face-to-face middle level social settings
as the Old West End is to accommodate a common and dominant aspect
of many non-privileged and vulnerable local subcultures.

Our own interpretation suggests that there are fundamental differences in the quality of deep unconscious experience encultured within
modern subcultural cohorts, (e.g., cohorts of peoples representing different social classes, ethnicities, races, religions, or "places") resulting
from complex interactions among one's basic temperament, early childhood experience, and the press of coping within an exploitative, strati-
fied, hierarchical corporate social class system. From this point of view,
being local and poor is likely to persist as long as the price for changing
requires that one's lifelong social character must also change from seeing
one's life as self-in-community to seeing one's life as an autonomous, independent, mobile individual.

We argue that there must be middle-level mediating institutions, as
well as modern corporate institutions and places, in order for there to be
an adequate range of roles or vocations or "ways of being" to accommodate the breadth and diversity of types of social character. We also argue
that a major factor which can make a role or vocation congenial is not
only its middle level place, but the quality of bonding that goes with it—
qualities that tie diverse people together within a common setting. This
takes us back to Service's description of the significant primal bonds that
held early humans together. We would speculate that the archetypal
communitarian consciousness of many modern humans did not suddenly vanish with the industrial revolution and the market economy. It
did not vanish for the Old West End Italian community of Boston. It did
not vanish for most of the local peasant-farmers in Fromm and
Maccoby's Mexican village. We suggest that it is still present in the loneliness and longing of many privileged modern people (We would note
the title of Riesman's classic study already mentioned called *The Lonely
Crowd*.) The basic problem is that such a communal consciousness makes
individuals vulnerable to stress and exploitation when forced to work

within settings—even village settings—controlled by those with an individualistic, exploitative, object-centered consciousness. The question is how to change the power structure from one of individual self-interest to one of communal caring to relieve people from this threat of exploitation.

ANALYSIS OF THE TWO SOCIETIES: EXPLOITATIVE OR BALANCED

Thus far we have discussed the relationship between *social character* and the availability of various societal forms or places in which people with diverse social character types might play out complementary (rather than competitive) positive social roles. In addition to these theories, there are a variety of other theoretical schemes dealing with diverse temperaments developed mostly by individually oriented psychologists—the Piagetian theory of epistemological "progress," the Kohlbergian cognitive moral stage theory, Briggs and Myers' (Jung's) personality types, Gardiner's "frames of mind" or multiple intelligences—all of which describe significant aspects of human diversity. All of these clinicians or scholars and their followers see themselves as pragmatic scientists. Here, however, we are less concerned with explaining or predicting individual human behavior based on epistemological stages, moral stages, character traits, or types of intelligence. Rather, we are exploring a deep and intuitive connection between individual and group diversity and the kinds of communal or social settings that allow for the positive, multiple, and/or interdependent expressions of this diversity.

We assume that in a balanced or genuine culture one's social character will be adequate to deal with the various qualities of bonding, vocational choice, and coping and that various settings will be available to make such choices possible. This is a premise, not an hypothesis to be proven. Therefore, the culture will naturally include people whose social characters are most effective as "householders," villagers, professionals, corporate merchants, managers, etc. This observation is consistent with the way Fromm and Maccoby frame the historical relationship between social character, the quality of social bonding, and socio-economic privilege or oppression. They talk, for example, about the new corporate merchant class that developed in 17th and 18th century Europe and America as having a "hoarding-productive" social character. This social character was "adapted to the need for capital accumulation (rather than consumption), personal industriousness, sobriety, the obsessional drive for work, and the absence of compassion. Only those who shared a sub-stantial quality of this 'obsessional-hoarding-productive' character syn-drome could become successful under the new conditions of developing capitalism."[19] What they do not say (and we would add) is that members of this new early developing merchant industrial class had a risk-taking exploitative element in their character that made them venture beyond their village or native city into the world of strangers in search of objects, products, and wealth for their own self-interest and profit.

At this point we would claim that for society to be balanced and nur-turing it must honor a broad range of temperaments and consequent so-cial character types. The self-in-community solution to the presence of what Fromm and Maccoby call "non-productive" receptive or hoarding character types is, in most cases, not coercive reenculturation or resocialization so that everyone will become progressive, upwardly mo-bile, affluent, modern, exploitative, and middle class. It is the creative movement toward a culture which will include places and environments that have productive roles for the natural diversity of humans that are in-cluded within our species.

Beginning with this approach, one can envision two types of society. The first is a social status system based on utilitarian and meritocratic considerations with external controls that maintain a decent minimal standard of living for those people with dysfunctional non-productive social character types. In such a system, a small economically successful elite makes the basic decisions. The elite consists of those with produc-tive-exploitative or productive-marketing social character types, or those lucky enough to be born to privilege, or to stumble into it. And it is these successful types who will decide how the "deficient" or unsuccess-ful people can be rehabilitated or accommodated. This, of course, is the commercial industrial corporate model with special institutions to pre-vent untoward human suffering for people with those character types who cannot cope with this system.

The second kind of society—which we advocate—would consist of a balance among different levels of societal forms and places. These might include households and small neighborhood guilds with local cottage industries, local village stores, restaurants and shops, and the corporate entities of local native cities with the responsibility for maintaining a ser-vice infrastructure, providing schools and health care for local people, and providing for those who have difficulty coping in the market economy. Within these local institutions, everyone's talents would hopefully be used and their needs would be known and accounted for.

Within this second system, people who want to compete on a strictly meritocratic basis in the cosmopolitan commercial industrial market-place would be welcome to do so. But beyond this an equally valued culture might be nurtured which gives priority and preference to the needs of community and the particular talents and needs of local people who live there. This would require, of course, that the basic necessities within the local place be regulated in some way such that the value of sustaining the local and the particular were counted above the values determined by the cosmopolitan market. Concepts like "modest and affordable housing" and "the minimum wage required to stay above the poverty line" would have to be translated into governmental policies of the native city. And the native city itself would have to become a critical institution much as the earlier city-state of the late medieval period. This harks back, we might add, to the great experiment in pluralistic democracy envisioned by Jefferson two centuries ago and restated below by Dewey:

> … In his theoretical writings chief importance is attached to local self-governing units in something like the New England town meeting plan. His project for general political organization on the basis of small units, small enough so that all its members could have direct communication with one another and take care of all community affairs was never acted upon. It never received attention in the press of immediate practical problems. But without forcing the significance of this plan, one may find in it an indication of one of the most serious of present problems regarding democracy.
>
> I spoke earlier of the way in which individuals at present find themselves in the grip of immense forces whose workings and consequences they have no power of affecting. The situation calls emphatic attention to the need for face-to-face associations, whose interactions with one another may offset if not control the dread impersonality of the sweep of present forces.
>
> … I venture to quote words written [by myself] some years ago: 'Evils which are uncritically and indiscriminately laid at the door of industrialism and democracy, might, with greater intelligence, be referred to the dislocation and unsettlement of local communities. Vital and thorough attachments are bred only in the intimacy

of an intercourse which is of necessity restricted in range.... Is it possible to restore the reality of the less communal organizations and to penetrate and saturate their members with a sense of local community life?... Democracy must begin at home, and its home is the neighborly community.[20]

The concept of "local" or "neighborly community" assumes that issues of privilege, conflict and interdependence which inevitably surround the facts of age, gender, race, and class diversity are mediated and negotiated within institutions in the balanced center, places in which there is room for all. Segregating different human types, whether on the basis of merit or presumed personal defect, is not seen as an appropriate mechanism for dealing with human difference. Even in the early years of modern industrialization, local New England towns did not warehouse and segregate the poor away from the lives of others; rather they built poor houses and poor farms often in the center of the community for those who could not cope or compete.

Two examples below based on age differences illustrate this difference in point of view. Small children are commonly seen by modern people as having potential value because they will some day become adults and contribute wealth to the society. Children within organic communities simply "are." In terms of the social requirements of the community, they have intrinsic value by just "being;" they cement a variety of human relationships together; they allow strong adults to express tenderness and deep nurturing tendencies; they stimulate spontaneous generosity; they give the community a tangible vision of immortality. There is no need to ask, as modern societies often do: What are we going to do with our troublesome and non-productive children until they grow up?

A second example:

The worth of the aged are seen by modern people as an even more serious "challenge" than the worth of children. In Fromm and Maccoby's terms, they are often non-productive receptive or hoarding character types. Yet there is the archetypal fear of ignoring or exterminating them, since the "productive" adults may well some day share that same fate. Like children, they are increasingly segregated within specialized places where they can be cared for at minimal cost. In so far as they can be commodified and become a profit-making industry, their value is maintained. Within more balanced communities which value cyclical time and the intrinsic seasons of life, elders, along with children, often carry with them the living history and traditional wisdom not available to busy "productive" adults. So one does not think to ask the young or the aged how they can be useful. One simply values special moments in which we look at the present world through the innocent eyes of the young or the more judicious of the old.

There are many other examples: Why support flaky poets? Why listen to utopian philosophers or cynical story tellers? How to compel unproductive dreamers like Thoreau to do a days work? Etc. From the point of view of organic balance, one begins with cultural assumptions that are fundamentally different from those intrinsic to the modern commercial corporate market. For example, if a commercial farmer cannot make a profit, he will let an inferior or unprofitable crop rot in the fields or plow it under. The balanced organic assumption is that humans are not like crops which are valued only for the price they can bring in the market price. From this point of view we do not let unproductive people rot in the field or plow them under. All are simply needed. Being is relational and reciprocal: mothers nurture children and children give intrinsic meaning to the lives of mothers; jokesters and musicians lighten the load of the taskmaster who, in turn, is grateful and occasionally rests; old people die and their spirit moves the community toward the constant renewal of what is best in the past for the future. But the most sober insight we would share is the notion that local institutions within face-to-face communities may well provide the continuous contact and intercourse which alone makes the frustrations of our rich and sometimes abrasive human diversity tolerable and the values that diversity inevitably yields manifest.

These models of society will be presented and discussed at greater length in Part Four below. But before we begin this conversation, we need to deal with one more culture error of our modern era: the rapid rate of economic, social, and cultural change built into the modern system and the consequent pathology it engenders.

NOTES

1. The extent to which humans inherit a genetic predisposition toward a self-in-community identity as opposed to an individualistic identity is the subject of a careful study by Maryanski and Turner of the evolutionary roots of human social bonding. They argue that sociologists commonly portray modern industrial society as somehow violating or suppressing basic social tendencies in

human nature. Their work ends with the conclusion that "humans are not collectivists; indeed, at a biological level, we would not be all that social were it not for the effects of socialization into culture." They argue that even with all the constraints and "obvious problems of industrial society" we need to maintain it and work toward, "a system allowing for more choice, freedom, autonomy, and individualism...." As they say "We do not wish to sound like apologists for 'The System' ... [b]ut our review of the 'evidence' ... suggests that a society which allows choice and restricts inequality and power is more compatible with human nature than the ones it succeeded ... as that nature evolved in the primate order over the last 60 million years." (Alexandra Maryanski & Jonathan Turner, *The Social Cage: Human Nature and the Evolution of Society.* (Stanford University Press, 1992), 168-169.

2. David Riesman, *The Lonely Crowd* (New Haven: Yale University Press, 1950), 13.

3. Elman Service, 1962/1971, *Primitive Social Organization*, (Second Edition) (New York: Random House) pp. 35-37.

4. Here he refers to the work of Erich Fromm in *Man for Himself* (New York: Rinehart, 1947), 50-61.

5. Riesman, *The Lonely Crowd*, 4-5.

6. Eric Fromm, "Individual and Social Origins of Neurosis," *American Sociological Review*, IX, 1944, 380.

7. Riesman, *The Lonely Crowd*, 6.

8. Ibid.

9. Eric Fromm, & Michael Maccoby, *Social Character in a Mexican Village* (Englewood Cliffs, NJ: Prentice Hall, 1970), 20.

10. Ibid., 17.

11. Ibid., 72.

12. Note on the "Productive Orientation." We assume that genuine culture is one which will make available places and cultural patterns for the positive or "life loving" forms of these diverse social character types. We would construe patterns which tend to enculture and press people into "life negating" non-productive forms of social character as "cultural mistakes." In short, we assume that genuine culture involves a constant process of active negotiation in which individuals and sub-groups search for various ways in which our potential diversity can be accommodated such that human differences complement and support one another in positive ways within common social settings rather than act in destructive and exploitative ways.

13. Fromm & Maccoby, *Social Character in a Mexican Village*, 79.

14. Herbert J. Gans, *Urban Villagers*. (New York: The Free Press, 1982).

15. Ibid., 80.

16. Ibid., 81.

17. Fromm & Maccoby, *Social Character in a Mexican Village*, 16.

18. Edward Banfield also writes about the limitations of primitive village life in his important study of a poor village in an Italian town called Montegrano. He sees the dominant ethos as one of "amoral familism." In Montegrano, each family unit is so obsessively inclined to maximize its own self-interest that the whole community is economically paralyzed and unable to cooperate in ventures that would benefit both the separate families and the community as a whole. We should add that when families were locked into a system of hierarchical feudal obligations, both inside and outside the preindustrial city, there was always the question of who would benefit from cooperative shared ventures—the individual families, the whole village, or the landlords. E. C. Banfield, *The Moral Basis of a Backward Society* (Chicago: The Free Press, 1958).

19. Ibid., 234.

20. John Dewey, *Freedom and Culture* (New York: Capricorn Books, 1939), 159-160.

PART FOUR

Reconsidering the Significance of Self and Place

CHAPTER EIGHT

Social and Technological Change and the Significance of Self

The foregoing chapters provide us with a more comprehensive way of looking at human nature and cultural diversity and suggest that a balanced culture must take into account the rich and varied qualities of social character which require a diversity of roles and social forms within which to express the fullness of our humanity. In this chapter, however, we argue that as modern people, we have become encultured into a rapidly changing and relatively impersonal set of institutions which encourage highly individualistic and opportunitistic tendencies.[1] Diverse social roles associated with sustained local communal institutions have become limited and prevent many humans from living within a continuing connection to their primary and middle-level cultural roots.

We suggest that this loss of feeling for one's primary roots then results in reducing one's sense of personal relational identity. This relational identity once came from sustained engagement partners and work associates, from neighbors, and from primary places such as households and villages, churches and sodalities. The loss of these primary and middle level connections in the face of sustained rapid changes in our whole way of living tends to rupture our feeling for a sense of place, a sense of home, a sense of continuing vocation, and a sense of familiar stories, familiar rituals, and familiarity even with the mysteries of life, death, and the wonders of the natural universe—and most profoundly, it under-mines our feelings of personal significance.

In an effort to redeem this loss, modern people tend to reach out to various sources of power and material products as alternative sources of value. But the result tends to be a very transitory satisfaction as "popu-lar" products, personalities, and ideas rush through alternating cycles of "fast forward," leaving the old and familiar behind. The quick, sharp technical fits of the mind used to execute feats of reason, try out various vocations, and purchase consumer products, will not do. We seek and need continuing frameworks and symbols of history to ground our iden-tity, our values, and our sanity. In Suzanne Langer's words:

> [When we are oriented by stable symbols] doubts of the "meaning of life" are not apt to arise, for reality itself is intrinsically "mean-ingful:" it incorporates the symbols of Life and Death, Sin and Sal-vation. For a balanced active intelligence, reality is historical fact and significant form, the all-inclusive realm of science, myth, art, and comfortable common sense....

> The mind, like all other organs, can draw its sustenance only from the surrounding world; our metaphysical symbols must spring from reality. Such adaptation always requires time, habit, tradition, and intimate knowledge of a way of life. If now the field of our un-conscious symbolic orientation is suddenly plowed up by tremen-dous changes in the external world and in the social order, we lose our head and our convictions, and therewith our effectual pur-poses.... All old symbols are gone, and thousands of average lives offer no new materials to a creative imagination. This, rather than physical want, is a starvation that threatens the modern order ... the tyranny of the machine.[2]

ORGANIC AND MODERN MECHANISTIC CONCEPTIONS OF SOCIETAL CHANGE

An organism achieves homeostasis by maintaining a balance between environmental and physiological stability, and change within and be-tween its parts, i.e., organic equilibrium. We assume all societies and their cultural practices are in a continuous process of change over time based on shifts in the environment and on the new and accumulated technology and knowledge which humans generate. With the added ex-perience of each new generation, societies not only replicate but modify the culture of the previous generation. Social memory coupled with complex speech and communication technology means that information can be stored and recovered even after individual humans have forgotten it or died. So in cultural memory there is always slippage and creative invention; for better or worse, there is always some degree of continuing cultural change in any group or society.

But in the modern era, the rate of economic and environmental change resulting from technology is unprecedented in human history. The process of modernization has brought about in Wilbert Moore's, words "the 'total' transformation of a traditional or pre-modern society into the types of technology and associated organization that [we now identify with] the 'advanced' ... nations of the Western World."[3] This "total transformation" involves not only dealing with new types of organizations, i.e., contract-based bureaucratic organizations that we now know as the political state and the commercial-industrial corporation. It also means gradually reducing in significance three or four layers of direct face-to-face relationships in social settings or "places" which once allowed common people in their everyday lives the opportunity to participate continuously and informally in negotiating the traditions, the meanings, and the changes in their own local culture.

When this technological revolution began, it was assumed that rapidly changing traditional-to-modern societies would evolve toward a more stable condition in which middle level institutions (such as the extended household, the sodality, or village community) might be sustained. Moore recalls that while sociologists and economists assumed that developing societies would pass through radically different phases (e.g., from heavy capital industrialization, to "economic take off," and finally to the dramatic availability of consumer goods), it was also assumed that societies in the end would slow down and stabilize. That is, the traumas and uncertainties associated with rapid industrial and technological change would abate, and the pace of everyday life would recover an acceptable level of human equilibrium. As "underdeveloped" societies transformed into "mature advanced" consumer-centered societies, experts predicted that the more "advanced" societies would level off and serve as models of sustainable progress.

As early as 1963, however, even common folks began to conclude that modernity as a socio-economic system involved continuing exponential change.[4] In Moore's terms:

Modern industrial societies are continuously dynamic, and indeed appear to change at a steadily accelerating rate. The crude experiences of everyday life, the things that "everyone knows," confirm the changeful qualities of social structure and patterns of behavior more nearly than do the expert treatises of sociologists.... [The assumption that] full industrialization ends the dynamic processes [of modernization] ... [o]nce stated baldly ... becomes ridiculous.[5]

Given the fact that Moore's early observation, published a generation ago, now seems commonplace, we summarize below some of the basic continuing economic characteristics that drive these continuing rapid changes and their effect on efforts to sustain local traditions or patterns of cultural continuity.[6]

1. Constant human and technological specialization and segregated cohorts of specialists in the search for greater efficiency and productivity are a major source of perennial rapid change that directly affects people. As Moore points out, "[o]ne crude index of specialization, the number of distinguishable occupations, continues to grow in all industrial societies.... Although some specialities may finally disappear and some differentiated tasks may be reassembled as a more complex occupation, the overwhelming trend toward greater differentiation continues (106).

This kind of specialization is celebrated in the modern corporate system with its association with efficiency and its impersonal and highly centralized hierarchical supervision and power arrangements. Specialized corporate units carry out research and development, build new markets for products, generate capital, make and break contractual obligations, etc. In short, commercial systems of exchange are so complex and abstract that they exclude most humans from active engagement or participation in decision making and the entire process is often fraught with mystery. The more arcane the system, the more the elite protect their self-interest, distancing common folks in the middle and on the bottom increasing their feelings of alienation and powerlessness.

2. Economic growth depends on highly mobile workers willing to improve their status by periodically searching for new jobs with more security or prestige. Humans tolerate this kind of migratory or nomadic way of life when they travel in communal bands, but

we wonder whether or not they may sustain a sufficiently stable culture to tolerate such mobility when they are forced to live as isolated individuals or in small, fragile, and often disintegrating families among strangers.

3. The "innovative personality" is celebrated in the constant drive to create attractive "products" for profit—from computer technology to cinematic special effects to seductive styles of music and entertainment. As indicated in Chapter Seven, the less aggressive or more receptive personality is considered ill-fitted for full participation in this kind of progress. Such people tend to end up doing routine work and participate in the innovative economy mainly as consumers.

Given these powerful forces toward rapid social change, even if one were to choose to slow down one's life or become less materialistic, the forces of change move so rapidly that few can afford to stop participating in the process. The economic system drives us ever more toward the mix of individualistic and corporate cultural patterns so that so the face-to-face institutions that might balance the culture are eroded and reduced to accommodate these forces. Under these conditions, reclaiming local or middle level institutions in the balanced center comes on as unrealistic, idealistic, and impractical.

THE FORMATION OF A RELATIONAL IDENTITY IN THE FACE OF RAPID TECHNOLOGICAL AND SOCIAL CHANGE

One may ask how and where all this began. Robert Nisbet discusses the dilemma of "identity" within the broader Western European historical context in the move from Medieval to modern cultures. Nisbit argues that when looking at medieval society:

> there is agreement upon certain social characteristics ... irrespective of the moral inferences to be drawn from them. The first is the preeminence ... in its economy, religion, and morality—of the small social group. From such organizations as family, guild, village community, and monastery flowed most of the cultural life of the age. The second fact deriving from the first, the centrality of personal status, of membership, in a society.... The reality of the separate, autonomous individual was ... subordinated to the im-

mense range of association that lay intermediate to individual and ruler....[7]

According to Nisbet, the construction of the sovereign state and the legal powers delegated to the private corporate institutions forced a change in one's sense of self or identity, and people began to consider themselves as "separate individuals." Individuals gradually lost their feeling of deep and permanent connection to local mediating institutions—households, churches, villages, guilds, native towns and cities, etc.—institutions that stood between the individual and the centers of corporate power. This process of replacing the local-self-in-local-group identity with an individualistic, self-interested identity coupled with a corporate self-interested identity happened in a relatively short time period.

Many modern people feel this loss of relational communal connectedness yet they barely notice its underlying source—the huge gap in significance between the individual/nuclear family on the one hand and the impersonal centralized corporate institutions that so dominate the modern system. We are arguing here that the cultural creation of this new hyper-individualistic self is a major cultural error since we lose our continuing commitment and capacity to participate in and negotiate culture within a fuller range of middle level face-to-face groups and communities. Moreover, with the loss of this commitment to and participation in group life, local groups themselves atrophy or die. We are then left with a much more limited quality of "self" or "being," to wit: (1) the proud, controlling, egocentric, independent, self-interested individual and (2) the dependent individual-subordinated-to-a-self-interested-contract-based impersonal corporation. Or as Nisbet says, quoting in part the social psychologist Kurt Lewin, "'Only by anchoring his own conduct ... in something as large, substantial, and super-individual as the culture of a group,' can the individual stabilize his new beliefs sufficiently to keep them immune from the day to day life fluctuations of moods and influences of which he, as an individual, is subject."[8]

Within the constraints of balanced primal to modern institutions with many informal face-to-face groups, the rate at which culture changes tends to be sufficiently gradual so as to maintain a level of individual sanity. But as familiar places, people and routines disappear, layers of deep relational personhood are disrupted and replaced with hierarchical instruments of power supported by more superficial symbols of authority. Bateson speculates on the consequences of this disruption in his discussion of alcoholic addiction, which he uses as a metaphor for the obsessive, self-destructive effort to "control life" exhibited by individuals in search of authentic symbols of personal significance, power, and self-control.

In Bateson's terms, the modern meaning system has made a critical epistemologial error. The issue with which Bateson is most concerned is "that group of premises upon which Occidental concepts of the 'self' are built, and conversely, with premises which are corrective to some of the more gross Occidental errors associated with the concept."[9] Bateson maintains that whether or not a rapidly changing and potentially disorienting condition will self-correct for a society or personality, (i.e., maintain a sufficient degree of stability to prevent self-destructive behavior or what he calls "runaway") depends upon the extent to which action or information in subparts of the system take into account what he calls the "mind" or "information" in the larger system. He argues that the fundamental error in the modern Western notion of "self" is the assumption that "self" exists only in the brain of an individual. As he says:

> ... we may say that "mind" is immanent in those circuits of the brain which are complete within the brain. Or that mind is immanent in circuits which are complete within the system, brain plus body. Or, finally, that mind is immanent in the larger system—man plus environment.[10]

Bateson then elaborates what he calls the "total self-corrective unit" within which individuals function and process information in adapting and attempting to control their self-in-environment. The limits of this total self-corrective unit within which one thinks or acts or decides, he says, "is a system whose boundaries do not at all coincide with the boundaries of the body or of what is popularly called 'self' or 'consciousness....' This network of pathways ... extends to include the pathways of all unconscious mentation—both autonomic and repressed neural and hormonal.... The network is not bounded by the skin but ... includes the pathways of sound and light which travel along and transform differences originally immanent in things and other people—and especially in our own actions" (319).

Contrary to this more holistic, integrative, and layered view of reality as multiple organic relationships and connections, modern people rather see reality-as-substances or things. Mind and information circuits are situated in the self which leads to an inflated and exaggerated notion of the "force" of separate personhood. To illustrate this point, Bateson introduces the idea of egocentric "pride." In his terms, this particular type of Pride is the "obsessive acceptance of the challenge to control [conditions in one's environment and] a repudiation of the proposition 'I cannot'" (319). This leads to compulsive risk-taking actions which pit one's conscious sense of personal pride against the "other" which includes one's own unconscious, deep feelings of insignificance.

When the "self" is set or lives within multiple frames of Place—in households or sodalities connected with vocation and extended family or even in the mysteries of the unconscious and its connection to the unseen world—the illusion of "separate mind" as the central controlling agent is subject to a constant process of social correction. The person is obviously part of and related to the human, the natural, and the metaphysical cosmos. But when the narrower and more inflated view of "mind" and "self" infects a society, the self-contained "essential" hyperindividual replaces the kin or clan or communal network as the unit of "reality" and the feeling of constraint that comes from the broader conception of "mind" atrophies. The significance of one's extended or relational self is then replaced by the isolated, insulated, and inflated sense of self, self-pride, and power.

Bateson calls this the "poison of pride" and goes on to describe his therapeutic response as the "theology of Alcoholics Anonymous" (321). The antidote for the poison of pride is essentially the recognition of a power greater than self that includes a connection to an intimate self-confessional group and the loving power of a larger Source. As he says, "The self is a false reification of an improperly delimited part of this much larger field of interlocking processes [which include all the informational pathways relevant at any given moment to any decision]..." (321).

When alcoholics refuse to acknowledge their own repressed fear of insignificance and continue to maintain a posture of pride, they court disaster. But this pattern of thought and action is not unique to the alcoholic. It is characteristic of many modern people—both the high and the low—who struggle within a powerful hierarchical technological culture in which humans see themselves as pitted against alien environmental forces and people that must be controlled. As Bateson observes, "Every battle that [they win] brings a threat of disaster. The unit of survival—either in ethics or in evolution—is not the organism or the species but the largest system or 'power' within which the creature lives. If the creature destroys the environment, it destroys itself" (332).

The experience of power that is reconstructed in Alcoholics Anonymous, however, is not "power over"—not power to control or dominate the forces of people or nature in the search for personal prideful significance. The power is seen as a relational binding of the members into a larger unity of common groupness and a unity with God. "In sum, the relationship of each individual to 'Power' is best defined in the words 'is part of'" (333).

Finally, Bateson notes that Alcoholics Anonymous may be effective partly because it deals with only a single focused addiction; it is problematic whether or not it can influence the personality in other domains. Although it may transform the power of alcoholic addiction from one of dominance into an alternative one of relational connection to a group and even a god, one wonders whether similar therapeutic or culture-building techniques can transform, for example, the power of compulsive gambling (in everything from business ventures to slot machines to adulterous risk taking) or compulsive merchandising or consumerism in search of a similar cure for one's deficit in feelings of "personal significance."

More recently Arjun Appadurai has made similar observations which connect addiction (in the form of obsessive modern consumer behavior) to "inculcated pleasure," which he maintains arises from the tension between the nostalgic longing for the stable past and a craving for the fantasies of the future. His theory suggests that pleasure comes from fleeting moments of novelty as one moves from one "worn out" consumer item to another novel one—what he calls the "valorization of ephemerality." One comes to live within a compressed, swiftly changing time frame so that "tradition" is distorted to mean the fashion that one momentarily embraces but which one is now leaving to embark on the next exciting adventure—the new momentary fix. Appadurai suggests these "ephemeral" moments are represented, for example, in the short shelf life of products, the speed of fashion change, the instantaneous use of credit, the fleeting nature of TV, and the quick changes in imagery on mass media.

Translating his language into our terms, humans require a cultural balance between the stability of "traditional" primal and middle level cultural institutions on the one hand and the novelty and excitement of imaginative probes into the unknown on the other (which may or may not have time to become enculturated). We would argue that authentic personal significance is grounded in the balance between relational middle level connections and traditions and the personal capacity to effect new and exciting changes in one's life as one embraces the strangeness of novel people, places, and events. But genuine pleasure requires a more sustainable long-term cycle of stability and novelty. The addiction to the "ephemeral" comes when such cycles come in all too brief and fleeting moments—when "progress" comes and then retreats too fast.

From the point of view of an organic balanced culture, change has to be grounded in sufficient stability and continuity such that one knows the difference between constructive technological change and novelty as opposed to the potential for mindless escape or "runaway." One has to know the difference between the deeply sensed history of the cultural past and the glitzy history portrayed in a modern theme park. Our hunch is that cultural runaway is the condition in which we compulsively pursue alcohol, diets, food binges, TV personalities, fast cars, fast computers, competitive events, rapid money-making, etc. to the point of being disoriented and unable to discern the truly important moments that define complex, genuine forms of being and significance. The result is often tortuous, mindless, or even destructive episodes of boredom.

FROM THE LOSS OF PERSONAL SIGNIFICANCE TO THE LOSS OF CULTURAL SIGNIFICANCE AND EPISODES OF ETHNIC VIOLENCE

The argument is often made that small, local and perhaps isolated communities are prone to narrow minded ethnocentrism leading to hostility and acts of violence against the "outsider." Anecdotes are commonly told about primal or "primordial" familistic or clanish people and the atrocities that follow from their sense of their own personal and ethnic significance. This narrow sense of place and culture signals to the cosmopolitan mind the loss of tolerance toward individual rights coupled with the fear that non-locals (cosmopolitans) will be viewed as somehow "alien." The classic American story and film "To Kill a Mocking Bird" is but one of these parables illustrating this latent fear of violent scapegoating of outsiders.

It is assumed that an irrational "nativistic" bonding develops within local communal groups which threaten the expression of diversity and individuality within and outside the group. We would not deny the legitimacy of this concern; fear and distrust of strangers is certainly a commonly expressed and powerful aspect of human nature. We would, however, note that local people living in traditional modest places may well be less likely to attack the outsider than are larger and more powerful universalistic institutions, e.g., feudal lords, religious zealots from various "world" religions, dictators of imperial or fascist sovereign nation-states, intelligence agencies or security forces from democratic nation-states, and CEOs and security agencies from powerful commercial industrial corporations. Little has to be said about the blatant imperial exploitation by Western nations and corporations against native peoples on virtually every continent of the planet over the last 500 years.

To offer a concrete contemporary example one need only recall the events of 1993 in Waco, Texas in which a compound housing a hundred or so fundamentalist Christians, called "Branch Davidians," (including men, women, and children) was literally fenced in, guarded by military contingents of the United States Government (the FBI, the ATF, and the United States Army) for seven weeks until attacked by a military force including army tanks and antipersonnel gas, and finally burned to the ground in a fire of suspicious origin, killing virtually everyone inside. One hardly need argue this as a case of modern paranoid overreaction toward "outsiders," since the violence was carried out by a highly organized governmental military force rather than by an irrational local lynch mob. The reasons for such overreactions require special attention, since they have been common in the history of modern nations. (We might note the fact that events from the massive irrational violence of World War I and the Vietnam War fought largely by modern nations for dubious causes as well as the bizarre "war" to capture Pancho Villa in 1915 all have the stamp of a compulsive pathological need to "control a dangerous outsider.")

Appadurai also provides insight into this kind of deep primordial fear of local "cultish communal life" by members of well educated modern power elites, especially when tinged with non-modern, "folk," "populist," "communalist," or religious overtones.[11] Appadurai argues that often when such situations occur it is because the dominant modern society fuses or "collapses" two very different ideological "poles" of ethnic irrationality:

> one ... is the pole of group violence, *ethnocide*, and terror. The other pole is constituted by any form of behavior that appears *anti-modern*, whether it involves sluggish participation in elections, corruption in bureaucracy, resistance to modern educational techniques, or refusal to comply with modern state policies, ranging from birth control to monolingualism.... In recent efforts to explain ethnic violence, the two explanatory targets of primordialist theory have become subtly fused, so that the primordialism of resistance to modernization and the primordialism of ethnic violence have become loosely identified [with each other].[12]

Appadurai argues that "Western models of political participation, education, mobilization, and economic growth which were calculated to distance new nations from the most retrograde primordialisms" (141) have often had the opposite effect. He cites as evidence the use of the armed forces in modernizing countries which "have turned out to be brutal, corrupt, anti-civil, and self-expanding" (141). He notes that there are some nations "that have had time to work out the Enlightenment project of political participation—based on the idea of creating a population of educated, post-ethnic, calculating individuals, subsisting on the workings of the free market and participating in a genuine civil society" and therefore able to avoid the violence and irrationalities of ethnic and kinship bonding. (The Waco case is, of course, a notable exception, since it took place in one of those presumably "post-ethnic" nations.) He also adds that many of these cases have required "a strong dose of state authoritarianism" (142) as well as various forms of economic subsidy by the United States and other colonizing entities to maintain order.

His critique is particularly relevant to our thesis since it applies most particularly to those who would blame ethnic violence on some form of primordial or primitive ethnic bonding persisting in the minds and hearts of traditional or premodern peoples who are still "trapped" within an "unenlightened" tribal and village mentality (which we have here generally celebrated). He suggests that if this were the case, one would predict that as the world became more "modern" irrational ethnic outbursts should subside. Yet this does not seem to be the case. As he says, "Given the widespread commitment to the idea of democracy in a very large number of societies since World War II, including those in the socialist bloc, which placed heavy emphasis on the project of modernity (technology, modern science, mass participation in politics, massive investments in higher education, and immense propaganda for new ideas about citizenship ...), why are ethnic primordialisms more alive than ever?" (144)

Our own analysis, already discussed above, suggests there is a natural human tendency to create familistic and communal institutions for sources of security, cultural bonding, and conviviality. These primal and middle level epigenetic tropes are far too deep within most humans to be extinguished by the normal socialization and educational institutions available to the modern secular nation state and its stepchild, the commercial corporation. And, as indicated above, efforts by the modern state to discourage various forms of local parochial ethnic bonding in favor of a more universal loyalty to the secular state often leads to a set of confused loyalties—an explosive atavistic drive to defend the "blood" clan coupled with the exhilerating sense of power that goes with modern military technology. With Appadurai we think this yields an even more dangerous form of primordial violence. We would note (as does Appadurai) the experience of Nazi Germany under Hitler who used mass primal face-to-face rallies, terrorist police raids and beatings on visible neighbors portrayed as "enemies" as well as modern media-driven propaganda techniques which exploited abstract primordial ideas of blood, soil, and fear of the outsider including displays of massive weaponry to support a vision of global conquest.

This dangerous fusion of governmental media-generated primordial ethnocentrism with commitment to the ideology of "progressive modernism" is an explosive combination. It has, in fact, led to the use of the social and technological instruments of violence including support for monopolistic privileges for large corporations (which presumably guarantee jobs for all) and an efficient and effective military force readily available in the service of the state to maintain law and order to enforce corporate contracts and, when needed, to effect aggressive war and mass murder. (We would note the Pullman Strike, the Haymarket Riot, and the Homestead Strike as earlier examples of this kind of violence in American history.) This scenario, which has been played out numerous times in the recent history of the state hardly places the root causes of modern primordial ethnic violence at the doorstep of small locally-driven populist village peoples.

After this analysis Appadurai adds a note of explanation regarding the paradox of the most brutal violence being perpetrated against one's "neighbor:"

> The rage of those who kill, maim, and rape seems to be tied up with a profound sense of betrayal that is focused on the victims, and the betrayal is tied up with the relationship between appearance and reality. When the neighborhood merchant is revealed to be, in his heart, a Croat, when the schoolteacher turns out to be sympathetic to the Hutu, when your best friend turns out to be a hated landlord—what seems to follow is a sense of deep categorical treachery, that is, treachery about group identity as defined by states, censuses, the media, and other large-scale forces.
>
> ... This sense of treachery, of betrayal, and thus of violated trust, rage, and hatred has everything to do with a world in which large-scale identities forcibly enter the local imagination and become dominant voice-overs in the traffic of ordinary life.... This discourse brings together uncertainty about categories and intimacy among persons—the key feature of the new violence....
>
> If the hypothesis of treachery is plausible, it has much to do with the large scale identities created, transformed, and reified by modern state apparatuses ... and circulated through the media. When these identities are convincingly portrayed as primary (indeed as primordial) loyalties by politicians, religious leaders, and the media, then ordinary people self-fulfillingly seem to act as if only this kind of identity mattered and as if they were surrounded by a world of pretenders. Such representations of identity (and identification) seem even more plausible in a world of migrants and mass media, which subvert the everyday certainties that come from face-to-face knowledge of the ethnic Other. (154-155)

Although happening 150 years earlier than the time-frame of Appadurai's work, much of his argument could be applied to our own American Civil War, which was notoriously savage, brutal, and filled with moral ambiguity. Most recently we have the Bosnian and Kosovar examples in which a very modern political leader in a modern Western-style state attempted to "cleanse" the Serbian state of dangerous backward peoples who happened to value their own "backward ethnicity" above that supported by the aggressive modern corporate state.

Appadurai's argument relates to the process by which legitimate, "real," or deep understandings of one's identity or the "significant self" is created. He suggests that the most malevolent kind of violence comes from confusions over who are one's neighbors, who shares one's primal identity, who is the outsider, who is an impostor, and who really is a danger to that identity, significance, or security of the village and, more importantly, of the state.

The issue of "significant" identity is similar to that described by Bateson, except that Appadurai applies it on a cultural or societal level rather than to individuals. When one is insecure about the fundamental source of one's significance, one often tests the ambiguity of one's significance by exercising power against outside forces in an effort to dominate and/or control them. For the alcoholic, the testing leads to self-destructive binges when the "power" over self fails. The AA solution is to reconnect those addicted to "runaway" excessive "pride" or "weak significance" to a primal communal group and a larger spiritual reality. In the case of confused ethnic identity, one tests the loyalty of one's fellow ethnics by daring to risk gross violence waged against an ambiguous ethnic or unmodern other. But in this case, the situation is fraught with mixed messages from both primal and modern sources—from the people in one's village, from one's shared economic interests and the sources of one's livelihood, from the state, from authoritative well-spoken voices in the media, or from leaders who presumably know more than the local people. The point is that a weak or superficial identity and a feeling of marginal significance caused by any of a variety of modern conditions (migration and loss of roots, economic precariousness or loss of work, feelings of powerlessness before rigid and impersonal bureaucracies, etc.) results in irrational and destructive violence launched against a morally ambiguous other or an outside "enemy."

What Appadurai (and we) are suggesting is that as the larger and more universal forms of social structure (governments, economic corporations, media, schools and universities, etc.) gain virtually monopolistic control over the livelihood and information provided to common people and their meaning-making organs of communication, the opportunity to participate in constructing and negotiating one's culture and identity within local to middle level settings is reduced and with it one's multilayered and authentic relational identity. The world then comes to be constituted only of powerful corporate places populated by really "significant people" in "important but distant places" who appear in the newspaper or magazines or on the TV screen or even the internet who drive the rapid changes. And all of this drama is virtually inaccessible to marginally significant or insignificant "local places," i.e., one's private dwelling or neighborhood or church or coffee break at work.[13]

THE DEEPER QUESTION:
THE DIMENSIONS OF AUTHENTIC "BEING"

There is a deeper question to be addressed beyond the issue of how or whether or not one grounds one's significance in a relational personal, local or corporate identity. This goes back to the ontological question of what constitutes "being" itself. Here we can make useful distinctions among various layers of what it means to "be oneself." There is the sense of "essential being" which separates one from all the other beings in the universe. There is the sense of "relational being" or "conditional being" which ties one's identity to other people, place, one's history, etc. There is also a "whole-part" being in which one's identity is tied to a complex communal whole or, in more religious terms, to a whole universe and, perhaps, finally to the "all" of godness or the Tao. Bateson's work pushes us toward larger and more inclusive units of being, suggesting that "mind" and the informational feedback system that goes with "mind" must be broad and holistic enough to connect with and feed back information across all of these layers of reality.

Whitehead is one of the few modern philosophers to actually make the distinction that Bateson suggests—that the value or "significance" of any "being" is relative to the fullness or the breadth of context within which that separate being or occasion exists. The special problem for our species is that humans have no "built in" set of specific instincts which let them intuitively know that they must keep their immediate ego-centered experience in touch, explicitly or tacitly, both more comprehensive domains and deeper contexts. This automatic instinct or epigenetic theorem that humans lack would, in Whitehead's words, run something like:

> The contrast of finitude [the sense of immediate fact] and infinity [the sense of an ultimate contextual background] arises from the fundamental metaphysical truth that every entity involves an indefinite array of perspectives, each perspective expressing a finite characteristic of that entity. But any one finite perspective does not enable an entity to shake off its essential connection with totality.[14]

That is, no matter how significant or essential is a single, seemingly stable, being, it is never free from the varied meanings implied by an ultimate set of contexts of which it is a part. Individual occasions of being are always connected to some understanding/feeling of a totality, no matter how vaguely apprehended. Whitehead then goes on to name the two ends of this metaphysical dimension, which are required to conceptualize the larger sense of the whole. One end is the world of actual fact, of activity, the world of emergent multiplicity, the world of active creation, the world of the "creative now." The other end is that "which emphasizes persistence"—the world of value. "The value inherent in the universe has an essential independence of any moment of time; and yet it loses its meaning apart from its necessary reference to the world of passing fact" (88). And so each of these two parts of the World—the "mortal" immediate transitory fact and the immortal perennial value are only parts. The whole of an entity or occasion happens when they are combined. "The two worlds of Value and of Action are bound together in the life of the Universe, so that the immortal factor of Value enters into the active creation of temporal fact" (90). Fact is not significant without value; value is not actual without fact. Whitehead then moves on to argue that:

> [t]he survival of personal identity within the immediacy of a present occasion is a most remarkable character of the World of Fact. (92)
>
> … The many become one [a unity], and by this miracle achieve a triumph of effectiveness—for good or for evil. This achievement is the essence of art and of moral purpose. The World of Fact would dissolve into nothingness of confusion apart from its modes of unity derived from the preservation of dominant characters of Value. Personality [of meaning or individual or group or society] is the extreme example of the sustained realization of a type of value. The co-ordination of a social system is the vaguer form…. The topic stretches from the physical Laws of Nature to the tribes and nations of Human Beings. (94)

Whitehead wonders at the "miracle" of "Personality," [i.e., individual identity or being] that is "a most remarkable Character of the World of Fact." And the background for this miracle "stretches from the physical Laws of Nature to the tribes and nations of Human Beings." In short, he and we assume that most individual humans require an identity within a "unity" of a specific "tribe" or culture in which there is a diversity of contrasts against which one can compare similarities and differences and maintain a sustainable feeling of significance. Particular cultures "manufactured" by the transitory information in the mass media are shallow and dangerous. They are shallow because they can easily be constructed by propaganda and repetition. They are dangerous because they can easily be manipulated to deal only with superficial issues of the moment by people who have only their narrow self-interest at stake.

Here we confront a myth and a paradox. The myth is that "local" peoples are those most likely to embrace irrational or superficial forms of nativistic behavior. The paradox is that it may require continuing experience and enculturation within middle level local institutions in the vital balanced center to deal directly with "others"—close up and face to face—to effect honest and authentic relationships which curb narrow bigotry and intolerance. And it may be that it is the members of powerful elite groups in any society—those who have the power to segregate themselves from others and with whom they have little or no direct contact—who do not really understand what it takes to "love one's neighbor," especially neighbors who are not like oneself, because they are separated from many of their neighbors by power, physical distance, and socio-economic barriers. They can afford to live tolerant "non-primordial" lives in the midst of material affluence and decontextualized abstractions. And it may be that the more brutal instances of modern primordial atavistic behavior, (e.g., Adolf Hitler's Germany or Robert McNamara's Vietnam or Milosovich's Bosnia and Kosovo) are more likely to be avoided when genuine participatory local institutions are combined with a perennial simple "common sense."

SUMMARY OF PART THREE

In summary, it is worth repeating the lesson that Part Three teaches in understanding the limits of human nature and the multilayered requirements of whole cultures. Roger Masters provides compelling evidence that culture overlays particular and enduring schemas on the biological substrate of the human brain. The result is that one's understanding of the "nature" of the individual in a particular society as well as the "natural" social and psychological patterns of that society are deeply learned so that much of their meaning is not under conscious human control. Service expands upon this observation by pointing out that humans choose from a relatively limited set of biological options concerning male-female relationships, nurturance, aggression or group bonding, but that culture has the capacity to invent a wide variety of patterns by which those roles and relationships will be expressed.

The cultural error that is perpetuated in the modern view of the human condition is the assumption that our nature is sufficiently flexible to successfully "ride through" the traumatic radical transition from close-knit kinship groups and small village societies into a reality of private, isolated nuclear families and impersonal corporations which will enculture highly individualistic, independent, self-sufficient "selves." Given the level of tension, insecurity, and violence that penetrates our modern way of life as we move among these transformed egocentric selves, we think this assumption no longer seems plausible. It is simply not in our nature for most of us to leave so many elements of our primal past behind and still know who we are as human beings.

NOTES

1. Of course the modern classic which documented the rapid pace of change in recent modernity is Alvin Toffler's *Future Shock* (Random House. New York, 1970). Our treatment focuses on one limited aspect of this problem—the psychological and cultural consequences of this rapid change. We would note here that Toffler's overall solution to the problem suggests a radical "opening up" of the channels of communication to create a perennial global town meeting of all the developed nations in the world. He has little faith in the future performances of myopic elites who, he says, suffer from the virus of elitism. The support for our claim that modern people feel that change is out of control is reflected in the incredible popularity of Toffler's long and complex book. When published in paperback, it ran through twenty-two printings in one year—1971.

2. Suzanne Langer, *Philosophy in a New Key. A Study in the Symbolism of Reason, Rite, and Art* (New York: Penguin, 1948), 235, 237-238.

3. Wilbert E. Moore, *Social Change* (Englewood Cliffs, NJ: Prentice Hall, 1963), 89.

4. The social theorist Peter Berger also questions and critiques the notion that mature developed societies "leveloff" in *Pyramids of Sacrifice* (Garden City, NY: AnchorBooks, 1976) which deals with perennial crises associated with modernization in Brazil and China.

5. Moore, *Social Change*, 105-106.

6. Ibid., 102-105.

7. Nisbit, *Quest for Community*, 80.

8. Ibid., 230.

9. Gregory Bateson, *Steps to an Ecology of Mind* (San Francisco: Chandler, 1972), 314-315.

10. Ibid., 317.

11. Appadurai, *Modernity at Large*, 140.

12. Ibid., 140.

13. The tremendous danger in this situation, of course, is that ordinary people lose their common sense of truth and dignity based on the rich immediacy of experience in local places. The grounds upon which Janet Reno, the Attorney General of the United States, made the decision to attack the compound of the Branch Davidians in Waco, Texas was FBI "information"—received in Washington, D.C.—that the children in the compound were being abused. She never took the trouble to personally or directly contact the Branch Davidians. Important people do not have to face such insignificant people. And although the attack by the army, the FBI, and ATF agents resulted in most of the children being burned to death, no one in the United States government really thought to hold anyone accountable, either for the uncorroborated information or the disastrous error in judgment which brought about the tragedy. The focus remained on the dangerous "Other"—the Branch Davidians—rather than the "legitimate" and powerful political and military figures who actually launched the attack. And Janet Reno remained a symbol of "the" powerful person, the United States Attorney General in Washington, D.C. who was too significant and proud ever to acknowledge the error until caught in the deception some six years later. This is a powerful lesson for common citizens regarding how power and the obsessive need to control can legitimate irrational acts of violence.

14. Alfred North Whitehead, *Science and Philosophy* (New York: Philosophical Library, 1948/1974), 86.

CHAPTER NINE

The Commercial Corporation and the Living Place

FROM CATEGORIES TO PLACES

In moving from Part Three to Part Four, our focus changes from a reconsideration of the way modern people construe abstract categories such as reality, human nature, and culture and diversity to the more concrete places humans inhabit. In this chapter we discuss two very different understandings of place. First is the modern economic view of place which has value in terms the goods and services that are produced and marketed there. The underlying metaphor for the modern economic place (or set of places) is something like a machine which efficiently provides "products" for the health, wealth, and happiness of individual people in society. So the nuclear family, for example, is an efficient institution (machine) by which to provide a resting place between times of paid productive work as well as to provide, in some degree, for eating, sleeping, recreation, child care, etc.

Our second understanding of place includes a set of complex levels of place which cannot be reduced to their utilitarian economic value. The underlying metaphor for this conception is a living organism. The parts of this organism may include such places as the extended household or home place, what we call the cultivation/nature place, and mediating local places, such as neighborhoods, local markets, work groups, and civic institutions which provide for common public services. Below we present a description and analysis of the contexts within which these two understandings of place may be better understood.

THE ORGANIC LIVING PLACE

We assume that living in a local place has been and is for most humans an important element for creating and internalizing something we have been calling "genuine culture." This does not mean "any local place." At this point we would venture to call such a place an organic "community" or a "living place," which implies a particular complex of interrelated living entities. The idea of "living place" we borrow from the work of Aldo Leopold. In his words, a living place is, "A thing ... [which] tends to preserve the integrity, stability, and beauty of the biotic community." In the words of his daughter:

> The vital new idea for Leopold was the concept of biotic health, a shift from the older conservation idea of economic biology, to a new biotic ecology. Here was a biota so complex by interwoven cooperations and competitions that "no man can say where utility begins and ends." With this experience, he gained a new humility about the possibility of ever understanding how the whole system functioned. He realized that science leads to structural under-standing, and with luck this may result in a stronger basis for an ethic.... Leopold experienced a profound humility as he became acutely aware of the complexity of factors involved in life and death, growth and decay. Ethical and aesthetic values guided his decisions.[1]

For humans, however, living places are more than simply biological and physical spaces. The living places which sustain genuine culture must be guided by ethical and aesthetic values and grounded in a hu-man-in-nature ecology. Moreover, as Leopold's biotic community was local, so is our human living place. In Table 5 below we have sketched some of the major social forms necessary for such a living place, adapted to the categories and institutions which are familiar to contemporary people.

At the bottom of Table 5 is the grounded center—the organic natural world. Radiating from this are elements in the natural world which our living place cultivates and develops to provide sources of food, energy, shelter, and other necessities and comforts for human life.

On the right of the middle section is the Extended Household as a so-cial form which traditionally included families, extended families, and friends, servants, or hired workers who are closely connected to the kinship network and/or economy within the household. Radiating out from the household are a set of institutions related to and supported by multiple households. These include neighborhoods, sodalities (religious, charitable, mutual aid groups, etc.) In the middle section on the left is the social form we call the Native City. Radiating out from the Native City is a set of civic institutions such as a legal/court system, schools, public roads, a water supply, etc. In the upper center is a commercial-industrial quadrant, the activities of which include production, trade, and a balance between local and distant markets.

Table 5. The "Local Living Place" as the Dominant Social Unit

Universalistic Commercial Corporation

artisans
trades people
local merchants, etc.

Native City	Local Mediating Social Forms	Extended Household
courts	sodalities	nuclear families
police	mutual aid	extended families
roads	neighborhoods	cottage businesses
schools	local markets	

Organic Natural World

air, water, soil, predation
timber, fish, minerals, etc.

Although this conception of the Living Place begins locally, we assume that it is surrounded by a larger, more universalistic system. Our theory suggests that genuine culture flourishes when there is a balance among the institutions in the local system as well as a balance in its relationship to larger, more universal outside institutions. Thus the Living Place is not driven mainly by the market demands of the larger commercial economic system, but rather is a balance among the several subsystems including the political civic system, the parochial concerns of the households, and the contingencies associated with the natural world.

It is easy, however, to imagine such a system being out of balance in a variety of ways. The civic institutions might well be controlled by despots; the commercial institutions might be controlled by greed-driven profiteers; the members of extended households might be continuously agitated by jealousy and mutual suspicion; the world of nature might be constantly on the verge of overwhelming the living place with floods, volcanoes, drought, etc. The challenge for any living place as a personified reality is always to "negotiate" as best it can some balance through the complexities of such difficulties. But, as Leopold says, such a place can never be fully understood or controlled by anything like science or human intelligence.

WHEN THE LIVING PLACE IS DOMINATED BY THE COMMERCIAL INDUSTRIAL PLACE AS THE CENTER OF HUMAN LIFE

This hypothetical view of the "Living Place" has happened, at least in a rough way, historically in some parts of the world. In Western Europe and the United States such local places existed for brief periods of time during the transition from what we now know as the late feudal period or the late middle ages and the onset of the industrial-technological revolution, leading to what we are here calling modernity. Table 6 is a graphic description of "place" dominated by the contemporary commercial industrial conglomerate and illustrates basic differences between this modern place and our version of the balanced living place given above.

Within the framework of the commercial industrial system, or "place," the significance of local places is greatly diminished. The extended household is reduced in size to the small nuclear household, which is continuously on the move in search of educational and employment opportunities. The "home" part of place is diminished in importance both because people spend less time there—the goal of the system is full employment and work is often done away from home—and because there is less attachment to place by transient populations. There is less investment in the specifics of one's vocation since it often changes. There is minimum contact with the raw natural world as a particular place since it is highly "managed" and is an essentially industrial or "recreational" enterprise.

Table 6.
The Commercial Industrial Place as the Dominant Social Unit

Centralized Merchandising

Local Trades People and Merchants Franchised by Centralized Corporations

Short-term Employment; Fast Turnover; Short Product Life

State-Supported Global Trade Agreements Enforced by Economic and Military Sanctions

Centralized R&D

High Technology: Rapid Change

Commecial: Industrial Corporations

Small Mobile Household Units

Nuclear Family

Service Work

Low-Tech, Low-Paid Service Work: Hotels, Child Care, Nursing Care, House Cleaning, Construction

Cultural Meaning-Making

High Paid Centralized Mass Culture Entertainment, Schooling, and Education

Large Scale High Tech Monoculture

Single Crop Agriculture, Forestry, Fishing, etc.

Single Product Factories

Specialized Mono-Care Schools

Specialized Mono-Care Nursing Homes, etc.

Organic Natural World

Human Control of "Wild" Natural Places

"Uncultivated Places" Waiting to be Developed

THE IMPACT OF MODERN ECONOMICS

It is here that our modern conception of economics becomes central to human existence. In the product-centered technological context, economics is understood as a scientific field which attempts to predict and describe the physical and material requirements of human existence within universal or global places by applying general principles and laws. Economists presumably discover the laws related to acquiring, developing and expanding the material resources needed for human society. They assume moreover that humans are essentially egoistic, self-interested individuals ever eager to negotiate the conditions of everyday life unrestricted by "irrational" or superstitious religious rituals and imaginary, outdated, "mythic" cosmologies. Within modern economics, there are no specific local human beings, but rather "generalized" human beings who function in a perpetual condition of scarcity. It also assumes that humans have the technological capacity and motivation to create wealth or "products" in ever more efficient and progressive ways.[2]

Modern people move from Living Places, which are local and contain human scale institutions, to a system that depends on wealth-creating places. Wealth-creating places are primarily concerned with developing "capital." Earlier views of production saw "capital" as the equity and machinery required for creating wealth (along with land and labor), but more recently "capital" is construed as a set of multifaceted abstractions that include all of the requirements for creating products and wealth. We now speak of *natural capital* (that which is extracted from the natural environment); *manufactured capital* (tools, equipment, or the money to buy such equipment); *human capital* or *human resources* (human beings with various degrees of physical and intellectual skills); *cultural capital* (symbolic artifacts and knowledge which have particular value within a society); and even *social capital* (non-work life and recreational activities which are needed to provide rest and renewal so that one can face the strains and fatigue of returning each day to the "productive" work place).

Perhaps the most problematic aspect of modern "economics" is revealed in these abstractions. In this way modern people "exchange" the vivid textured lives of humans-in-action or humans-in-the-midst-of-complex-local-settings for humans as abstract categories which can be quantified. It is this contrast which appears to lie at the epistemological center of the concept "significant place." Significant places for modern people are all those places in which products are created and made available for purchase or consumption. "Significant Place" thus represents more than a simple biological or physical place; it is centered on the "hard" facts which yield to rational quantification and precise predictions regarding how to maximize the quality, quantity, and efficiency in the research and development, the production, the marketing, the distribution, the sales, and the final trashing and recycling or dumping of goods and services. The more primal metaphor of "a living place" in which people cooperate and negotiate with their neighbors and with the physical and biological environment is thus transformed into settings where products are created, purchased, sold, consumed, and trashed.

THE DALY-COBB CRITIQUE OF MODERN ECONOMICS

Herman Daly and John Cobb (an economist and a theologian) critique the way we understand this transformation from holistic organic local places to product-making and product-buying places.[3] Their critique is based on the Whiteheadian concept of the "fallacy of misplaced concreteness"—the misguided assumption that one can legitimately construe precise, abstract, often mathematical generalities such as "capital," for highly contextualized living places without risk or serious distortion. Daly and Cobb maintain that when economists, scientists, lawyers, business people, and administrators describe complex human events by means of abstract quantitative and/or theoretical models, they simply "miss" many, if not the most, significant dynamic events or "facts" in the evolution of the human condition as well as in the historical development of human culture itself.

In order to illustrate this distinction between the abstract and the concrete we might describe two different ways of looking at an activity that was once central to the early industrial commercial revolution in New England—whaling. In economic commercial terms, fragile ships and whale boats were not distinctive and particular places—they were "manufactured capital." The whales who were killed as prey for the sailors were not large living creatures with pods or families living in the deep ocean—they were "natural capital." The men who manned the ships and often were maimed or killed were not humans—they were "human capital" or perhaps simply "personnel." The skills and experiences of the sailors which allowed them to carry out these dangerous exploits would be considered "cultural capital." And the home life to which the sailors returned and which provided the incentive for undertaking this most difficult and precarious of human activities for three to six months of the year were not "home places"—they were "social capital."

All of these forms of capital were susceptible to quantitative calculation within the micro-economics that "business" used to obtain whale oil. Moreover, all of this "capital" stands for and replaces the concrete reality of organic living places. The quantification of capital allows for a more precise calculation of the cost of producing or harvesting whale oil as it masks the risk and suffering of the "actual" experiences that were described only in picture, story, and song when the ships returned. From the point of view of local whaling families, for example, the pictures, the stories, and songs provide essential meaning for the community of whaling people—the cosmological bonds that connect people to the culture of whaling in the New England city. For the economist, the stories simply become entertaining books available for sale in a global market place.

Daly and Cobb acknowledge that while economists and business entrepreneurs may have understood the more contextualized meaning of "place" in the earlier days of the commercial industrial revolution, in more recent times this sense of place and the actuality of place has been all but lost. Today most of the metaphors that define modern western society's concept of a significant "place" are heavily weighted with abstract considerations of capital cost and profit and the mathematical calculations of such costs. As Daly and Cobb note:

> The evolutionary or historical character of the economy has never been denied or wholly ignored. Hegel and Marx gave it a rich attention in the nineteenth century. Alfred Marshall, the founder of neoclassical economics, was highly sensitive to the historical character of the actual economy. Nevertheless, economists on the whole wanted economics to become increasingly scientific, and their idea of science was based on physics rather than evolutionary biology. That meant that economics had to focus on formulating models and finding laws "governing" present economic behavior rather than seeking laws "governing" the changes of economic systems or asking about contingent historical matters.[4]

Daly and Cobb conclude by observing that while modern models and economic laws may have made the field somewhat more precise, overall it has obscured the connection between the abstractions and the sense of whole organic places upon which the abstractions are based. The hard fact is that academics and entrepreneurs who describe complex occasions and places with quantitative abstractions (engaging in the fallacy of misplaced concreteness) distort the ability to see vivid and significant ontologically or historically based places. In the human-centered cosmos of the modern economic corporation, individual people are somehow significant mainly because of the wealth they create as opposed to the deeper context within which the products are created or the natural world from which they and their products come.

In the final analysis, modern people tend to believe that products and "capital" are interchangeable or substitutable for one another. Thus they come to live in a world in which oil as a fuel to heat one's homes can be substituted for wood; atomic reactors can be substituted for oil; assembly lines of robotized humans or robots themselves can be substituted for skilled people fashioning their world; walking on treadmills can be substituted for the physical activity required to hunt and till and build and nurture; abstract communication via writing on paper or through electronic messages in "chat rooms" can be substituted for convivial face-to-face conversation. The motivating force in all of these substitutions is the drive toward economic efficiency, which is achieved by the careful calculation of the cost of all these various forms of capital: "natural capital," "manufactured capital," "human capital," "cultural capital," and "social capital." From a modern economics point of view, living units of reality, from Whitehead's emerging "occasions" to Leopold's Living Places, are seen not as having intrinsic or grounded qualities of being that have evolved over millennia, but rather as interchangeable and substitutable "things" or as capital needed to create "products."

PIETILA'S TRIANGLE OF HOUSEHOLD, CULTIVATION, AND INDUSTRIAL PRODUCTION

Hilkka Pietila, a contemporary Finish economist, provides us with a radical departure from conventional modern economics. She begins with the simple statement that economics includes "all work, production, actions, and transactions needed to provide the livelihood, welfare and survival of people and families, irrespective of whether they appear in statistics or are counted in monetary terms."[5] She then suggests that there are actually three economic "places," each having different sources of moral glue and different orientations toward the human condition.

Her three places or sectors of economic activity include:

1) The "household economy," which includes a group of people having a household together, "irrespective of whether they are kindred or not; or even a group of small households living close enough to create a unit..."

2) The "cultivation economy," which includes "production based on the living potential of nature, which is the interface between economy and ecology, [and] human culture facing ... ecological laws" (p. 114). We assume that the "cultivation economy" includes not only the immediate connection (interface) between nature and human culture but also those continuing aspects of growth, decay, and change within nature that have direct if not immediate implications for the needs of all life.

3) The industrial-commercial, economy which has traditionally been "based on manufacturing from nonrenewable natural resources—minerals and fossils—which are extracted from the earth, though raw materials produced by the cultivation economy are also processed by industry." (124)

Pietila's work supports Daly and Cobb's observation, noted above, that economics as a discipline has patterned itself after the natural sciences in order to create knowledge related to the "production, extraction, and manufacturing from 'dead elements', minerals and fossils" (124). She points out that when the concepts and methods of "manufacturing economics" are applied to the household and cultivation economy, they run into considerable difficulty. For example, when commercial industrial economics is applied to agriculture, modern people find themselves in the peculiar position that "in industrialized countries, in spite of the application of the most advanced technology and significant subsidies, [agriculture often faces] ... collapse under the burden of debt and the effects of insane cultivation practices" (124).

We see a direct relationship between Pietila's three economic sectors and our primal-to-modern dimension in the evolution of human societies. After the shift to village society, which developed into the preindustrial feudal system and later the "native" city, elements of the commercial industrial system enter the picture. (The term "feudal" actually relates to the term "feud" or "fee," which refers to payment for the use of land and implies a contract.) Here the moral glue which holds societies together becomes more abstract and includes the impersonal, calculated self-interested negotiation of a commercial contract. And finally, with the advent of the modern urban conglomerate all four overlapping sectors or economies shift their relationship from tribal to village to preindustrial feudalism to the commercial industrial society. Here the moral glue shifts to egocentric self-interest embodied in legal contracts embedded within governmental and legal institutions, including the modern sovereign state. As Pietila says:

> In the course of history, most societies have ... been agrarian societies consisting primarily of fairly self-sustaining farming families.... The basic structure of the society at that stage is the often quite extended private family, which provides for most of the basic needs of the family members: food, clothing, shelter, caring, entertainment, etc. On a modest level, the family is a fairly autonomous unit, depending only on the provisions of nature and the capabilities of its members. (115)

In terms of gender roles, Pietila emphasizes the fact that although local societies may have been largely patriarchal, women played a central role because of their vital contributions to the livelihood of the family. However, as she says, "[i]n the process of so-called modernization, industrialization, monetization, commercialization of the society, many traditional functions are transferred outside the family. Making of furniture and clothing, growing of food, child and health care, training and education, even entertaining, have been transferred outside the family and monetized. They have become either public services, provided by the society, or commodities purchased on the market...." And, as she says, we pass from a culture in which the skills required to sustain household functions are lost in a commodity-based economy which may well end up with "the total abolition of work and skills in families" as they are "absorbed in the market economy, [and] time outside the economic system is reduced to pure unskilled leisure-time "(115).

Pietila describes what we have already identified as the process of substitution. Moral functions such as raising children and caring for the sick and elderly are removed from households and taken over by corporate, governmental or private entities. As the fundamental nurturant and life-sustaining activities are moved from the household to the market economy, many women (and unskilled men) move out of the home into supervised low-paid jobs. Children move from home to school; food production moves from family farms to agribusiness and monoculture;

clothing production moves from sewing rooms to sweat shops; entertainment moves from households, churches, and village squares to mass
media; etc. As a result, many people whose roles were critical in the
household (especially women) end up at the bottom of the commercial
industrial economy. The drive toward economic efficiency moves the
commercial industrial place toward ever increasing specialization and
leaves artisans and householders with a more limited role in the local
place.

Pietila also notes that new commercial industrial institutions to which
household work is transferred are "designed, planned, and built up exclusively by men who possess neither the particular gifts nor the experience which women have acquired over centuries of managing the
private family and nurturing its members." It is this imbalance between
women and men which she cites as one of the major sources of the "social,
economic, human and international problems which we face today" (116).

But not only is much household work transferred to the commercial
industrial economy, the majority of the work remaining in the household
economy is without remuneration. Using statistics from her native Finland, Pietila estimates that the amount of unpaid household work in the
years 1980 and 1990 was about six to seven hours per day, the great majority of which was done by women. Quoting a United Nations report of
1995 she notes that if women's unpaid work were given its proper
weight within a world-wide context, women might well emerge in most
societies as the major source of family support.[6]

PIETILA'S FREE, FETTERED, AND PROTECTED ECONOMY AND THE INTERMEDIARY MIDDLE LEVEL ECONOMIC SECTOR

As a Finnish citizen, Pietila is motivated both by the necessity of limit-
ing the growth of a relatively affluent society (Finland) as well as by the
effort to include the non-monetary home economy in calculations of
wealth. In place of the current modern system, she suggests an economic
model in which the center is the "revival of the self-reliant, non-monetary, local as well as household-based" production of goods and services
(119). She calls her tripartite economies "the free economy," "the protected sector," and "the fettered economy."

The "free economy" (which should not be confused with "free trade")
includes the household economy plus an extension into its nearby envi-

ronment. It is the "non-monetary" core of the economy and society, i.e., the unpaid or "free" work for one's own and family needs, community activities, mutual help and cooperation within the neighborhood." Much of the work in the free economy is motivated by sentiment and mutual consideration rather than for commercial trade, production, or money.

The "protected" sector consists of production and work for the home market as well as public services (such as agriculture, food production, construction of houses and infrastructure, administration, schools, health, transport and communication). This is essentially the tax-based public economy in which the cost is somewhat independent of pressures from the competitive world market. It is in the "protected sector" that we see a moral mix of enlightened self-interest, civic sentiment and pride, and public responsibility.

The "fettered economy" represents large scale commercial industrial production for a global market so that the viability of products is tied to or "fettered to" the pressures of international competition. Pietila notes that the larger the part the "fettered" economy plays within a nation, the more dependent is the public economy on outside factors, since the two sectors are inextricably linked. Surprisingly in 1980 the "open" global market economy in Finland "accounted for only 10% of the total working hours and 19% of the value of production." The fettered economy is, of course, motivated by the drive toward efficiency and specialization in which the process of increased production and profits is sacrosanct regardless of how it impacts the free household or the native civic protected place.

Despite the potentially limited significance of the "open fettered" or global commercial economy (at least in a welfare-oriented nation like Finland), this economy is often considered of prime importance by economists and politicians all over the world. As she says, "The pressure for economic competitiveness has become ever stronger during the years, and now it has even spread to other fields than economy, e.g., hospitals and universities, irrespective of whether it fits or not. The rule of 'management by (economic) result' is devastating for caring institutions, cultural activities, environmental issues, etc., and for the whole idea of welfare in the Nordic meaning" (120).

In contrast to this global reality, Pietila argues that the priorities given the two economies should, in fact, be reversed:

> ... the Household economy (both monetary and non monetary) is, from the human point of view, the primary economy. It works directly for the satisfaction of essential human needs—material, social, and cultural. It also produces things that are not available on the market and cannot be purchased for money, such as the feeling of "being somebody," closeness, encouragement, recognition and meaning in life. All this is realized in connection with living and doing things together: cooking, eating, cleaning, playing, watching TV, sleeping, sharing joy and sorrow, and transferring human traditions. In this sphere, every man, woman, and child is a subject, recognized as a person; everyone is indispensable.

> If the human maintenance—mental and physical—and the nurturing of human beings are not taken care of, no other economy is possible. Thus the household is basic not only for the economy, but for the whole society—for the survival of the human species. Therefore, the picture of the human economy should be turned the right side up: the industrial and commercial economy should be seen as auxiliary. (121)

While Hilkka Pietila's critique of modern economics makes an enormous contribution to our reconsideration of what modern economics "means," her article is particularly significant in describing a number of practical programs and proposals which follow through on her initial vision. More specifically she suggests that an *intermediary level* of society is needed between the small and vulnerable individual households and the corporate institutions in both the public and business sectors. She suggests that the "essential functions of living should be brought near to each other. There should not be too much distance between dwelling, work and recreation, between production and reproduction, between age groups and genders" (121).

For the people living in these "Intermediary Level" units of society, she says, they might "gain control over their own lives and break dependency on market products and services over which they have little or no influence" (122). She notes, in fact, that there has been for some time a "village action movement" which has "revived the 'free economy' to quite an extent in the direction proposed above." The model for this movement is the effort to transfer functions from the nuclear household to a "village" Intermediary Level and to reclaim some of what were traditional household functions from the business and public sectors. Activities in the Intermediary Level would include, for example, self-management, care of children and the elderly, paid and unpaid production, housekeeping, gardening and cultivation.

RECONSIDERING ERRORS IN OUR MODERN CONCEPTION OF ECONOMICS: A SUMMARY

We conclude this critique and reconsideration of modern economics, its conception of place, and limited understanding of of such categories as nature, wealth, production, and technology with a summary of what we consider to be three of its major cultural errors: the error of substitutability, the error of non-sustainability, and the error of fragmentation.

THE ERROR OF SUBSTITUTABILITY

The first error is the assumption that aspects of human life can be interchanged or substituted for one another in the act of producing greater quantities of goods and services with little or no consideration for the environmental, social, or meaning-making context within which people live. Thus modern people can substitute the places people live, the work they do, they way in which they bond and relate to one another, the range of meanings that are necessary for their equanimity or sanity irrespective of limits on their underlying nature. And if people do not adjust or adapt to these new "substitutions," they can be taught or persuaded with money or marketing or education or Prozak or, perhaps, in the future, with the manipulation of DNA to make positive adaptations to these substitutions. Following is a brief list of such substitutions:

- Accepting as our major work-places distant mines, factories, offices, vehicles, etc. as a substitute for remaining within and working near one's household or neighborhood.
- Accepting a life of moving about from place to place and being among casual acquaintances or strangers for much of one's life as a substitute for living among friends and acquaintances for substantial periods of time within a native place.
- Accepting as food that which is created in massive monoculture, agribusiness, and food processing institutions in which animals

and plants can be efficiently managed and/or chemically processed as a substitute for obtaining food from local gardens and farms.

- Accepting the enculturation, socialization, and education as it is provided for one's children through efficient multi-service human resource institutions run and supervised by child care workers and professional social workers as a substitute for being near and teaching and rearing one's own children among friends and relatives in one's own neighborhood.

- Accepting living in private homes or in clusters of private homes or apartments in relative isolation among people whom one barely knows as a substitute for living among long-time neighbors.

- Accepting wealth, a well-paying job, and an abundance of material products as a major indication of one's personal significance as a substitute for the significance of being an individual in whatever way that is construed by living and doing what is required by simply being "home."

- Accepting the stories and myths which are invented by clever, distant and unknown professional story and script writers and film makers, etc. as giving significance and meaning to one's life as a substitute for stories and myths that describe one's own culture and the meaning of one's local or regional life created by indigenous story tellers.

- Accepting living almost exclusively near and within plastic, concrete, asphalt, and steel enclosures as a substitute for living near to raw or marginally cultivated nature.

- Accepting the exchange value of money or tokens in the market as the final determination of what is most useful or valuable as a substitute for considering as useful or valuable objects which provide visible and immediate evidence of the necessities and comforts of life.

- Accepting as the major mode of thought the rational calculation of one's own self-interest within product-based material contractual terms as a substitute for a more pluralistic view of experience which would also include the value of searching for and perhaps feeling a mystical world of vague and unseen forces as indicative of a vivid past and a novel future.

Of course, the list could go on until humans reach the point of asking what to substitute for a deep story that connects such powerful events as birth, suffering, creative work, and death, or what to substitute for clean water and radiation-free sunlight when these essential elements are lost in efforts to create cheaper and more marketable products. The obvious answer might be that modern people will develop a technology which reduces all matter to their recombinable components, e.g., electrons, atoms, molecules, DNA, at which point humans can reconstitute (or substitute) everything and anything they might need to survive and prosper as biologically viable beings. As Freeman Dyson has speculated, for example, when fossil fuels run out modern people might well recombine DNA so as to transform some trees into gasoline pumps to keep their internal combustion engines running.[7] This then moves us back into the question of how flexible is human nature and within what limits it can be authentically expressed within the cultural and environmental possibilities available to our species.

In his book *Consilience* the scientist/philosopher Edward O. Wilson looks forward humans will completing the Enlightenment Project when they will "succeed in breaking a human cell down into all its component parts, track down the processes, and accurately model the whole system from the molecules up ... and finally when the developmental biologists, whose focus is on tissues and organs, enjoy similar success." At that point "[t]he stage is then set for the final assault on the still more complex systems of mind and behavior. They are, after all, products of the self same kinds of molecules, tissues, and organs."[8] (We would note the metaphor "assault"—one of control and domination rather than relational inclusion.)

Beyond this futuristic vision there is, of course, the work of those who are actually creating the fully flexible and substitutable human. One of these visionaries is Ray Kurtzweil, who elaborates his view of the future in his book *The Age of Spiritual Machines*.[9] One reviewer summarizes Kurtzweil's futuristic scenario:

> In Kurtzweil's vision, there is no conflict between human beings and machines, because we will all soon, within the lifetimes of most people alive today, become machines. Strictly speaking we

will become software. As he puts it, "We will be *software*, not *hardware*" (italics his) and can inhabit whatever hardware we like best. There will not be any difference between us and robots. "What, after all, is the difference between a human who has upgraded her body and brain using new nanotechnology, and computational technologies and a robot who has gained an intelligence and sensuality surpassing her human creators?" Among the many advantages of this new existence is that you will be able to read any book in a few seconds.[10]

From our point of view, the essential qualities of our nature invite us to reclaim and construct a genuine culture, one that reflects the range of primal to modern multi-layered primal-to-modern biosocial potentialities we have inherited both from our biological past as well as from the multiple layers of our historical and cultural pasts. So to imagine a future that leaves much of this past permanently behind (or recreates it in the form of "virtual reality" or recombined DNA) is not only unrealistic but "unhuman." There are qualities of our nature for which there are no substitutes. They are qualitative, not quantitative; and they are qualitative and limited.

THE ERROR OF ECONOMIC AND ENVIRONMENTAL NON-SUSTAINABILITY

Modern economists have never really faced the challenge presented by the Club of Rome in *The Limits of Growth*—the environmental limits of the planet in supporting the more fragile forms of life on the planet.[11] The issue of sustainability is now a central if not critical concern in the thinking of biological scientists all over the world, while economists still work out schemes, for example, whereby the production of waste products from CO_2 to nuclear debris might somehow be transferred or transported around the planet to keep the expanding industrial machine in operation. Pietila again makes a critical distinction between what she calls the "cultivation economy" and the "industrial production economy." As she says:

> Economics as a science is based on the logic of industrial production extraction of and manufacturing from 'dead elements,' minerals and fossils. When the logic is applied to the cultivation economy, when the same demands of efficiency and productivity are imposed on agriculture and husbandry as on industry, the sys-

tem is bound to run into difficulties. It is absurd to impose the demand for international competitiveness on agriculture, animal husbandry, fishing and forestry, since natural conditions vary enormously from place to place on the earth's surface.

The crucial question is whether the cultivation economy can survive, if the requirements of the industrial economy, i.e., a constantly increasing profitability and efficiency and international competitiveness, are imposed upon it.[12]

There are a number of issues embedded within Pietila's three sector "triangle of the human economy," all of which are closely related to our previous discussion of metaphysical and cultural errors and to the "organic theory" of culture which follows below in Chapter Ten. First is the recommendation that the commercial industrial product orientation toward economic issues with its stress on competition, monetization, and the creation of commercial products for sale is too narrow to deserve the general term "economics." Second, the commercial industrial product orientation virtually ignores the critical local context in which human beings live, love, and struggle to cope with each other, and with the world of nature. And finally, each of these economic orientations contains deep meanings associated with their different contexts. As Pietila says, "Each of these components operates by its own logic and the terms of the industrial economy are well known. The other components need to be further analyzed and defined.... [What we see is] the need for a new theory of the totality of human actions for sustainable livelihood."[13]

THE ERROR OF FRAGMENTATION

From the perspective of our own work the major power of Pietila's critique is that she connects problematic aspects of modern economics (the global competitive industrial model) with specific proposals in which that system may be brought into better balance with regional and local institutions. Some of these relationships are described in Table 7 below. Here is included, for example, a Protective Public Sector (comparable to what we will call throughout this work the "native city") which stands between the voracious commercial system and its destructive effect on the other four sectors.

Table 7. Five Socioeconomic Sectors within a Cosmic Reality
Human Cultural Engagement in the Natural Universe

Commercial-Industrial Sector

Natural capital fed into manufactured capital using human capital—creating products—for money

Physical material wealth, value based on monetary exchange

Metaphors: Efficiency, Substitutability, Production

The Protected Public Sector

Nation state and local native city-state
Economy, society, culture protected by social contract
Food, housing, administration, health, education, etc.

Metaphor: Civic Life

The Nature-Cultivation Sector

Respect for the continuing living potential of nature
Interface between economy and ecology
Human nature restricts culture; human culture restricted by ecological laws

Metaphors: balance, sustainability of natural forms, complementary across living forms

The Household Sector

Households or groups of households
Direct production of essentials of unpaid work
Direct exchange in gardening, cultivation

Metaphor: Family

Middle Level Sector

Institution
Face-to-face neighborhood life
Guilds, sodalities, etc.
Care of children, spouse, elderly, etc.

Metaphor: Community

Instead of seeing modern economic institutions dominating the whole society, we would see it balanced against other subsystems under the control of local and middle level places. This requires that we not only reconsider the meaning of such fundamental categories of thought as metaphysics, reality, layers of reality, human nature, culture, human diversity and the human self and soul; it also requires that we reconsider our deeply internalized "scientific" understanding of modern economics. We must think in terms of the specific *places* in which people live, work, and make their homes and the social bonding and meaning-making institutions that are required to support these local intermediate places.

Here we would argue that Table 7 above, which borrows much of its material from Pietila's work, moves beyond the narrow reductionistic limitations of modern economics. While the upper quadrant consists mainly of neoclassical economic terms, the left hand quadrant reflects what might be called the interventionist civic institutions into the economic sphere—the welfare political economy pioneered within some Western European and several Scandinavian countries. The moral basis of this Protected Civic Native Place might be institutionalized by means of a new social contract with the more Local Places in order to protect and sustain them. This proposal is considerably more radical than the old welfare state. While modern people are currently accustomed to governments working out arrangements to support or control some aspects of global trade, the explicit notion that both national and regional governments might protect the social, economic, and cultural patterns of local places such as households, villages, and native cities has of late been largely ignored. The Middle or Intermediate Sector in the center of Table 7 suggests that humans need to take into account the interaction between economics (in the traditional sense) and government, biology, and various ways to strengthen and sustain regional institutions and local places.

Finally, although not explicitly in the Table, the metaphysical categories suggested earlier in our work by such concepts as "source" and "the unseen world" assume that within the cosmos there is a continuing process of novel creation in which all beings participate. Yet this creation exists within patterns, some of which humans understand, some of which they can manipulate and control, and many of which are (and may always remain) as mysteries. These transcendent layers of reality represent, in some degree, this quality of mystery. Our feeling is that theology and philosophy as disciplines are as much needed as economics, sociology, and anthropology to provide a humble search for areas of knowing and being that transcend our more focused pragmatic tendencies toward literal knowledge. Philosophy and theology are excursions into the unknown with the understanding that they may forever remain there.

Daly and Cobb enjoin us in the beginning of their work, like Pietila, to critically reconsider economics as the dominant discipline of modernity. Such a reconsideration, they suggest, might well force us "both to think through the discipline of economics as well as beyond into biology, history, philosophy, physics, and theology."[14]

And so while we have attempted to clarify and extend the meaning of various modern metaphysical, cultural, and normative categories in the work presented thus far, below we venture into an effort to begin the project suggested above—that is to provide a more comprehensive and transdisciplinary theory of place and the preconditions of genuine culture that may be required to make such a place truly live.

NOTES

1. Nina Leopold Bradley, "Aldo Leopold," *Wild Earth*, Fall, 1999, 11-14.

2. In general economic-technological terms, "inputs" require resources ("land"), human activity ("labor"), and the accumulation of equity (money), manufactured tools and equipment (capital) to create "output." Output is defined as "goods and services" which are counted as "wealth" after they have been exchanged in some known "market" and counted by the official record-keeping organs of corporate institutions. (See O'Hara, S. "Toward a Sustaining Production Theory," *Ecological Economics* 20, (1997), 141.)

3. Herman Daly & John Cobb, *For the Common Good* (Boston: Beacon Press, 1989).

4. Ibid., 30.

5. Hilkka Pietila, "The triangle of the human economy: household - cultivation - industrial production. An attempt at making visible the human economy in toto," *Ecological Economics*, 20, (1997), 113-127.

6. See also Marilyn Waring, *If Women Counted A New Feminist Economics* (San Francisco, CA: Harper and Row, 1988). And Waring's Video: "Who's Counting."

7. Freeman Dyson, TV interview on PBS MacNeil-Lehrer News Hour

8. Edward O. Wilson, *Consilience* (NY: Knopf, 1998), 94.

9. Ray Kurtzweil, *The Age of Spiritual Machines* (NY: Viking, 1999).

10. John R. Searle, "I married a computer," *New York Review of Books*, 46, no.6, (April 8, 1999), 34-38.

11. Donella H. Meadows, Dennis L. Meadows, Jorgen Randers, and William W. Behrens, III, *The Limits of Growth* (Washington, D.C.: Potomac Associates, 1972).

12. Pietila, "The Triangle of the Human Economy," 124.

13. Ibid., 126.

14. Daly and Cobb, *For the Common Good*, 2.

PART FIVE

An Organic Theory of Place and Culture

CHAPTER TEN

A Balanced Culture Within a Living Place

CREATING CATEGORIES TO DESCRIBE AND EVALUATE PLACE AND CULTURE

CULTURAL RELATIVISM AND THE PROBLEM OF COMPARING PLACE AND CULTURE

In Chapter One we began making normative judgments when we compared cultural institutions of modern society with anthropological and sociological interpretations of cultures within tribal and village societies. This is, of course, a risky business since it requires that one evaluate the quality of life across different levels and types of society from the perspective of one who is already situated within a particular culture. Goldschmidt notes that anthropologists have generally been reluctant to make such normative judgments. They are caught up in what he calls the Malinowskian dilemma; that is, they insist that "every culture be understood [only] in its own terms; that every institution [or cultural practice] be seen as a product of the [unique] culture within which it developed.... It follows from this that a cross-cultural comparison of institutions is essentially a false enterprise, for we are comparing the incomparable."[1] The result is what Goldschmidt considers the ambiguous or "double edged" contribution of contemporary anthropology to an understanding of modern ethics and morality. As he says:

> Anthropology has had a great impact on the moral philosophy of our time, an impact out of all proportion to the numerical and fiscal strength of the discipline. It has moved us away from biological thinking and toward an appreciation of the force of culture; it has

made us aware of our own customs and beliefs as one of the many and apparently arbitrary modes of thought. In doing this it has promoted a cultural relativism....

But ... we cannot escape the fact that this is essentially a negative achievement. The positive accomplishment of a [normative or moral] theory of man has not been developed, and there seems to be little evidence on the horizon that it is developing.[2]

But as Goldschmidt says, it is now time to move beyond this relativistic phase of social science "in order to relieve social philosophers of the habit of evaluating cultures in terms of our own culturally determined predilections." As he says, " By now we can certainly appreciate the contextual value of infanticide without advocating it, or can see the merits and demerits of polygyny without concern over our own convictions or regulations. What we must do now is examine the consequences of particular institutional devices for the stability of the community and the physical and mental health of its constituent members."[3]

We would now translate what Goldschmidt calls the "phenomenon of dysfunction" into what we have earlier referred to as cultural errors and his phrase "relevant criteria for functional efficacy" into an invitation to develop normative standards to which Sapir referred with his concept of "genuine culture." Inspired by this call for a less relativistic orientation toward culture, this chapter sketches out a theory of human society in which we articulate various qualities of place and cultural patterns by which to describe these "places." It is from these descriptions of place and culture that we then move to the normative concept of "balance" as a major construct by which to judge quality of life. Not surprisingly, our theory focuses on the balance between the primal to modern dimensions of various places and patterns of culture.

INTRODUCING A HOLISTIC SOCIAL THEORY

Our theory of holistic society begins with the idea of a "living place" (to repeat Leopold's term) that is inhabited by psycho-biological and spiritual humans functioning within a complex evolving ecosystem consisting of various levels of place and meaning. We assume that humans within these places have been encultured into a structured coherent way of life, and that such cultures have, at least potentially, habitats which may balance primal-to-modern cultural patterns which support and sustain these habitats. The question then is how to proceed from these more general statements regarding organic "living places" and "balanced cultural patterns" to a more finely articulated, systematic, normative theory.

As indicated above, when we follow Pietila's line of argument we see society as including such places as the household, the cultivation place, the protective city, the corporate mercantile place, and a variety of middle level or mediating local places we shall call the balanced or vital center. We must confess that describing and comprehending this layered contextual view of society is not easy within our modern linear way of thinking. Ironically, however, the point of this multi-level, multi-layered view of society is to allow us to see the human condition in more unitary holistic terms—as a single, more or less balanced and integrated organism. We assume, of course, that all societies cannot be characterized as having "living places"—some are seriously flawed and are better characterized as filled with dying or lifeless places and unbalanced cultures. A theory which allows us to describe a living or balanced society and culture should, however, also allow us to identify flawed and unbalanced places.

THREE LEVELS OF SOCIETY

Our theory in its present form distinguishes among three levels of analysis, and within each level we posit further layers or categories.

- Level One denotes *place or habitat* within which we distinguish three layers: a) abstract geographic or mathematically delineated places described, for example, by surveyors or mapmakers, b) actual natural geological places, e.g., valleys, hillsides, etc., described from the "outside" by scientists, developers, engineers, and their inhabitants in terms of the separate beings or events that happen there, and c) organic "living places" or ecosystems which sustain an interrelated set of mutually interdependent living beings who experience place as an inner intrinsic part of their own being.

- Level Two denotes a set of *adaptive functional cultural patterns* which sustain life within these places and which reflect the potentialities and requirements of our human nature as well as the nature of the other inhabitants of these places.

- Level Three presents *primal to modern balance* as the normative principle we are using to discuss quality of life within such places. From this point of view, balance requires a range of primal to modern places and primal to modern cultural patterns that characterize these places.

The central reason for distinguishing among these levels or layers of society is to provide a foundation for positing that primal and middle level face-to-face institutions are an essential precondition for any meaningful discussion of the errors and promise of a more balanced modern world.

THE CONCEPT OF ORGANIC HOLISM

In constructing a theory in society we use the organic metaphor to make explicit our assumption that humans are capable of distinguishing between healthy and sick or dysfunctional societies just as they are able to distinguish between healthy and sick individual organisms. Like individuals, we assume that societies are born, mature, grow old, perish, and are, in mysterious ways, sometimes reborn and renewed. This organic view of society is thus explicitly normative in that it associates "goodness" with health—but not necessarily with continuing progressive change or improvement, or advancement toward perfection. Rather we see "goodness" as associated with the *availability*, integration, and balanced wholeness of a range of places and primal-to-modern cultural patterns. It is important to point out that our theory includes balance between deeply encultured traditional institutions and modern, novel, pragmatic modes of functioning. It is, in fact, the compulsive modern use of our rational pragmatic gifts as we engage in the constant effort to progress and "improve" things which may undermine the quality of life and sustainability of many "living places."

Below we elaborate these three central categories of our theory: Living Place, Culture, and Normative Balance.

A LIVING PLACE

Our initial understanding of place consists of historically evolving places which include the wilderness, the household, the sodality, the village, the corporate work place, the native town or city, and the nation state. (Our list is meant to be suggestive and is in no sense assumed to be exhaustive or complete.) The term "evolving" suggests the importance of the historical dimension, from primal to middle to modern. We see society as a set of places (or social forms) having evolved through the primal and archaic layers to contemporary times. (Redfield and Singer discuss this evolutionary history in the following chapter.) As each new place evolves, it carries within it elements of prior forms just as any complex individual organism carries within it many of the more elementary organic forms that persist in the process of evolution, (e.g., mitochondria in cells, *E. coli* within the bowel, etc.). Our hypothesis is that although these basic forms of place exist (or once existed) "out there," their schematic potentiality may remain deeply embedded in the substrate of our human nature and reach out to construct the cultural patterns that shape our lives in the actual world of "societies-and-cultures-coming-into being."

In our view, societies consist of places in the process of being born, renewed, and, possibly, perishing. Whole societies or part-societies often contain dysfunctional places which only marginally support human life and the human spirit, and it is no great task to feel the difference between a living vibrant place and a sick or dying place.

Table 8. Layers of Human Habitats or Evolving Places		
Primal	Middle	Modern
wilderness bands in		
familistic households in		
local sodalities, churches, schools in		
farms, shops, villages, plantations in		
individuals in urban conglomerates in		
nation states, etc. in planetary places		

ENCULTURING MULTIPLE LAYERS OF PLACE

When we observe birds building nests and mammals creating lairs—in habitats or "places," the notion of place as home seems like common sense. The bird, for example, has an inner place in the "nest" as an intimate part of its own being; there is the immediate environment in which it feeds; and there may be expansive areas over which it flies during migration or otherwise. There is no doubt that these "places" for birds are both "in" the being of the bird in some physical (and perhaps metaphysical) way as well as "outside" in the world that the bird comes to inhabit. But we suspect that as modern people we often have difficulty acknowledging the various place-based layers of our inner and outer being. As Bateson says, we tend to see ourselves only "inside" the skin of our bodies; see place or places as "outside," as separate from ourselves, as "out there" to be observed as spectators.

Place can thus be encultured at several levels. First it can mean what astronomers or physicists talk about when they measure, map, and manipulate *space* as a mathematical abstraction. Once measured, space or place in this sense can be bought and sold as a commodity. The value of place then can be given value in monetary or bartered units. Modern people may then look at an "empty" field or wood lot and note that there is "nothing there" now, but that it can be "developed." There is then a more vivid sense of place in which humans and other living creatures cope and live in the everyday world. Such places may have significance for humans in that they provide for the economic necessities and comforts of life. Place can also have deep emotional and metaphysical connotations.

Thus, we have the human nature/cultural potentiality for seeing and feeling "place" in these various ways. For example, one's archaic inner sense of household or communal life can either be "fixed" and made central to one's identity or attenuated by cultural conditioning to appear in our consciousness as only a weakly defined grounded sense of home. Our guess is that for most humans to sustain themselves and truly engage the world, they may need to be encultured to experience some part of the world as a "living place," as "home." From this perspective humans (and many other mobile living species as well) are little different from plants which cannot be continuously moved out of their original or native habitat without considerable risk. Not to be "at home" (or not even to know where home is) for many humans may well result in subverting a fundamental part of their nature and an essential aspect of genuine culture.

WALTER'S THEORY OF LIVING PLACES

E. V. Walter describes this deeper understanding of place in what he calls "placeways."[4] Central to his analysis is the concept of "haptic" or a "grasping" perception—the notion that the living organism directly "feels" and connects with its environment (with place) based on a long history of environmental and cultural adaptation. Within this theory the "body feels the articulations of shapes and surfaces in the world by means of its own inner articulations."[5] Walter suggests that humans can actually register relationships with the topography of the ground and the environment in "our bones." As he says, "This powerful and elaborate perceptual system is not located in a clearly definable anatomical group with an exact inventory of nerves and sensations … [but rather the senses organize them as] a unity of function from anatomical diversity."[6]

Evidence for this theory is adduced from a variety of sources, including the work of James J. Gibson, an environmental physiologist, as well as from the writings of the architectural historian Vincent Scully, the urban historian Lewis Mumford, and from considerable experience with native peoples, especially the Australian Aborigines.[7] Walter distinguishes between the mythic (archaic) metaphysical feeling for "a sense of place" and the scientific notion of physical space defined in abstract mathematical terms. He argues that:

> Modern space is universal and abstract, whereas a "place" is concrete and particular. People do not experience abstract space [as] … they experience places. A place is seen, heard, smelled, imagined, loved, hated, feared, revered, enjoyed, or avoided. Abstract space is infinite; in modern thinking it means a framework of possibilities. A place is immediate, concrete, particular, bounded, finite, unique. Abstract space is repetitive and uniform. Abstraction moves away from the fullness of experience. Abstract space against concrete place contrasts abstract representation with the pulse of life feeling.[8]

Walter describes the intuitive expressive dimension of place by referring to the way people feel and think and imagine—"perceptual reality signifies things they [directly] perceive, and cognitive reality, things they understand."[9] "Direct perception" means that we are "in" the place and the place is "in" us, and the whole environment is around us, in us, and alive. Direct perception suggests that cultures must support the basic need for humans to "grasp" places as we do in the synaptic process when actuality emerges from the Void. That is, the underlying substrate of human nature reaches out to connect physically with the quality of a place which is then cognitively elaborated, "fixed," and given meaning within the framework of a particular culture. It is assumed that as long as humans (or any organism) remain within a social and environmental "place" or habitat for a substantial period of time, the understanding of that place will remain fixed as a quasi-permanent cultural code. Place thus carries with it moral and empirical information that shapes and is shaped by the culture of the people who live there. Keith Basso gives a striking example of this phenomenon in his experience with groups of Apache. Basso has observed that the Apache see the landscape as filled with specific named locations where, as he says, "time and space have fused and where through the agency of historical tales, their interaction is made visible to human contemplation." He says, the Apaches

> view the landscape as a repository of distilled wisdom, a stern but benevolent keeper of tradition; an ever vigilant ally in the efforts of individuals and whole communities to put into practice a set of standards for social living that are uniquely and distinctively their own. In the world that the Western Apache have constituted for themselves, features of the landscape have become symbols of and for this way of living, the symbols of a culture and the enduring moral character of a people.[10]

If humans can be so profoundly "marked" by a particular place, one is then compelled to ask: What happens when humans turn their cognitive abilities to radically changing or "improving" their places and lose their grip on their capacity to "grasp" the place directly? Walter answers this question by describing the experiences of humans who left the more loosely structured wilderness places in which they evolved (perhaps for thousands of years) and constructed settled places. He calls this a "topomorphic revolution" in which the change in human settlement patterns brought about a profound change in cultural meaning.[11] He maintains that everything we know about the paleolithic peoples— "from their view of symbols, pictures, and perception of space"—would lead us to understand that they lived with "a pervading sense of interdependence among creatures, things, heavenly bodies, and cosmic forces—an inseparable oneness of the universe."[12] As he says, "The terror of wild beasts is not paleolithic—it belongs to the agricultural era. In the Old Stone Age humans defended themselves against predators, but they did not imagine hearth and home as a separate place apart from the beasts. The primeval hut was not topistically different from other lairs or nests."[13] And continuing:

> Whereas the art of agricultural civilizations represented the differences between men and beasts, paleolithic artists showed the connections. They imagined an unsegregated community of humans, beasts, and spirits, belonging together. In southern France and northern Spain, therefore, prehistoric cave pictures reveal a primeval structure of mutual immanence—a system of effective presences dwelling together in the long prehistory before the agricultural way of life. (47)

Walter points out that the new, stable village and its agricultural economic base changed humanity's deepest view of reality. The wilderness and settlement became polarized opposites. The village became a place of "cultivation" that was set apart from "beasts" (47). "Domestic" animals were attached to the *domus* or extended household while "wild beasts" became alien and were spatially segregated from the human settlement.

But fundamental changes in human habitats did not stop here. Walter describes a second and much later topomorphic revolution toward the end of preindustrial "civilization" during which the town or city-state was transformed into the commercial industrial city and the nation-state. Here he points to a very different kind of segregation—instead of the wilderness and beast becoming separated from the village and the town, the poor become segregated from the rich. Using paintings from early literature as evidence, he argues that in preindustrial medieval towns and cities, at least in Europe, the rich were never radically separated from the poor. They were, as he says, "thrust into each one another's life space of communal interdependence" (40).

> The rich accepted the relentless presence of the poor, who attended, assisted, and harassed them continually as slaves, servants, clients, employees, petitioners, sycophants, supplicants, and spectators. The city in those times remained a unified urban experience for all conditions of men and women, whereas now it tends to decompose into little more than an administrative matrix for a range of differential urban experiences, alien to one another, with different moral values. (40)

Walter contrasts this mixing of socio-economically diverse peoples within ancient and medieval cities with the revolutionary changes wrought by the commercial industrial revolution. One of these changes was the segregation of various parts of the city into wealthy and slum neighborhoods.

Walter describes the slum as a "specific condition ... shaped by a process of exclusions, enclosures, and dissociations" in which cities were transformed from common places into a revolutionary new system of segregated places. Central to this revolution at the end of the eighteenth century was the creation of the "industrial slum—an environment of factories, hovels, and the workhouses" (37). The modern urban slum, of course, includes much more—rail yards, warehouses, trucking centers, massive highways, shipyards and loading docks, public housing, and a variety of commercial markets.

Walter concludes his argument by suggesting that the human perception of reality is heavily conditioned by an encultured experience of place which requires that humans have some notion of the "fully human environment"—Stuart Hampshire's term. The obstacle to creating a "fully human environment" for modern people is what he calls "ungrounded reason" (212). Walter agues that modern people need to regain "the unity of a place as a location of [direct] experience and a matrix of energies." They need to balance their capacity for reason as a utilitarian tool with deeper symbolic feelings for place.

> ... The mind includes more than intellect. It contains a history of what we learn through our feet. It grasps the world that meets the eye, the city we know with our legs, the places we know in our hearts, our guts, in our memories, in our imaginations. It includes the world we feel in our bones. (213)

But how does the modern person reclaim some sense of "the fully human environment?" How does one regain the fullness and balance and integration of the *domus* or homestead, the sodality, the village, and the native city?

Walter encourages us to believe that the archaic ways of seeing, thinking, and caring about "place" are not lost; that they are somehow still buried in the deep schemata or "unseen world" that is part of our nature. But the cultural patterns and forms which allow humans to express this nature are increasingly overpowered by the transitory, fragmented places in which modern people live and the social structures and symbols of the modern market. With Walter, however, we should remind ourselves that the memory of "grasping" time and place, feeling kin and friendship, and connecting with place is still there. Millions of humans still inhabit extended households and villages and native cities and contribute daily to the archaic living memories and images and energies needed to reclaim the conditions of genuine culture.[14]

CULTURE

The second level of our theory consists of what sociologists and anthropologists commonly refer to as "structural-functional systems" or cultural patterns invented/discovered by human beings which allow them to live and "function" within community and society. Such systems or patterns of culture require a language by which to identify and interrelate the various "functions" required for humans to adapt successfully to their world.[15] Obviously the number and particular layers or functions one selects to describe a society are in some degree arbitrary since it follows from one's particular theoretical focus. Because our concern is for the relationship between primal and modern aspects of human nature and their relationship to primal to modern places and cultural patterns, our interest is in building a more adequate theory of *cultural balance* and finding ways by which to maintain cultural continuity across this dimension. Thus our special interest is in defining those cultural functions which allow us to clarify and develop our theory of primal-to-modern balance and discuss more specifically institutions related to the vital mediating center between these poles.

TWO FUNDAMENTAL ASPECTS OF CULTURE: DESCRIPTIVE PATTERNS AND CULTURAL DEPTH

Before continuing with our functional analysis, however, there is an important ambiguity in the concept of culture which must be clarified. Culture refers first to the various descriptive patterns of action, relationship, and meaning which allow us to characterize a group of people inhabiting a particular place as doing something "in common"—as engaging in a set of common adaptive habits or "cultural" behavior. Tables 9 and 10 below provide a language for describing such patterns and relate them to the primal to modern dimension of place and human nature. So, for example, there are patterns of human habitation, patterns of work, patterns of social bonding, patterns of meaning making, etc.

But there is a second important quality of culture. This is the relative depth with which cultural patterns are embedded within individuals and within communal actions and experience. This dimension relates to what we commonly call "tradition" on the embedded side and existential rational pragmatic "problem solving" on the short term existential side. Deep traditions last through generations. Short term pragmatic cultural patterns are generated to meet the unforeseen exigencies of daily life. Some come and go with the fluctuating problems of life; others persist across generations to meet long-term needs and eventually become traditions.

Below we shall first present a set of categories by which to denote descriptive cultural patterns of action, relationship, and meaning. This will give us the language by which we can also make normative quality of life comparisons so as to evaluate substantive aspects of people's lives as they work, and cope, and play, etc. Later in this section we shall discuss at greater length the complex dimension of cultural depth.

DESCRIPTIVE CULTURAL CATEGORIES OF ENVIRONMENTAL/ECONOMIC PATTERNS, PATTERNS OF RELATIONSHIP AND BONDING, AND PATTERNS OF MEANING-MAKING

Our analytic scheme begins with the assumption that certain functional patterns must be fulfilled in order for humans to create viable living places. We posit the following three superordinate cultural categories both as basic patterns to fulfill the requirements of our human nature as well as being useful for issues of balance within place and culture.

- Environmental/Economic Patterns by which humans find and create within a habitat successful modes of economic sustenance and environmental adaptation;
- Socio-Political Relationships and Bonding Patterns by which humans cooperate and form various forms of communal or corporate life; and
- Meaning-Making Patterns by which humans create various modes of discovering, learning, and creating images, metaphors, stories, interpretations, and rituals to express the various levels of meaning of their humanity.

Table 9 below lists these three major cultural functions (designated by Roman numerals) and the elaboration of these patterns (designated by letters) followed by illustrative examples.

The first cultural pattern listed under *environmental-economic* is "the sense of place." As indicated above, a culture might conceive of environment or place simply as a geometrically defined area on the planet or a piece of real estate, while another culture might consider "place" as a deep metaphysical or spiritual entity called "home." We assume that the former would be considered as a more modern aspect of culture while the latter would be considered more primal. From our organic perspective, a *living place* is defined as having a range of possibilities within its cultural repertoire which contribute to the adaptive efficacy of the society.

Table 9. Cultural Patterns Reflecting the Adaptive Potentialities and Requirements of Our Human Nature

Environmental/Economic Cultural Patterns

Sense of Place (physical, metaphysical-spiritual)

Types of Vocation (breadwork, artisanship, industrial)

Levels of Technology (simple tools, complex)

Specialized Work Groups (socio-economic classes, gender, races)

Socio-Political Relationships and Bonding Patterns

Forms of Bonding and Social Glue (kinship, friendship contract, etc.)

Sources of Power and Control (shared power, hierarchical power over, etc.)

Social Structures Based on Diversity (race, gender, temperament, etc.)

Meaning and Meaning-Making Cultural Patterns

Conceptions of Personal Identity (essential being, relational being, holarchical being, unitary being)

Time (linear, cyclical, dream, etc.)

Experience (emergent, narrative, interpretive, mythic, etc.)

Enactment (festivals, games, sacred events , etc.)

In a second example, we see cultural patterns requiring high technology and a high degree of specialized work as more "modern," as opposed to primal patterns requiring simpler technology and less specialization. Again, the point is that one kind of cultural potentiality is not *ipso facto* superior to the other. We assume that a genuine culture will have an adequate and balanced representation within a *range of primal to modern adaptive patterns.*

Similar comparisons may be made within the superordinate function relating to *socio-political relationships and bonding*. Within this category we see, for example, forms of bonding relating to family, kinship, and friendship as more primal, and forms of bonding relating to bureaucracies and legal contracts as more modern. Likewise we would consider cultural patterns relating to power which involve relatively egalitarian ways of negotiating shared power as more primal, while more complex hierarchically centralized ways of delegating and negotiating power within large organizations would be considered more modern.

Other comparisons can be made in the third major function relating to *meaning and meaning-making*. As indicated in Part Two, we consider enculturation at the emerging or prehending phase of "experience" along with a symbolic or metaphorical understanding of reality as more primal, while cultural elements related to complex, explicit, literal interpretations of story or data are seen as more modern. Likewise we consider sacred rituals in which individuals seek to integrate a more intimate connection with the unseen metaphysical world with the actual stories of everyday life as more primal as opposed to modern secular rituals in which individuals engage in sports, recreation, or the arts.

Table 10 below elaborates the information in Table 9 and presents the relationships among the primal to modern dimension as it applies to evolutionary layers of place and to more specific patterns of culture. Each major pattern set is expanded to include several relevant subordinate patterns along with suggestive examples which illustrate the norms and requirements for both place and culture. Our theory assumes that healthy places (and consequently healthy cultures) require that an adequate range of balanced and integrated patterns be available across the primal to modern spectrum to meet the needs of genuine culture. Especially important are the patterns in the center of the Table which allow humans to mediate and balance their lives in both primal and modern ways.

Within each of the three superordinate functions, primal places have a tendency to provide the physical conditions under which primal patterns will be encultured. In Pattern Set I (Environmental/Economic Patterns), for example, primal or middle level places are more likely to allow for the construction of such cultural patterns as a sense of place, artisan-type vocations, while modern places are more likely to provide the conditions that encourage physical mobility, commercial entrepreneurship, and the development of complex technology.

The point of this organic approach in studying human society is that we are prompted to articulate the connection between the presumed primal-to-modern *functional needs* of our human nature and the *cultural patterns* that are constantly evolving to meet these needs within actual places. In doing this, we hopefully tend to "notice" various aspects of places or habitats we may otherwise ignore or underestimate in importance, and

Table 10. Cultural Patterns Across the Primal-To-Modern Dimension and their Relationship to Types of Place

Primal	Middle And Vital Center	Modern
wilderness		
household		
	sodality	
	native city	
		industrial, commercial
		private dwelling

Environmental/Economic Patterns

A Sense of Place

Primal	Middle And Vital Center	Modern
Deep Sense of Connection		Flexible, Highly Mobile

Types of Vocation

Primal	Middle And Vital Center	Modern
Hunting-Gathering	Mother Work	Entrepreneurship
Mother Work	Artisanship	Engineering
	Agriculture	Management
	Local Markets	Routine Jobs

Level of Technology

Primal		Middle And Vital Center		Modern
Hand Tools	Animal Power		Water/Steam	Fossil/Atomic

Specialization and Socio-Economic Cohorts

Primal	Middle And Vital Center	Modern
Simple Specialization	Various Levels of Artisanship	Segregated Affluent Elites
Agriculture		The Poor, Middle Class,
Villagers	Nobility and Retinue	Underclass

Social-Political Patterns and Forms of Bonding

Forms of Bonding and Social Glue

Primal	Middle And Vital Center	Modern
Kinship/Mating	Friendship Communal Cooperation	Contract and Self-Interest

Sources of Power, Control, and Decision Making

Primal	Middle And Vital Center	Modern
Age, Size, Competence	Relational "Power Within"	Economic "Power Over"
Agonistic Displays		Control of Property and Capital
	Informal Negotiation	
		Skill Training, Education, Legal Sanctions and Institutions of the State

Table 10 Continued		
Meaning and Meaning-Making		
Conceptions of Personal Identity (Being)		
Implicit Within Kin/ Place/Vocation		Education/Corporate Success/Power
Participation of Self-in-Community		Importance of Individual Self-in-Corporation
Time		
Linear	Organic/Linear/Cyclical	Linear/Progressive
Seasonal/Cyclical	Seasonal/Dream/ Eternal	Past-Present-Future
Dream/Eternal		
Experience		
Emergent	Pragmatic Problem Solving	Science
Narrative History		Technology
Preconscious	Philosophy	Fiction and Arts
Primacy of Myth, Metaphor		Private Personal Experience
Cosmology		
Enactment		
Engagement in Unconscious Unseen World	Sacred Ritual Embedded in Everyday Life	Secular Festivals and Games
		Mass Media
	Sacred Communal Feasts	Cult of Personality
		Secular Entertainment

we look to these places as potential venues to meet significant functional needs. We thus probe the extent to which cultural patterns actually respond to various human requirements or needs built into our nature.

THE DEPTH DIMENSION OF CULTURE

THE IDEA OF CULTURAL LOGIC OR GRAMMAR

The concept of "cultural logic" suggests that one cannot understand the various levels of culture without taking into account its deeper metaphors and themes which provide a holistic, integrating logic or grammar. The term "logic" stresses the fact that various aspects of culture "hang together." That is, the deeper processes of enculturation tend to precondition our understanding of the more superficial manifestations. Thus, we are limited or restricted in the extent to which we can self-consciously change or repair specific cultural patterns by the extent to which any particular pattern is embedded within a whole constellation of cultural actions, relationships, and meanings.

In language, for example, the semantics or the range in use and specific meanings of words are more flexible and culturally changeable than the syntax which determines different underlying functions of language. Or, to change the modern emphasis on linear time, for example, would require that we alter in some fundamental way our understanding of "work" which is highly scheduled, supervised, and paid in objective monetary units. So in any culture there is a deep logic or "grammar" which conditions how we understand and think about the more superficial patterns expressed in the vocabulary of that culture.[16]

LEVELS OF CULTURAL DEPTH: ENCULTURATION, SOCIALIZATION, AND PRAGMATIC REASON AND CONSCIOUS MEMORY

In our terms, cultural depth refers to various levels of patterning that shape and condition individual people within their social milieu. The deepest level of patterning is probably related to what we commonly mean by instinct, e.g., the tendency of newborn babies to nurse. At the next level there is the *imprinting event* which happens almost instantly when the organism is presented with a critical cue or stimulus after birth. A mother's identity, for example, is presumably imprinted on her baby early in life by smell and/or tone of voice. These two processes of patterning might be considered as precultural.

Perhaps the first level of cultural conditioning emerges from what we have referred to as tropes—tendencies embedded in our human nature which require only slight or moderate cultural conditioning to be expressed as an actualized pattern. These latent or "tropic" tendencies, we are speculating, are similar to what the sociobiologist Edward O. Wilson refers to as *"epigenetic rules."* In Wilson's terms, "Genes prescribe epigenetic rules, which are the regularities of sensory perception and mental development that animate and channel the acquisition of culture."[17] Wilson gives several examples applied more specifically to body language or paralanguage to illustrate his position—e.g., spitting as an

aggressive display of rejection; flicking the tongue around the lips as social invitation.

We would add two major qualifications to the epigenetic aspect of culture-making as precondition for the creation of stable patterns of behavior. First, some epigenetic rules or latent tropes provide single direct
routes to human enculturation; others provide multiple, various, and alternative routes. We may, for example, have deep structural rules that
guide the learning of human language, but we have the potentiality to
invent dramatically varied kinds of language, and taking one route (creating one language) may well preclude the possibility (or probability) of
taking on others (creating second or third languages within a single culture). Second, there is the somewhat disturbing fact that humans seem to
have the rather perverse capacity to enculture in some degree patterns
which either fail to flow from strong, positive epigenetic tendencies, or
which contradict epigenetic tendencies altogether—what we have referred to earlier as "cultural errors." In short, humans have the somewhat dubious "gift" of being free in some cases from the rigid strictures
of instinctive behavior which allows them to enculture through seduc-
tion, perversion, and/or coercion, patterns which violate the more "genuine" qualities of our human nature. One thinks, for example, of the
common Western pedagogical practice of coercing young children to sit
in hard wooden or plastic desks in school for long periods of time doing
seat work or book work or computer work in order to learn what are presumed to be the necessary canons of the culture.[18]

It is important to stress that all three tropic capacities for shaping human behavior—instinct, imprinting, and tropic-level enculturation—
are profound forms of "learning" or patterning. When we say they are
profound, we mean that instinct, imprinting and enculturation effect
fundamental changes and are difficult to unlearn and change. When different cultural patterns challenge them (as when one moves into a new
culture), there is usually great stress in the process of adaptation.

A second level of cultural conditioning is socialization usually associated with the learning of social conventions which operate at or near the
subconscious level, but which are relatively easily brought to consciousness. We see a significant distinction between tropic enculturation and
socialization. Whether one sees oneself, for example, as "self-in-community" versus seeing oneself as an "independent autonomous individual"
is the result of deep tropic enculturation. Selecting styles of clothing

would be more in the realm of socialization. Food habits are somewhat ambiguous. For many Americans, for example, learning to eat certain insects or dog meat might well require repatterning at the level of enculturation while giving up potatoes or bread to pursue a low carbohydrate diet might be done within the framework of resocialization or even within the framework of pragmatic reason.

A third level of culture-making is that which comes from pragmatic reason and the resulting subconscious or conscious memory that follows its application. As humans go about their daily affairs, they draw on the routine memory of the way things normally are or have been. This applies to everything from preparing a meal to driving a car. When faced with "blocks" or glitches in everyday life, humans rely on patterns of behavior that have worked in the past. (If the car does not start, we call the garage or jump start it from a friend's car.) But this large repertory of pragmatic solutions to life's problems as well as creative strategies for constructing new solutions to such problems are built on the foundation of deeper, often unconscious, patterns of tropic enculturation and socialization. Thus, the selection of problem-solving strategies in a given situation is limited by earlier processes of tropic cultural conditioning and socialization already given to our deeper psychic and communal being.

For example, when a young person is faced with the problem of leaving home and finding a job or attending a distant school, much deeper qualities of learning come into play. For the affluent, cosmopolitan young person who has been to summer camps or traveled to distant places alone or with friends, "leaving home" means something very different from its meaning for a traditional kin-oriented or "village" person who has always lived close to an extended family and friends. At the level of socialization, the cosmopolitan person feels comfortable with the routines of packing, moving, making new friends, etc. These are not strange and difficult routines to follow. At the level of enculturation the cosmopolitan person may suffer from home sickness or loneliness for periods of time, but s/he knows that the parental bond inevitably has to be loosened and one is supposed to leave home and be on one's own. To live at home or, in some cases, even to stay in one's "home town" may well signify a kind of personal failure. This, of course, relates to several common contemporary cultural dilemmas. A permanent pattern of life as "self-in-community" or "self-within-one's-native-family" is seen by the affluent upper-middle class culture as an unacceptable way to be.

One must create a separate, independent, autonomous identity. Living with long term ties to a particular place and a particular group of people is seen as provincial, narrow, parochial, even "uneducated." The status acquired simply from home or family membership is never enough; it must be achieved through one's exceptional performance in life. So the affluent individualistic person and the more modest "local" person may cope with the problem of "leaving home" in quite similar ways, e.g., long telephone calls or e-mail messages, but the deeper "cultural" meaning of these actions may be radically different.

BALANCE AS AN ETHICAL-CULTURAL NORM

PRIMAL-TO-MODERN BALANCE AS A PRINCIPLE FOR QUALITY OF LIFE

The third level of our theory presents the principle of *balance* as a central concept by which to make value judgments regarding quality of life. Below we shall develop five areas or levels within which to reflect upon and judge the quality of life for living places and genuine cultures. First, society must have "available" multiple and adequate of places (e.g., households, villages, native cities, local and cosmopolitan markets, etc.) within which to balance primal to modern patterns of culture. Second, there must be balance across basic (or superordinate) functions, i.e., balanced emphasis across environmental-economic functions, socio-political and bonding functions, and meaning-making functions, so that societies are not narrowly concerned with one or two qualities of human activity. Third, there must be balance across each of the more specific primal to modern cultural categories or dimensions. Fourth, there must be balance in the degree to which settings or places focus on highly specialized and compartmentalized activities and fragment society into segregated cohorts versus the degree to which settings or places integrate and connect various types of activities and types of humans within a society. Finally, there must be a balance between the depth, authenticity, and sustainability of a society's traditions versus the extent to which cultural patterns change in response to pragmatic rational strategies required to critique perceived "errors" or violations of human nature within its traditions.

ELABORATING NORMATIVE CATEGORIES OF BALANCE

1) Adequacy and Availability of Balanced Places

The adequacy and availability of places deal with the extent to which a given society has a sufficient number and type of places within which individuals can express the fullness of their human nature potential. We might ask, for example, whether or not a culture has constructed adequate primal institutions such as the domus or household with family members and workers in the home who can devote time caring for children and families. Or we might ask whether or not there are significant modern places in which both men and women have the opportunity to choose vocations that are consistent with their diverse temperaments.

2) Balance Across Basic Cultural Functions

Modern philosophers and social scientists often speak of the human condition in one dimensional terms—as the "economic human" or the "religious human" or the "playful human" or the "tool-making human" or the "territorial human," or the "aggressive human," etc. We can recall the Freudian dictum that the central motivations of humans are "love" and "work," which, of course, leave out human concerns for the stability of "place," the need for simple friendship, and the search for meaning itself—and much more. From an organic, holistic perspective, this exercise is much like asking which organ of the body is most significant or essential: the brain, the heart, the kidney, the genitals, the arms and legs, etc. The answer is that all are essential and important but in different degrees depending on the individuals involved, and the time and place and need. Moreover, individual humans construct a tremendous variety of "living places" in order to accommodate their multiplicity of talents and temperaments and their broad range of cultural activities.

Thus, the idea that a place or society should give priority to one major type of cultural function over others is problematic at best. While social commentators may attempt to identify the single kernel or core of human nature, we are more concerned that there be cultural patterns across a broad set of functions. Rather than pushing people to determine which function (or subfunction) is central to our humanity, we think it more useful to think in terms of a compelling *set of functions*. In other words: Do the various place-based activities of a culture represent adequate ways by which the full potential of our nature can be expressed—not just for a privileged elite, but for the great diversity of humans within any "normal" community? Do cultural patterns of a place represent a balance of functions both within a single function, e.g., within environmental and economic coping, as well as across functions, e.g., across the functions of economic coping, human and environmental relationships, and meaning-making? Are the activities of poets and mystics, of mothers and fathers, of the very young and the very old represented as well as the activities of gifted athletes and common villagers and the professionals and the "public intellectuals?"

We would reiterate here that modern societies seem focused on developing and merchandising increasing quantities of products to satisfy every conceivable appetite of humanity as long as the product can be sold for profit. Thus we see various types of human relationships sacrificed or diminished—for example, the availability of long term kinship or friendship connections are sacrificed as people move about constantly searching for jobs that will provide an ever increasing number and variety of products. We also see modern social relationships (within our second major functional level) judged in terms of whether or not a "connection" or relationship will promote one's self interest. And we see modern meaning-making (within our third major functional level) judged within the narrow standards of pragmatic economic efficiency, successful merchandising, and the success and gain that come from such activities. Modernity is hardly a balanced culture across our three major superordinate categories.

3) *Balance* Within *Primal to Modern Functional Patterns*

Our principle of balance suggests that there should be adequate balance along the primal-to-modern dimension *within* specific cultural functions. Thus we might look within a society for primal to modern balance across types of vocation or types of human bonding. For instance, local family farming is an example of a relatively balanced activity in terms of a primal-to-modern vocation. Farmers live close to the land and the other organic beings in the world. Limited types of modern scientific information and small scale efficient farm equipment also make it less punishing as a type of "hard" labor. Yet, it is economically difficult for modern people to enter this work since the vocation itself is increasingly taken over by expensive large-scale technology which often exceeds the resources available to small farmers.

Another example is the work of small independent artisans and business people who tend to develop more balanced lives than people who are required to work in large corporate offices or factories. Artisans often own their businesses, their tools and shops, and work out of their homes. They also work within a relatively narrow geographic range so that they come to know their customers more intimately over long periods of time. But these vocations, like farming and plumbing and carpentry, are under siege by corporate conglomerates and chains who own and manage multiple franchises which advertise in cosmopolitan newspapers and electronic media and increasingly use "outsourcing" arrangements to avoid long-term responsibility to their employees.

4) Balance In the Degree to Which Settings or Places Focus on Highly Specialized and Compartmentalized Activities and Fragment Society into Segregated Cohorts of Specialized Workers versus the Degree to Which Settings or Places Integrate and Connect Various Types of Activities and Various Types of Humans

An example of integrating different functional types of activity within a single setting is the extent to which *supervised focused work* can be mixed with more convivial social relationships in a single setting. This is commonly done within households in which different members of a family might help prepare a meal. In a second illustration we might imagine a group of carpenters framing a house (an economic activity) having a conversation about the meaning of "dating" or the appropriate behavior for courtship (a mixed social and meaning-making activity). We might then imagine the foreman or contractor approaching and insisting that the carpenters stop talking and work in silence in order not to interfere with the efficiency of the job. The activities of talking-and-carpentering represent a more integrated cultural norm while the silent (and perhaps more efficient) carpentering alone represents a more specialized cultural norm. We are here suggesting that activities with more diverse and integrated cultural patterns often represent a richer quality of life.

5) Balance Within the Depth Dimension of Culture

Finally, a fifth aspect of balance is the extent to which living places can maintain a balance among sustained actions and experience based on deeper processes of tropic enculturation and the traditions they sustain as opposed to more superficial processes such as socialization and pragmatic reason and self-interest. Deep, sustained cultural patterns must be valued and weighed against the advantages that come with the questioning of these patterns and their reconsideration through more existential, rational, pragmatic processes of meaning-making. Of course, there is no way of correcting serious cultural errors without an appeal to meta-cultural pragmatic insights which can be used to challenge destructive, irrational, or outdated cultural patterns.

SUMMARY

This chapter begins by raising the thorny problem of cultural relativism and asking how we might approach the issue of evaluating quality of life issues across different societies or within sectors of a given society. In order to lay the groundwork for determining the preconditions of a healthy society, we presented a holistic social theory which relates "living places" to the balanced cultural institutions required for their survival, sustenance, and constructive change. The major point of the theory is to provide a language from which to speculate about the quality of life in a place or society by applying the concept of *balance* to various levels of place and patterns of culture.

We assume that the depth of human patterning flows on at least five levels—from deep instinct to the relatively superficial experiences which are the product of socialization and practical reason which constitute an inevitable part of one's daily behavior. The "logic" behind this patterning is related to our earlier discussions of the ways in which cultural groups intentionally construct their individual realities. For instance, there is a deeply imprinted logic about how humans use language or how they experience time. Because these patterns are so resistant to change, disrupting the "cultural logic" means changing patterns at every other level.

A critical aspect of our organic holistic approach and its relevance to issues of cultural change is that it assumes from the outset that each of various cultural patterns is not only interrelated within a single social system, but that it is in some degree built into the substrate of human nature. The use of the word "organic" implies that humans are able to distinguish between nurturing places and toxic places just as they are able to recognize instinctively caring relationships from coercive and abusive ones. Organic holism defines the criteria for quality of life in that it seeks to place humans within a balanced constellation of "places" in which they can grow and thrive.

In Chapter Eleven we move from a theoretical language for describing norms for a living place and genuine culture and present a more elaborated version of the role of the Vital Center as a critical connecting link between more primal and modern cultural institutions. For without this connection, we feel, humans gravitate toward unbalanced societies and are prevented from expressing the fullness of their nature.

NOTES

1. Goldschmidt, *Comparative Functionalism*, 8.

2. Ibid., ix-x.

3. Ibid., 138.

4. E. V.Walter, *Placeways: A Theory of the Human Environment* (Chapel Hill: Univ. of North Carolina Press, 1988).

5. Ibid., 134.

6. Ibid., 135.

7. James J. Gibson, *The Ecological Approach to Visual Perception* (Boston: Houghton-Mifflin, 1979); Lewis Mumford, *The Culture of Cities* (New York: Harcourt Brace Jovanovich, Inc., 1938); Vincent Scully, *The Earth, the Temple, and the Gods* Rev. ed. (New York: Praeger, 1969). We would also note that the theory of "whole body" perception is consistent with Whitehead's process philosophy in what he calls "perception in the mode of causal efficacy."

8. Walter, *Placeways*, 142-143.

9. Ibid., 143.

10. Keith H. Basso, "'Stalking with Stories': Names, Places, and Moral Narratives Among the Western Apache," *On Nature*, Daniel Halpern, ed. (San Francisco: North Point Press, 1987), 114.

11. Walter, *Placeways*, 23.

12. Ibid., 6.

13. Ibid., 40.

14. It is important to state in the most emphatic way at the outset that the theoretical constructs presented below which are closely related to what sociologists call "structural-functional theory" are not intended as a proposal by which elitist professionals might "reform" or "develop" new social institutions. It is intended to make a very different point. Its major purpose is to alert scholars and others who would care to study it of the profound difficulty of significantly altering the problematic institutions of modernity with our current simplistic understandings and assumptions regarding "the way the system works." It is meant to show that we need a more radical and complex way of moving out of the quicksand of social engineering and technological DESIGN. We would however, acknowledge our debt to the brilliant efforts of Talcott Parsons and Robert Bales, for example, who raised and dealt with the problem of looking at societies and their interdependent layered constituent parts as a whole. [Talcott Parsons, Rob-

ert F. Bales, and Edward A. Shils, *Working Papers in the Theory of Action* (New York: Free Press, 1953).

15. The inability of sociologists and anthropologists to agree on anything like a common or uniform set of such socio-cultural categories noted by Goldschmidt and Lenski may well be the major reason that social scientists moved toward small technical studies and away from the kind of broad theorizing we are undertaking here. Our own sense is that avoiding the issue of seeing the human condition within broader systems of analysis, however, leads to fundamental distortions in the direction of reductionism and fragmentation that are more serious than creating a less than totally satisfactory system of such categories. The major categories of the organic functional scheme presented here are adapted from the work of Lenski. Gerhard Lenski, *Human Societies* (New York: McGraw Hill, 1970), 34-47.

16. We are here using the term "grammar" as Tyack and Cubin apply it to explain the difficulty of effecting sustainable experiments in school reform. David Tyack & Larry Cubin, *Tinkering Toward Utopia* (Cambridge, MA: Harvard University Press, 1995).

17. Wilson, *On Human Nature*, 157.

18. We note that biological flaws within a species are common, often resulting in the extinction of species. Even within the human species at the most micro level, the creation of proteins as long strings of amino acids folded into three-dimensional shapes—a process which is essential for the formation of all of our complex organs—there are flaws or mistakes. At this micro level in which millions of cell reproductions take place in nanoseconds, there are mistakes which result in diseases such as Alzheimer's and cystic fibrosis. Our conclusion from this remarkable finding is that even in the most swift and micro level of reality, nature creates tendencies toward life and health—but nature also makes mistakes, creating tendencies toward pathology and disease. Why then should cultural patterns constructed by "natural" human beings be exempt from such errors? Source: National Public Radio forum "Talk of the Nation, Science Friday," October 23, 1998, 4:00 pm.

CHAPTER ELEVEN

The Vital Center

A central error of modernity is to assume that the "progressive" or "modern" characteristics of humans lead (metaphorically) "forward" to a "higher" civilization and should be pursued even at the expense of the primal ones, which are generally considered "primitive," "backward," and of secondary importance. Redressisng this error, we argue, requires that we sustain or reclaim local mediating or centering institutions which express aspects of their nature along the primal-to-modern dimension. So we ask: How can we protect those places in which we are able to think, and feel, and act out the fuller range of our human potentiality? There is, of course, no easy answer to this question, since these middle level institutions are under increasing siege by the global processes of migration, commerce, mass media, and universal forms of knowledge and technology rather than local qualities of reality.

Part of the difficulty of sustaining local places is expressed in our theory of society, which assumes that various cultural patterns *mutually reinforce one another.* This means that once a healthy society gets out of balance, the chain reaction of feedback loops set up by new "progressive" institutions create ever more imbalance. So, for example, once large-scale commercial urban conglomerates stifle or destroy the *sense of place* for those living in native cities or local villages, a number of things happen. In terms of *vocations,* modern people move either toward abstract technical vocations or toward low skill mass production jobs rather than toward middle level artisanship; in terms of *bonding,* they move toward impersonal contractual relationships and bureaucracy rather then kinship and friendship. In terms of *meaning-making* they move toward objective instrumental forms of pragmatic knowledge (e.g., science and journalism) as primary rather than narrative, myth, and spiritual insight.

Our project in Chapter Ten was to provide a language through which we might understand the relationships among these various layers of culture. The focus of this chapter then is to provide a fuller description of mediating institutions within all three cultural patterns. We shall therefore go somewhat systematically through our major superordinate patterns and detail some of the issues related to what we are calling the "balanced" or "vital center."

THE BALANCED CENTER AND ENVIRONMENTAL/ ECONOMIC CULTURAL PATTERNS

PRIMAL PLACES, MODERN PLACES, AND THE BALANCED CENTER

Places that are associated with primal environments include the wilderness, savannas, and jungles. In these environments, nomadic tribal societies tend to live in encampments in which little is done to change the natural setting. The economy is based on gathering and hunting materials for food, clothing, shelter, healing, and the like. The mythology of the modern world sees this as an early stage of human life before "civilization." It is, however, also associated with mythic places (e.g, Eden) which presumably existed before humans were required to labor and struggle for survival and eventually die in the same "brutish" way as other animals. Modern people celebrate Thoreau and his time on Walden Pond as a return to the purity of nature—moving away from the crass commercialism of modernity. They see "camping" or "roughing it" as a return to the simplicity and challenge of being close to the spiritual roots of nature, thus perpetuating the modern ambivalence toward primal places.

The most common and pervasive "places" that surround modern people, however, are not primal but modern: buildings, vehicles, roads and streets, etc. designed and planned for systematic corporate work. These places are organized to minimize disruption and spontaneity. "Work stations" are designed to allow for predetermined activities which will achieve "objectives." Road signs and stop signs control the direction and flow of private and mass transportation. In stadiums, people sit in "stands," watching other people play games according to precise rules, although many of these games imitate the primal ritual of hunting and predation.

Ostensibly the home is a retreat from the highly organized work of the modern corporate place, the place where one rests and prepares oneself for work the next day. Children's homework is to "educate" them for a career (which may no longer be available). Beyond these "goals," the major objective of being "at home" is to consume the products created in corporate work places. As one watches TV or surfs the Internet one is constantly reminded of the products that are "out there for sale."

The balanced center is represented by households, sodalities and the simple village system. As "ideal types," villages and extended households have special characteristics. The "middle level" household once included (and many cultures still do include) an extended family, servants, artisans, hired farm hands, etc. Households are often set among woods and fields which are neither exclusively for work or play. Villages (often within native cities) are places in which public negotiation among neighbors can happen, either in the market or in disputes over privilege, property, or children. They are places in which mild sanctions of disapproval can be administered without the harsher treatments associated with loss of one's livelihood, imprisonment or public humiliation. They are places in which closeness and distance among acquaintances can be negotiated without people becoming permanently categorized as friends or enemies. They are places in which degrees of friendship and emotional attachment can be established without compromising the unconditional obligations of primary kinship or the ambiguities of employee-employer relationships. They are places in which voluntary associations of all kinds can be created and abandoned without seriously threatening the viability of the larger village polity. Perhaps most important of all, villages are places in which the emotional volatility inherent in the intimate nuclear family can be softened. Children who become alienated from parents can move in with uncles or aunts or grandparents. Job-related tensions can be shared and forgotten in various associations that give one significant and sustaining support by sodalities such as churches, lodges, sports clubs, etc.

VOCATION, TECHNOLOGY, AND THE BALANCED CENTER

Primal societies, even with limited tools and technology, successfully obtained food supplies, shelter, discovered knowledge and techniques for treating injury and disease, and otherwise provided for the necessities of life. And because these local societies were relatively isolated, there was little need for complex exchange techniques such as money to

calculate the common value of different activities or "products" resulting from their work.

When village peoples invented the wheel the impact on agriculture
was dramatic. Larger and larger tracts of land could be farmed with ani-
mal-drawn wagons and plows. Large-scale irrigation projects could cul-
tivate a wide variety of crops, including fruits and grains, which could
then be milled and stored in central facilities. To manage this increasing
production, people invented communication and exchange techniques,
including writing, mathematical notation, the solar calendar, and the use
of money. Work roles were divided into categories associated with age
and gender in activities such as child care, household work, field work,
etc. Specializations developed for various kinds of artisans and merchants who sold their products and services in local markets.

Feudalism then developed as a two-tier economic and social system
which separated the urban nobility with its elaborate retinue of privileged clerical, military, legal, engineering, and other members of the
court from the great numbers of disenfranchised poor, including servants, slaves, and agricultural villagers. One consequence of exploiting
slaves and women for the work they provided was productive leisure for
an aristocracy, which yielded a rich and creative output of art, science,
and philosophy. As a result, feudalism developed elaborate forms of
high culture in buildings and architecture, roads, storing of water, the
arts, religion, games and sports, and methods of human coercion, war-
fare, and control.

DIVERSITY, SPECIALIZATION, AND
SEGREGATED COHORTS AND THE BALANCED CENTER

Primal aboriginal societies living within wilderness environments
presumably experience a diverse social environment including an intimate mix of women, men, and children of different ages, genders, temperaments, talents, and handicaps. There are no sharp status differences
or power hierarchies based on a systematic and highly competitive sorting process. All members of the group or family share an intrinsic feeling
of significance simply because they "belong." There is, however, a degree of functional specialization and hierarchy related to age, gender,
temperament, special abilities as well as to kinship or family connections, but nothing comparable to modern socio-economic stratification.

The diversity and role expectations that are essential to the balance found in the vital center can be seen in the small village and in the native city. First of all the village society was larger than the gathering-hunting-society and may have included several hundred persons who engaged in a greater variety of occupations and activities. Although almost everyone cooperated in activities related to the survival of the village, there was a substantial division of labor involving specialized crafts. These included the age- and gender-based roles connected with domestic and agricultural work as well as more specialized vocations such as blacksmithing, building, healing, and ministering to problems of the spirit and the unseen world.

The presence of domestic animals brought with it the intimate mingling of human and animal life. Perhaps the quintessential institution representing this mixed human-animal place was the barnyard. Here one found chickens, ducks, geese, horses, cows, asses, goats, etc. as well as manure piles waiting to be carted to the fields or wood piles waiting to be cut up for fuel or lumber. The barnyard was (is), perhaps, one of the best examples of a complex micro organic society.

In the transition from the village environment to larger archaic towns, some humans seemed better adapted to a class-based high-cosmopolitan or to a low folk culture of the town while others seemed better adapted to the more mixed and ambiguous culture of the village. (One fact seems clear, however. Larger and more complex social structures evolved within the feudal period.) Some of these changes, in retrospect, seem very positive. These included the development of stable extended families and pride in the artistic and vocational achievement of everyday life, as well as substantial respect for the value of leisure (in the archaic city) as a precondition for fulfilling the unique and varied gifts and talents of the more diverse population.

During the past two hundred years, the native or archaic city has been transformed into the modern urban conglomerate, which has forced a dramatic increase in place segregation based on one's position in the socio-economic hierarchy. Modern urban centers are, of course, larger and more complex than those in earlier village or feudal societies. Simply because of their size, they contain an immense variety of human types and human conditions. If, however, one asks about the range of humans with whom one has personal or intimate contact or engagement for any sustained period of time, the picture changes radically. As Walter noted earlier, affluent people live near affluent people, go to similar schools, have similar jobs, drive similar cars, live in similar physical neighborhoods, speak a similar kind of language, including a class dialect, and have a similar level and range of conceptual grounding. And the middling and the poor are likewise segregated. There is also a rich and varied set of other groups beyond those identified with social class—racial, ethnic, gender-oriented, professional-artist, student, etc. These groups share similar kinds of ghettoizing and which, paradoxically, both increases and reduces that potential for diversity in urban people's lives as opposed to that experienced in middle level settings.

In work settings, the great majority of modern people have contact with those who do work similar to theirs and often have little sustained contact with people who do very different kinds of work.[1] We suspect that while most workers share a similar tropic pressure for "producing" something that will "make money" and keep them in business or keep their job, each individual feels a special identity with his or her particular work place and the social status that goes with that career. The fact that modern people work in small socio-economic segregated cohorts of individuals doing specialized work tends to heighten their anxiety over how important they are to the larger society. In this sense uniqueness and diversity are largely "internal" concerns and not commonly subject to public appraisal or discussion. A modern person thus becomes "just another" carpenter or "just another" technical writer or "just another" teacher unless they have attained some rare or rarefied "star" status (which may be short-lived) in a highly valued occupation.

Our point is that while we live within incredibly diverse places in modern settings, we often share our lives with a narrow set of similar people functioning within narrowly defined similar environments. And while our survival depends on a finely tuned and incredibly large and complex technical global economic system involving tremendous diversity, most elements of this diversity are geographically or psychologically invisible to us. Few of us are privy to the conditions that would allow us to understand (should we care to) just how "necessary" and important or "unnecessary" and trivial is the work we happen to be doing. And regardless of how critical our contribution may be to the health, safety, or survival of our particular society, most modern people understand at some level that they are replaceable parts in a faceless economic machine.[2]

This situation is substantially different in villages or even old city neighborhoods where the work of most members of a community is or was public knowledge. We often knew what healer helped or harmed which patients, which carpenter roofed which houses and whether they leaked or were tight. We knew the managers and perhaps the owners of local businesses and how they treated their workers. We saw and knew many of the people on the street as neighbors and acquaintances. We also knew the difference between the relative importance of those who cultivated the fields and brought food to the community or those who delivered the mail as opposed to those who did less essential work.[3]

THE BALANCED CENTER AND SOCIAL/POLITICAL STRUCTURES OF HUMAN BONDING

FORMS OF BONDING

Humans, like many of our animal cousins, live within organized social groups in which members perform somewhat predictable roles. These roles are woven into mutually reinforcing and interdependent patterns which commonly bind people to one another in ways that make it possible—and even necessary—for individuals to function as families, groups, and communities. For early peoples living close to nature within primal encampments, relationships depended heavily on the structure of mating, family, and extended kinship connections, and upon the sharing of tasks required for surviving and coping within a common place.

In the balanced center, the family is often structured in terms of interdependent roles for mothers and fathers, first-born children, boy and girl children, adolescents, aunts and uncles, and grandparents, which tell people when and how to relate to one another. These deeply encultured tropes are the formulae that specify how to stay together, how to live and work together, how to quarrel and negotiate differences with one another, how to be jealous of one another, and how to cooperate and make a life together.

The most important social structures and sources of bonding in the modern system are perhaps the nuclear family and the contract-based commercial corporation. Nuclear families commonly carry out a variety of primal activities related to the fundamentals of survival: eating, sleeping, shelter, nurturance, sexual relations, reproduction, health care, etc. In recent years, however, the long term commitment of family members toward one another has dramatically diminished. Divorce rates in the

United States are now over 50%. Children receive limited parental contact, both because of divorce and because many more adults work outside the home. Children are commonly left in corporate work environments called "schools" for most of the day or cared for by "extended care" and "day care" arrangements. In most cases children are expected to grow up, leave home and have limited parental contact, and become independent of parental help in their early twenties. At that point the nuclear family essentially dissolves. Children moreover often consider it an unreasonable burden that they be expected to provide any long-term assistance to infirm and dependent parents even in their old age.

We speculate that in the later stages of modernity, the middle social structures associated with the nuclear family and the extended household will lose much of their cultural tropic force. Most of their functions will be replaced by ultra modern corporate-entities such as "full service schools," work places with cafeterias, gyms, and health care facilities, and retirement and nursing homes for the elders.

PRIMARY AND SECONDARY GROUP BONDING

A common sociological perspective distinction is made between "primary" versus "secondary" groups based on the quality of relationships and the nature of the bonds that hold people together in group life. Primary group relationships and roles involve direct, intense, face-to-face, informal interaction. They tend to be more affect laden, more diffuse (people relate in a variety of ways for a variety of reasons, not simply to achieve an objective), more personal, and one's status is often determined by one's overall membership in a family or community rather than simply by one's specialized skills. Secondary group relationships and roles, on the other hand, focus primarily on the effort to achieve specific goals to maintain a corporate objective and groups come together for that purpose. Secondary roles tend to be focused more on achievement (thus requiring specialized task competencies), and are less concerned about (or tolerant of) informal non-task-based personal interaction.

Within this conceptual framework, the bonds for primary groups tend to be seen as based on kinship, friendship, and emotional dependence and interdependence, all of which require long-term human engagement. The bonds for secondary groups tend to be based on calculated self-interest defined by reciprocal arrangements or contracts that are enforced by a legal system with sanctions providing for carefully defined compensations and penalties when agreements are honored or broken.

The importance of presenting or acknowledging the primary group-secondary group distinction here is to show that it comes out of and illustrates the pervasive Lockean private-public dualism which allows modern people to perceive society as divided into two social realities—one dominant and one subordinate. So we come to see the corporate place or secondary group as instrumental, productive, and dominant and the family or primary group as only a private, personal, and non-productive/consuming entity—and thus of secondary importance.

The concept of the balanced center goes right to the heart of this distinction by rejecting this kind of dualism which is such a destructive trope in modernity. In authentic cultures, human social life must include at least three levels and qualities of cohesion: the intimate primary familistic group, the more formal work-centered secondary group, and the middle level communal group. It is the presence of a middle-level grounded set of intermediary institutions with unique qualities of bonding and cohesion that integrates elements of both primary and secondary groups. We are not implying that primary groups such as the nuclear family or secondary groups such as corporate work groups should somehow be replaced or take on essential communal characteristics. (We view the proposal to somehow integrate the corporate and communal forms of organization as unrealistic and romantic!) We are, however, suggesting that robust forms of middle level group life may transcend the narrow and parochial interests of families as well as protect both individuals and families from the depersonalizing tendencies associated with "objective" bureaucratic corporate institutions which focus so intensely on "keeping one's job," "getting work done," and "making money."

The concept of the balanced center relates to the several levels of habitat or societal form already presented and discussed: the extended household, the sodality, the village, and the archaic or native city, all of which allow for more primal types of bonding, e.g., bonds of kinship and friendship which may filter into non-corporate work done to maintain and sustain our human comfort and survival. These are places in which people can work without continual fear of losing their jobs, places in which both children and adults can play without the fear of being reprimanded for wasting their time, places in which mothers and adolescents can care for children without fear of being in the way, places in which lovers can quietly talk and touch without being considered obscene, places in which one can simply "be" and feel significant because one is at home, where one is supposed to be—in one's local place.

Despite its large size and degree of formality, the archaic or native city potentially represents an especially important mediating institution within our holistic theory because of its ambiguity—it is saturated with both primal and modern qualities. On the modern side, the development of a tradition of legal constitutional protections for the rights of both individuals and groups is an enormous achievement. Thus, it is a place in which one can retreat from the intimacy of close friends or family into risky and unconventional places and even venture forth and challenge conventional ideas and vocations without being criticized for being an outsider or forced into leaving the scene. One's idiosyncrasies are often tolerated simply because one is not "strange;" one's oddities and eccentricities come to be known and understood over time so that one is accepted simply because of "who you are."

FORMS OF BONDING THROUGH POWER RELATIONSHIPS

Power relationships provide another focus for looking at and understanding patterns of human bonding. In primal cultures, power relationships tend to be associated with kinship, gender, and age. Women may dominate in child rearing and agriculture; men in war and hunting. In general, older members of a society tend to be seen as more authoritative. When factions develop, however, as in time of uncertainty and crisis, primal cultures do not lack for skills in negotiation, manipulation, threats, use of magic, or the use of physical violence and other destructive ways of expressing power.

Middle level institutions in the form of local traditional village societies differ little from tribal societies in power relations except for the fact that they are commonly larger and there is more property over which one must preside and make decisions. Who actually controls various forms of property, how to protect the reasonable use of property, how to pass on property from one generation to another all become important and volatile issues instigating controversy and requiring societies to develop cultural practices in order to prevent (in so far as this is possible) destructive power struggles. In some circumstances, isolated villages and village cultures work out interesting and creative solutions to these issues, e.g., deeply encultured rules of inheritance.

During feudalism, territories—and the villages within their boundaries—were established, became connected to, and, in some degree, were controlled by a cosmopolitan military establishment often centered in a walled city or community. In return for meeting certain demands, e.g., forced labor, taxes, and service in the military, local villagers were promised protection from raids and predatory attacks by other military bands, warlords, or landlords. Under feudalism, while the military elite exploited local people and their institutions by levying taxes and conscripting labor, villages often created and maintained a significant local culture.

Our modern orientation toward power is considerably different. As long as local peoples engage in the "progressive" use of the planet's resources to increase the amount of "wealth" or products for consumption by humans and as long as powerful elites can gain from this process, power may be shared between power elites and those who are willing to cooperate with the system. Democratic participatory institutions such as a free press and media, academic freedom in education, elections and legislatures, and judicial processes have been developed in modern liberal societies to mediate conflicts among elites and between elites and those with less or little power. These institutions have served to soften and slow down the painful economic and technological disruptions in people's lives during periods of rapid social and environmental change. (Most of these institutions, e.g., elections, the press, judicial appointments, are also controlled by small and powerful elites.) As the material standard of living increases for some broadly based groups (known significantly as the "middle" class), people come to realize that there is too much to lose economically if one seriously threatens or engages in direct confrontation with the elite; so those with less power become accustomed to compromising or acceding to those who dominate and largely control the system.

The problematics of using and legitimizing power in mediating centers involves the subtle process of accurately feeling the force of the past moving into the present and the future. While the modern corporate culture celebrates the power of reasoned self-interest in negotiating "arrangements" and contracts to resolve power problems, the traditional person uses tradition or "culture" to honor the balance among the feelings and expectations of the whole community. As Whitehead notes, despite modernity's tendency to stress the even handed and progressive nature of the legal contract, the power significance that emanates from custom and tradition is not to be underestimated:

> The favorite doctrine of the shift from a customary basis for society to a contractual basis, is founded on shallow sociology. There is no escape from customary status. This status is merely another name for the inheritance immanent in each occasion. Inevitably inheritance is there, an inescapable condition. On the other hand, the inherited status is never a full determination. There is always freedom for the determination of individual emphasis.[4]

Thus we can conceive of three very different understandings of power:

- the power over others that resides in individuals and the resources they may control;
- the power that may be exercised in negotiating contracts among individuals in terms of their mutual self-interest; and
- the power inherent in complex social settings as this may be expressed by the various aspects of the setting, including non-personal aspects such as rivers, the land, tools, the regularities and customs or cultures of the people, their history, and the natural universe.

What Whitehead calls "custom" (what we would call "culture") may be thought of as a kind of transpersonal pattern established over time within a community of people which influences how members of the community or village exercise power. In this Whiteheadian or process sense, power is intrinsic to the occasion and is related to the desire of the fullness of the occasion to complete itself. This "feeling" for the idea of power within the emerging occasion is dramatically different from the more pragmatic "feeling" one has for the exercise of personal or corporate power based on the legal or physical resources one has at one's command which can be used to "rationally" control others.

Thus the context for using power and decision-making based on contract and physical power is very different from that based on custom expressed within the face-to-face contact among peoples with long-standing personal histories. As Whitehead suggests, custom or culture is not necessarily determinate. Culture is dynamic and constantly being negotiated within the constraints of human relationships on a day to day basis. To understand the dynamics of a living place and culture, we have only to imagine the circumstance of an elderly person being pressed to vacate her/his life-long home because s/he cannot pay taxes or rent to understand this distinction.[5]

Within institutions in the mediating center one does not negotiate in terms only of the pragmatic rationality required to maintain the predictability of social life or to increase the immediate comforts and conveniences provided by the purchase of consumer goods and services. History speaks and has power. Nor does one exercise power because it is supported by abstract rights and principles backed by governmental sanctions. One listens to the silent sounds from the unseen world of ancestors and the memories of the spirits which inhabit, protect, and give significance to a living, sacred, centered place.

THE VITAL CENTER AND CULTURAL PATTERNS RELATED TO MEANING AND MEANING-MAKING

BEING: CONCEPTIONS OF PERSONAL AND GROUP IDENTITY

The set of cultural patterns relating to Meaning which we refer to as "being," raises the question: What are adequate units to describe "being" or "beings" both in the actual world and in the larger cosmos? From the materialistic perspective of modern science, the issue is relatively simple. "Beings" are the units of reality humans manipulate and study in the actual world. The field of natural and human ecology has a more complicated answer. Here broader ecological systems are conceived of as the units. Within Leopold's understanding of "living places," unless ecological systems have an adequate diversity and integration of "beings," the larger unit or system changes and becomes something else and the old one perishes—along with the individual "beings" within it. A fundamental problem for the hard sciences is the fact that "beings" or "things" are always in the process of changing and becoming something else, and these "something elses" are usually engaged in a process of connecting to other "things" and transforming themselves into novel beings that are ever more simple or complex.

From the point of view of our primal human nature, we argue that units of being (as within gatherer-hunter societies and early horticultural peoples) tend to be more collective than individual. That is, they tend to be based on collective kin groups, usually a group of nuclear-to-extended families connected by geographic contiguity, blood, marriage, and immediate visible economic interdependence. While there is always the understanding that individual humans (and other beings) have an essential separateness, their connections to ancestry, family, tribe, and clan gave early humans a profound sense of identity as relational beings.

The unit of being within the balanced center is more complex in that it tends to combine and integrate the primal and the modern. The householder, member of a sodality, villager, or native civic person tends to develop a strong ethnic identity. Such people say: "This is my place, where my ancestors lived and died; these are my people of whom I am one. My being is defined this way because I am related by the historical fateful conditions that go with this place, with these people." But local people today rarely live in such communal places. They travel about as strangers and mingle with other strangers, which gives them a greater sense of separateness and individuality.

The idea of identity is radically different among modern people for whom ancestry simply provides the inherited DNA patterns that relate to one's personal health and longevity. The unit of being for modern people is the individual. In the West this sense of "being" rests both on the dogma of "individual freedom" (political, economic, personal) within the tradition of democratic liberalism as well as on actual or vestigial Judeo-Christian beliefs wherein each individual is given a separate soul and a separate destiny. Individualism is also synonymous with the personal "identity" of the business corporation which is now considered an individual legal "person."

TIME AND THE BALANCED CENTER

J. B. Priestly has developed a theory which includes three qualities of time. The usefulness of his theory is that it explains human experiences which extend beyond the limitations of linear time. As he says,

> I propose to call these ... time One, time Two, and time Three. As visible creatures of earth we are ruled by time One. We are born into it, grow up and grow old in it, and die in it. Our brains have developed through eons into marvelous instruments of time One attention.[6]

Time Two, Priestly explains, contains preconscious episodes of "dreaming" time. He documents vivid and compelling instances in which humans dream of an event that actually occurs later, or of possible tragedies that are prevented because of warnings provided by such dreams. He sees time Two as a poorly understood variation of time. Three that in some way connects the potential with the actual. He links this with imagination and sets forth the following thesis:

> Because imagination appears to be free of the limitations we know in time One, we think of it as being outside Time. It is there, however, that the nothings begin. We might do better if we thought of it as belonging to a different time order, to another time ... imaginative creation seems to imply not a second time order, contemplative and detached from action, but a third, in which purpose and action are joined together and there seems to be an almost magical release in creative power. If there is a part of the mind or a state of consciousness that is outside the dominion of time One and time Two but governed by time Three, then that is where the creative imagination is home and does its work. And it may be that there imagination is not something escaping from reality but *is itself reality*, while the world we construct from our time One experience is regarded there as something artificial, thin, hollow.[7]

We assume that throughout history humans have functioned within all three qualities of time with a greater emphasis placed on the demands of cyclical time. We hypothesize that the integration of imaginative dream time, organic cyclical time, and mechanistic linear time provides people with the insights of a middle level reality in which they mediate between the seemingly untethered and unseen quality of dream time and imagination and the inflexible disciplined quality of mechanical time. So when humans become deeply engaged in dream time (e.g., through dreaming, meditation, prayer, ritual transcendence), they gain profound insights about their place in a larger cosmic reality. Such experiences give our lives their most significant source of sustained meaning and inspiration. Yet dwelling mainly in dream time may cause humans to lose their ability to cope with the organic requirements needed for comfort and survival.

The balanced center contains both the tenuous dream time in the unseen world as well as the regularities and predictabilities of linear mechanical time. We know that "loving" and "singing" and "talking" to our children, to plants, to animals, actions which come out of the unseen unconscious world, affect the natural biological world. We also know that we can apply mechanistic processes to living things to both improve and distort the world around us. We are suggesting that we use our modern capacities for linear time to construct a technology of human scale within time dimensions that balance rather than outweigh deeper patterns of biological time.

Contemporary people practice and work in the linear mechanical time they associate with modern physics and technology. Time is measured most precisely by the rate at which nuclear particles break down and, in more common sensical terms, by the everyday clock. Modernity has given increasing priority to the pressure of mechanical technological time, which now "runs" most of our behavior in modern culture. (Note the anxiety associated with the impending Y2K day at the end of 1999.) Modern people get up "on time," go to work "on time," move and travel on time schedules, etc. While this does not totally stifle more primal forms of time, e.g., "unseen world time," dream time, cyclical time, since they operate at other levels of consciousness, linear time based on our reliance on modern technology has fundamentally changed our sense of human biological time in the natural world. Today we explicitly assume that modern technology can somehow defeat these great biological cycles and that humans will, in the end, "control" or "manage" time.

Likewise, when humans become deeply engaged in linear mechanical time, they become so focused upon the immediate material and cultural reality and the control and understanding of that reality that they may lose their sense of who and what they really are—transitory multilayered micro-beings connected to the All of a larger mysterious cosmos. So modern people begin to treat the natural world as an object to be monitored and controlled exclusively for their own human convenience. (Note our celebration when the astronauts could suddenly view the Earth as a separate object in space from which they were totally disconnected.) We have begun to worship ourselves and our cultural artifacts because we can predictably manipulate these particular aspects of the natural universe. Furthermore, humans come to believe that these separate beings, defined within the limits of mechanical time, constitute their total reality.

Mumford warns that when humans lose their feeling for that quality of biological time connected with the survival of their own person and community—giving primary focus to mechanistic physical time, they court disaster. In his words:

The conception of time as the flux of organic continuity, experienced as duration, as memory, as recorded history, as potentiality and prospective achievement stands in frontal opposition to the mechanistic notion of time simply as a function of the motion of bodies in space—along with its spurious imperative of 'saving time' by accelerating motion, and of making such acceleration in every possible department the highest triumph of the power complex.[8]

Mumford then makes a point regarding the critical balance between the natural pace of organic time and Priestly's more creative time associated with human imagination as a basis for cultural renewal. As he says, only when,

the organism has achieved the necessary preconditions for stability, continuity, dynamic balance, and self-replenishment [is] ... creativity ... assured; and the ability to transcend these conditions ... becomes possible. When, on the other hand, chance events multiply and a dehumanized social regimentation leaves no place for an organic response, disintegration and wanton destruction gain, as now, the upper hand.[9]

In short, creative advances may come occasionally to genuine cultures which briefly transcend the natural organic pace of time through flashes of intuitive imagination and/or new invention, but the preconditions for this change are the unhurried flow of organic biological time. As he says, regimentation leads to disaster.

EXPERIENCE, RITUAL ENACTMENT AND THE BALANCED CENTER

The subtle initial coming into being of human experience and the complex qualities of feeling and understanding that develop from that "thin" thread of initial information were discussed in detail in Part Two. They need not be repeated. Using organic holistic multilevel theory, we suggest that middle level cultural patterns in the center are required to sustain a balance for humans between the primal and modern aspects of our experiential potential. Within the framework of this theory, the personal/communal and historical narratives provide the grounded link which attracts or "pulls" the emergent "unseen" experience into a public arena. The focus of "knowing" in the mediating center is the Story. The work of transforming Story into a more enduring and explicit coherent cosmology happens in the native city as well as in the more cosmopolitan centers where concrete stories are "elevated" through scientific and philosophical abstractions and complex mythic cosmologies. In this latter phase of knowing and experiencing, the Story becomes not only public but subject to critical interpretation within a more universal cultural context and becomes abstracted into generalities. The Story can become generalized as scientific laws; it can become even more abstracted and generalized into broad theories of cosmic order, as is illustrated by this book. From these cosmologies, one can reflect back and add rich meaning to the local story of one's culture and the personal narrative of one's life.

In short, in the process of moving between the specific occasions that constitute narrative and the broader abstractions that constitute science and philosophy and cosmology *flows in two directions*. There is pressure to apply theory so as to interpret and enrich narrative; there is pressure to apply narrative to provide corrections, add to, and amend theory. The relationship between narrative and cosmology and the scientific and philosophical points in between are thus seen as interactive and reciprocal.

Our assumption is that people who live for significant periods of time in middle level balanced places participate in generating significant personal and mythic narratives. Without this capacity, the unseen world of emergence becomes disconnected from the constraints of nature, uncorrected by its lack of contact with the manyness of the natural world, and subject to illusory fantasy and imagination. (So the tendency of modern people is to make a sharp distinction between fiction and fact.) Likewise, without the "data" provided by a grounded sense of narrative (which hooks back into emergence and the source), nature becomes simply abstract secular "science." Modern people then run the risk of losing their epistemological humility which comes from the deep intuition that human experience is fundamentally limited by the nature or *umwelt* of our very being—a being that is only one of the myriad realities and beings that inhabits this vast cosmos.

RITUAL ENACTMENT: INTEGRATING PRIMAL AND MODERN PHASES OF EXPERIENCE IN THE BALANCED CENTER

Cultural patterns related to meaning and meaning-making are somewhat difficult to discuss, for most of what we consider "meaning" happens within the human mind (or soul or brain or nervous system) and is accessed mainly through inference from language, intuition, or feeling. (Of course, all cultural patterns are inferred, but the more accessible ones are induced from both language and physical actions.) The exception to this emphasis on language is what we call "enactment" in which meaning is transformed into disciplined ritual, physical movement, and action. We are referring to cultural patterns in the arena of sport, art, music, drama, meditation, ceremony, etc., few of which have any obvious connection with immediate requirements for survival, but which are necessary and even critical for human sanity and the sustainability of traditional culture.

We use the term "enactment" to describe the *fundamental cultural dramas* that are focused mainly on the reconstruction and recovery of deep symbolic meanings which integrate aspects of the unseen world with the more obvious aspects of one's more conscious or accessible world. Because enactment moves between the thin line that separates being from non-being, life from death, and spiritual or non-material reality from the actuality of the natural universe, enactment engenders human responses representing both the deepest and most volatile of feelings and emotions and conversely the purest and clearest visions, understandings, and conceptions of the cosmos.

Primal tribal peoples have no apparent problem generating a great range of meaningful cultural enactments which "call forth" qualities of reality that intensify their access to transcendent or liminal moments between layers of human reality. The power of these enactments comes from the sense that all speak to, about, and within domains that are "real." From our point of view, the transformation of the actual drama of life—whether it be in occasions of courtship, birth, predation, accident, or death—into enactment must have a fundamentally religious participatory and even dangerous quality. Enactment from the point of view of the mediating balanced places within a society means actually engaging and participating in the *re-creation* of these *fundamental dramas of life*.

Modern people, trapped within the narrow cultural trope of a subject-object reality, have built a barrier between the presumably real, the true, the actual facts on the one hand and fantasy, fiction, and "imagination" on the other.[10] Of course, modernity still has its nominal religious enactments, but they tend to be heavily laden with language-based intonations and abstractions. We note that perhaps the most authentically dramatic liturgical moments for modern people happen within what are considered more "superstitious" religious groups (e.g., the Pentecostals) who have not yet been totally converted to the unchallenged faith that progress happens when we line up in the service of modern work to produce, purchase, consume, trash and recycle the material products of the factory and the market and then go home to watch TV. Of course, the rituals of such groups often become quickly transformed into sensationalized commodities by the press and are discounted and/or corrupted. (We would note the play by mass media on such sensational rituals as handling snakes or speaking in tongues.)

SUMMARY

In this chapter we have explored the types of places and human relationships that are present in balanced or mediating centers of more complex societies: from primal to modern places and environments, from primal to modern forms of bonding, and finally from primal to modern concepts of meaning and meaning-making. Our examples are mainly our own and reflect our personal conviction that the archaic native city comes very close to being a place where the multiple primal and middle level social forms merge in a healthy way with the more modern industrialized corporate forms of the city. We argue that village life or even life in the preindustrial city, as opposed to modern life in the urban conglomerate, traditionally contained far more direct contact with authentic natural and human environments. Domestic as well as "free" plants and animals were an intrinsic and necessary part of village life. In villages and native towns or cities humans tend (tended) to live in less segregated cohorts among a broader range of people of different ages, vocations, temperaments and social classes. Complex urban/suburban/exurban environments, by contrast, tend to be populated by insulated cohorts of people often separated from the essential "bread work" of life, and many of these more privileged modern people lose contact with the harsher pressures of simply surviving. This then radically restricts the possibility of understanding the biological and social requirements of our modern existence.

In the next chapter we will present an evolutionary-historical scenario of the development of human places and a case study of a native city in which the vital center appears to be a vibrant and compelling presence within the whole community.

NOTES

1. Different occupational groups including executives, managers, secretarial or "support" staff, janitors, cafeteria workers, etc. may associate on a daily basis and, in some sense, do different kinds of work, but looked at from a distance it all amounts to "managing people" or "being managed" through verbal directives describing work to be done or through electronic or paper communication. We suspect that lawyers' offices, physicians' offices, insurance offices, professors' offices, real estate offices, although seemingly involved in very different kinds of activities, look quite similar at a deeper environmental and socio-cultural level. Likewise, if one looks at the life of an artisan working on high rise construction or engaged in building or repairing houses, within any particular category of task, the work looks much the same. Plumbers, plasterers, carpenters, dry wall workers, ceramic tile specialists, crane operators all share in considerable degree a work culture that rarely connects with people in the "office" world, except when they are required to negotiate across these worlds in some formal contractual way. We could, of course, go on reinforcing this point by describing other settings, such as production line work, service work (waiting on people in stores, restaurants, hotels, airports), etc.

2. The environmentalist Ramachandra Guha describes how Mumford talks about precisely this issue and his impassioned plea for what we would now call cultural and biological diversity. In Mumford's words:

> [The machine world] has insulated its occupants from every form of reality except the machine process itself: heat and cold, day and night, the earth and the stars, woodland, crop land, vine land—all forms of organic partnership between the millions of species that add to the vitality and wealth of the earth—are either suppressed entirely from the mind or homogenized into a uniform mixture which can be fed into the machine.

Guha then continues, "Against this deadly uniformity, Mumford called for us to cherish our own history by 'promoting character and variety and beauty wherever we find it, whether in landscapes or in people.'" Ramachandra Guha "Lewis Mumford, the Forgotten American Environmentalist: An Essay in Rehabilitation," 209-228 in David Macauley, ed., *Minding Nature* (New York: The Guilford Press, 1996), pp. 218-219.

3. Most modern people have little contact with the *basic source* of their food, their shelter, their transportation, their medical care, the disposal of waste, and the other essentials of life. They see only finished or "final" products in consumer distribution centers. The blood in a life-saving transfusion, for example, comes in a plastic bottle as does milk. The dangers inherent in this condition of alienated and "isolated and segregated cohort living" are already apparent in various environmental crises now upon us—overfishing ocean waters, overgrazing grasslands, slash and burn agriculture in rain forests, overuse of pesti-

cides and fertilizers and the wearing out of topsoils, and the increasing presence of toxic substances in the atmosphere.

Instead moderns live amidst superficial glitz. Massive abuse, exploitation, and destruction of peoples, plants, animals, and the natural environment are hidden in specialized places where only a few can observe and take note. Modern people cannot see rain forests being burned, fishing grounds being killed, atomic wastes being dumped, or even high rise office buildings filled with people mindlessly watching oscilloscopes and typing out invoices. Thus one critical difference between the vital center and the urban complex is the openness and permeability which the middle level face-to-face settings reveal. This is not to say that such permeability will reveal only positive aspects of culture. There are certainly many dark forces hidden in village life waiting to express themselves. The fact is, however, that there we are more likely to have personal, direct, and intimate contact with them. And we may be able to tolerate the pain that comes from this direct contact because we can immediately act and respond to what we see and hear. We are literally "in touch."

4. Alfred N. Whitehead, *Adventures of Ideas* (New York: Free Press, 1933), p. 179.

5. In a somewhat more common (and complex) example, one can imagine a parent in a household attempting to influence her small children to leave their play and come to supper. It is in the interests of the children, the family, the house, the meal, the whole context for this to happen. Efforts are thus made to make the supper meal a *customary ritual* rather than have consistent tense negotiated confrontations among adults and children. One can then ask: Where is the power to resolve this problem? The answer is not: Who is stronger, or who is older, or who is wiser, or who can instigate the noisiest tantrum. The answer lies in a set of carefully crafted subtle compromises among all the principals involved, even including, perhaps, how long the food would normally "choose" to stay warm and appetizing on the stove or the table. This setting probably deals with one of the most delicate and complex kinds of human negotiations for it involves fundamental issues of fairness, love, sustenance, patience, pragmatic calculations, and power. And if it is done well and consistently, it may result in an important, albeit marginally stable, ritual of life-long significance. And it normally happens and is learned in primal and middle level institutions.

6. J. B. Priestly, *Man and Time* (London: Aldus Books, 1964), p. 292.

7. Ibid., p. 293.

8. Lewis Mumford, *The Pentagon of Power* (New York: Harcourt Brace Jovanovich, Inc., 1964), p. 391.

9. Ibid., p. 393.

10. The dualism can be directly observed in "performances" of dance, drama, or sports, for example. Such modern rituals are divided into those "actors" or "players" who directly participate in the enactment versus those whom we call the "audience." So the actors enter into a primal drama. In football, for example,

the players stalk one another, throw their bodies on those of the opponent, and bring other "players" to the ground, much as a large cat stalks a deer. While this is happening, the audience claps or screams or cheers while sitting safely on the sidelines. For the audience this is enactment without serious risk. So we view as culturally defective a modern view of the arts, drama and story telling, and sport as *creating entertainment* by participants for a physically distanced (and often passive) audience. Such rituals tend to have limited power as a means of reconstructing the deeper symbolic meanings of the central myths of our cosmologies simply because they are treated as entertainment—to relax us or to keep us from being bored between the "important" business of "working."

CHAPTER TWELVE

Historical Perspective On the Transformation of Place

TRANSFORMATION OF VILLAGE TO THE CITY: REDFIELD AND SINGER

In this chapter we discuss Redfield and Singer's speculative history of two kinds of urban places which emerged from the village, followed by Mumford's description of a city in the late middle ages illustrating one particular kind of city. This brief historical introduction will provide us with a baseline and context from which to compare the modern commercial industrial corporate place with these earlier forms of place.[1]

Redfield and Singer's time perspective as they describe the evolution of place is more limited than that of Walter presented in Chapter Ten. They focus on the transition of human habitats only over the past 15 thousand years, during which villages evolved into the preindustrial feudal complex and then later into modern commercial industrial cities. They make clear that their account is a tentative "scheme of constructs" which uses particular cities or civilizations to illustrate and support their speculations.[2] They begin their analysis with a distinction between the folk society and the early city. The folk society is characterized as "a long established homogeneous, isolated and non-literate integral (self-contained) community; the folk culture is that society seen as a system of common understandings."[3] Such a society, they say, can be created in a tribal band or village, but not in a city. In the transformation from village to city, they posit the possibility of two radically different processes which yield very different types of "place":

a) an *orthogenetic process* in which "the local moral and religious norms [of the earlier village] prevailed and found intellectual development in the literati and the exercise of control of the community in the ruler and the laws;" and

b) a *heterogenetic process* in which "local cultures are disintegrated and new integrations of mind and society are developed..."[4]

The basis for the disintegration of the local culture in the heterogenetic process is the rapid influx of new and alien peoples who are introduced through trade, invasion, and/or voluntary migration. In the more recently evolved commercial heterogenetic city "the predominant social types are businessmen, administrators alien to those they administer, and rebels, reformers, planners and plotters of many varieties. It is in cities of this kind that priority comes to be given to economic growth and the expansion of power among the goods of life."[5]

Redfield and Singer characterize the earlier orthogenetic or native city as driven by a "moral order" (deep religio-cultural commonalities) as opposed to the heterogenetic city which is driven by a "technical order" (economic profit and technological efficiency related to commerce and industry). Cultural change and growth occur in both kinds of cities, but in the orthogenetic native city, commercial, industrial, and technological growth never overwhelm the religious and moral core of the native culture.

The orthogenetic model is thus the first phase of a two stage pattern of "primary" and "secondary" urbanization reflecting the development of two radically different types of cities:

> In the primary phase a pre-civilized folk society is transformed ... into a peasant society and correlated urban center. It is primary in the sense that the peoples making up the pre-civilized folk ... share a common culture which remains the matrix too for the peasant and the urban cultures which develop from it.... Primary urbanization thus takes place almost entirely within the framework of a core culture that develops, as the local cultures become urbanized and transformed, into an indigenous civilization (344).

This primary process can be rapidly interrupted or aborted when local peoples are confronted with conquest or intense migration by other peoples from alien cultures. Primary urbanization can also be interrupted more gradually when the core local culture simply expands to include other alien cultures on the edges of its territory. In either case, the result is that humans are confronted by a new societal form or place, a new kind of city driven by a new "secondary pattern." "This secondary pattern produces not only a new form of urban life in significant conflict with local folk cultures but also a new urban type. In the city appear 'marginal' and 'cosmopolitan' men and 'intelligentsia;' in the country various types of marginal folk: enclaved-, minority-, imperialized-, transplanted-, remade-, quasi-folk, etc." This process leads to secondary urbanization and depends on many factors including mainly the rate of technical development and the scope and intensity of contact with other cultures.

But primary urbanization and the orthogenetic process lead to a very different kind of city. The most important consequence of primary urbanization is the transformation of old traditions and meaning systems of local villages (which they call "Little Traditions") into a city's or region's "Great Tradition"[6] which, while bringing about a more cosmopolitan society, provides for continuity between the village and the city. The instruments for both conserving the village and creating the new native city are "embodied in 'sacred books', or 'classics', sanctified by a cult, expressed in monuments, sculpture, painting and architecture, served by the other arts and sciences.... [T]he Great Tradition becomes the core culture of an indigenous civilization and a source, consciously examined, for defining its moral, legal, esthetic and other cultural norms" (348).

In the process of moving from Little Traditions to a Great Tradition, humans develop "fixed idea-systems (theologies, legal codes)" and create "esoteric" (348) and intellectual forms that are both traditional and unique (the Italian Renaissance is given as an example) which separate the orthogenetic (native) city from the local villages. "In short, the trend of primary urbanization is to coordinate political, economic, educational, intellectual, and esthetic activity to the norms provided by the Great Tradition" (349).

The consequence of secondary urbanization is, of course, radically different from the urbanization leading to the native city. There is a weakening of local and traditional cultures resulting in:

- a technical order characterized by calculations of economic self-interest, development of impersonal bureaucracies and institutions, supported by sanctions of force;

- class and ethnic consciousness of subgroups within the heterogenetic cities;
- emphasis on the future advantages of change and progress rather than sustaining the traditions of the past.

Redfield and Singer suggest that there are other (and perhaps more salient) consequences of secondary urbanization, which may easily be understood today within our highly individualistic culture. First are the shifts in mental outlook including the creation of an ethos and personality that is more "depersonalized, individualized, emotionally shallow and atomized, unstable, secularized, blasé, rationalistic, cosmopolitan, highly differentiated, self-critical, time-coordinated, subject to sudden shifts in mood and fashion, 'other directed.'" Redfield and Singer observe that these radical shifts in ethos, character, and personality are not related to the more general process of urbanization but are "primarily a consequence of secondary urbanization and [happen] ... in a particular critical stage when personal and cultural disorganization are greatest" (351). (We would note the relevance of this analysis to Riesman and Fromm's concept of changes in social character discussed earlier in Chapter Seven.)

These traumatic shifts suggest, moreover, that it is important to look at the continuities and discontinuities in "outlook, values, and personality as we trace the transformation of folk societies into their civilized dimension." In terms of continuities, the "literati" of the native city who create and maintain the Great Tradition do not repudiate the values and outlook of the rural hinterland; rather they transform this outlook into a more complex abstract cosmology. Along these same lines the native city, like the original villages, continues to stress the importance of kinship and blood lineage as well as the unique mystical personality which evolved from Little Traditions and is now identified with the religious core of the high culture.

While there may be elements of cultural continuity between village and the native or orthogenetic city, as Redfield and Singer suggest, there is still an inevitable gap. As they say, "the literati of the city develop the values and world view of the local culture to a degree of generalization, abstraction, and complexity incomprehensible to the ordinary villager, and in so doing leave out much of the concrete local detail of geography and village activity" (351). Nonetheless, Redfield and Singer emphasize that primary urbanization holds together important elements of common understanding *between* the Little Tradition *and* the Great Tradition. These elements include: 1) sacred books, monuments, art, icons, scriptures, fixed points of worship for common people; 2) a special class of literati or religious people who can read, interpret, and comment on scriptures for the common people; 3) leading personalities whose charisma binds people from village and city together; and 4) a sacred sense of place, buildings, monuments, and celebrations. These institutions tend to bind together household, village, and city, giving all a "feeling of consciousness of a single cultural universe in which people hold the same things sacred, and where the similarities of civic obligations in village and city [lead citizens to] build ... public squares, plant fruit trees, erect platforms and shrines ... [that express] ... concrete testimony to common standards of virtue and responsibility" (355).

The heterogenetic or commercial industrial city and villages in the countryside do not rest on a common ethos or culture since there is none. There are only common economic interests, which, with the rise and domination of a commercial money economy, rest on common market interests rather than on any symbiotic connection between the food and resources provided by villages and manufactured goods provided by the city. "The city becomes only a 'service station,' an amusement center for the country" (356).... The great challenge for the heterogenetic commercial city is to maintain conditions that allow for peaceful and productive "foreign relations" among the variety of "strange" personalities and cultures with which one comes into contact. In the words of Redfield and Singer:

> We may call this an enlargement of cultural horizons sufficient to become aware of other cultures and of the possibility that one's own society may in some ways require their presence. To paraphrase Adam Smith, it is not to the interest of the (Jewish) baker, the (Turkish) carpet-dealer, the (French) hand laundry that the American Christian customer looks when he patronizes them, but to his own....
>
> ... When all or many classes of a population are culturally strange to each other and where some of the city populations are culturally alien to the country populations, the necessity for an enlarged consciousness is obvious. (357)

One is then forced to question what in fact is the experiential and moral basis of this "enlarged consciousness."

The thrust of Redfield and Singer's historical/evolutionary model suggests that humans have difficulty sustaining the integrity of balanced middle level forms of association because of the pressure of commerce and industry toward unrestrained impersonal merchandising. The heterogenetic city with its overwhelming drive toward self-interested economic gain is intrinsically unstable because it does not include or integrate within its fabric authentic local or centered places. The shallow culture characteristic of the heterogenetic city precludes the creation of elements of continuity and tradition that may be required for one to feel connected to one's kinship and history, and to one's native place.

In summary, Redfield and Singer describe of two different cultural phases in the evolution of place with radically different outcomes. Phase one includes and integrates two rather primal societal types of place: the extended household and village on the one hand alongside the more complex but still local form, the native city. While these places are quite different, both social forms or types of "place" exist within or near one another and are connected by a common moral order. Here a "Little Tradition" remains joined to a "Great Tradition" and the primal elements of one connect to the more abstract and corporate elements of the other. The second phase evolves from the commercial trading company, the industrial corporation, and finally to the heterogenetic city dominated by a technical order which evolves into the modern urban conglomerate and finally the multiple locations of the global corporation we know today.

Perhaps a more common sensical and somewhat illusory modern American understanding of what villages and contemporary cities look like prevents us from seeing the power of Redfield and Singer's distinction, for we commonly assume that there is only one kind of city which looks either like the alarming slums of 19th century Chicago or the awesome skyscrapers and high culture of contemporary Manhattan. Likewise, modern people may see the village as standing either for a narrow monotonous way of life or for the raw purity of the rural countryside.

MUMFORD'S DESCRIPTION OF THE MEDIEVAL "CHARTERED" CITY

The distinction between the native as opposed to the commercial industrial city can also be found in the writings of Lewis Mumford, a contemporary student of urban history. It is important to understand that Mumford's critique of the modern city comes out of his monumental work on the history of the city and especially his description of the late chartered Medieval city; what Redfield and Singer would call an orthogenetic city.

Mumford, predating Redfield and Singer by some twenty years, develops a position similar to theirs within the framework of the Medieval-to-Modern experience. He sees the village and the late medieval city not as two competing oppositional societal forms, but rather as places with an essential connectedness and interdependence much as Redifield and Singer see the connection between the Little and the Great Tradition. While the city person is able to express more complex potentialities in an urban context than the villager in the countryside, both places share a common root or source in nurturing their essential humanity. As Mumford puts it:

> Every phase of life in the countryside contributes to the existence of cities. What the shepherd, the woodman, and the miner know, becomes transformed and "etherealized" through the city into durable elements in the human heritage: the textiles and butter of one, the moats and dams and wooden pipes and lathes of another, the metals and jewels of the third, are finally converted into instruments of urban living: underpinning the city's economic existence, contributing art and wisdom to its daily routine.[7]

Mumford goes through the time cycle leading from the earlier orthogenetic to the modern heterogenetic city recounted by Redfield and Singer and arrives at a somewhat more jaundiced conclusion. "Layer upon layer, past times preserve themselves in the city until life itself is finally threatened with suffocation: then, in sheer defense, modern man invents the museum."[8] The city remains but its soul dies. This is the "technical order." In short, he observes that cities are living places with a natural life span in which time ultimately runs out and they die.

But Mumford presents the late medieval town or city not only as a lively social environment, but also as an adequate physical environment. He describes the various smells and sights that citizens endured with mixed judgment. They were in some ways offensive, but in other ways were well understood by our human senses, and stimulated the primal human nature. In terms of odors, he talks about "smoky rooms," "perfume in the garden behind the burgher's house," "fragrant flowers and savory herbs" widely cultivated, "the smell of the barnyard on the street," "the odor of flowering orchards in the spring," "the scent of new mown hay, floating across the fields in early summer," the common smell of horse dung and cow dung (49). In terms of sounds Mumford talks of the "crowing cock, the chirping of the birds nesting under the eaves," or the tolling and chiming of bells in the bell tower, the noises of craftsmen hammering or tapping. Then at night the complete silence except for the stirring of animals or the calling of the watch. In terms of visual stimulation, Mumford observes,

> Common men thought and felt in images, far more than in the verbal abstractions used by scholars: esthetic discipline might lack a name, but its fruits were everywhere visible. Did not the citizens of Florence vote as to the type of column that was to be used on the Cathedral? Image makers carved statues, painted triptychs, decorated walls of the cathedrals, the guild hall, the town hall, the burgher's house: color and design were everywhere the normal accompaniment of the practical daily tasks." (50-51)

Spatially, the late medieval city could be characterized by the clear functional delineation of major structures (the wall, the church or cathedral, the market, the town hall) and the human scale of these structures. The wall symbolized one's identity with place. The wall provided protection in that the design of the streets and ways made it easy to rally at the wall. In a siege or famine or other emergency everyone had the feeling of share-and-share-alike.

> First the cowering countryside, with its local production and mainly local barter: social life gathered in little villages or in "suburbs," as the agricultural settlements that nestled under the castle's walls were called.... Then ... the wall: protection made permanent and regular. [Here] local craftsmen and peasants and fishermen, under privileges wrung from their local lord, came together for a regular weekly or fortnightly market: presently they sought permanent quarters for themselves in a spot that combined so many advantages in living.... As social life became more solid and compact, this industrial and merchants' quarter, the suburb, became the town center; and the seats of feudal and ecclesiastical power tended to become more suburban. (16)

Near the center of the city, where several streets converged, was the principal church or cathedral. The church is, in fact, both a place and a town hall—as Mumford says, "not too holy to serve as a dining hall for great public festivals;" (55) with a parish church for every hundred or so people. Alms houses were built for seven to ten men; hospitals were built to serve about two to three thousand people. This decentralization was not only functional in terms of social needs, it tended to keep the buildings in human scale.

Individual houses were commonly built in rows around the edge of gardens or in blocks with inner courts and gardens. Heating was accomplished early on by an open hearth in the middle of the floor which later gave way to a hearth and chimney. The houses lacked differentiated space (separate kitchens, living rooms, bedrooms, etc.) which limited personal privacy. In many of the irregular medieval sites houses were built where they might be grouped by specialized trades or as religious compounds, and residents used footpaths to pass between these self-contained quarters.

The "household unit included ... not only relatives by blood but a group of industrial workers as well as domestics whose relationship was that of secondary members of the family." Women worked mostly in the home and men from both noble and common classes learned from members of the prior generation all they needed to know. As Mumford says, "The workshop was the family. The members ate together at the same table, worked in the same rooms, slept in the same dormitory, joined in family prayers, participated in the common amusements" (35).

Mumford recounts the distinction we have referred to earlier as "relational being" as opposed to "essential" or egocentric being, and it is the former that was a fundamental aspect of medieval identity. One was attached not only to home and family, but also to a manor and/or a monastery or guild. The guild was not only an economic social institution, but also a religious one which met to provide support in good times and bad. It protected its members from economic disaster and guaranteed all a decent burial. "It was a brotherhood adapted to specific economic tasks but not wholly engrossed in them: the brothers ate and drank together on regular occasions: they formulated regulations for the conduct of their craft: they planned and paid for and enacted their parts in their mystery plays, for the edification of their fellow townsmen: and they built chapels, endowed charities, and founded schools." (30).

There was, in fact, a general merchant guild that organized and regulated the economic life of the town or city, providing for consumer protection, honesty among craftsmen, and fairness in conducting one's business. The guild was not simply a labor union or trade association to protect and promote the economic interests of its members. It had broad social purposes as well, and it was in the fulfillment of its social purposes that the guild became a health and old age society, a dramatic society, an educational society. As Mumford further notes, once its economic purpose became focused and "all engrossing ... the institution decayed: a patriciate of wealthy masters rose within it to hand on the privileges to their sons and to work together to the exclusion and disadvantage of the poorer craftsmen and the growing proletariat" (31).

In these early European cities there was an ethos of *civic service*. When one became a member of a municipality, one no longer was required to pay feudal dues in return for which one assumed various civic responsibilities. These included military service in time of emergency and rotating policing of the community—being "on watch." "To patrol one's city at night: to know its dark alleys under the moon, or with no light at all except one's lantern, to enjoy the companionship of the watch ... [was] more useful, more humane, than any national scheme of military training" (28).

From the tenth century on, older towns and cities moved toward greater independence. Cities became "chartered" which meant they negotiated with a regional nobility to guarantee military security, which also gave those who stayed "in town" for a period of time freedom from obligations of serfdom. Gradually cities won the right to hold regular markets, coin money, establish and run their own courts and bear arms in their defense. This kind of "town building ... was one of the major industrial enterprises of the early Middle Ages" which resulted in the age-old problem of draining manpower from the countryside (37).

> As urban occupations step by step drove out the rural ones that had at first been pursued in the city with almost equal vigor, the antagonism widened between town and country. The city was an exclusive society; and every townsman was, in relation to the country folk, something of a snob.... This fact was eventually to contribute toward the undoing of urban freedom and government. (27)

Mumford states bluntly that "the one powerful and universal institution in the Medieval city was the Church." As he says:

The fundamental political divisions of society, surviving all other ties and allegiances, were the parish and the diocese; the most universal form of taxation was the tithe, which went to the support of the great establishment of Rome. No small part of the economic life was devoted to the glorification of God, the support of the clergy and of those who waited on the clergy, and to the construction and maintenance of ecclesiastical buildings—cathedrals, churches, monasteries, hospitals, schools. (28)

The church brought to the city a quality of life and consciousness characterized by the sense of withdrawal or retreat; the necessity of quiet contemplation and the nurturing of the inner life; the importance of prayer and inner communion. "In the Medieval city the spirit had organized shelters and accepted forms of escape from worldly opportunity. Today, the degradation of the inner life is symbolized by the fact that the only place sacred from interruption is the private toilet" (28).

However, because of its influence in every aspect of medieval life, the church was also closely identified with trade and commerce. Mumford notes that, in fact, much of the trade that existed was granted to the church rather than to temporal lords (18-19). According to Mumford, the increased trade was a by-product of the increased security provided by the wall. Moreover most of the new "wealth" was created by local craftsmen selling their own goods rather than from commerce by merchants. Much has been made of the medieval "Great Fairs" which stimulated early international capitalism through the exchange of luxury wares from distant places. But according to Mumford:

> if the cultural importance of international trade was high, its economic importance ... has been grossly exaggerated for the early Middle ages.... Even at a later period than the eleventh century the merchants with their retainers accounted ... for only a small part of the town's population: far smaller than today. For the producers in the early medieval town composed about four-fifths of the inhabitants, as compared with two-fifths in the modern city. (19)

Mumford further points out that capitalism actually had a disruptive effect on the internal life of the people in that a few groups competed with one another for goods and services based on the lust for profit and gain, while other groups of protected producers lived in a state of relative stability and equality. He describes the increase in both the extensiveness and efficiency of agriculture in the countryside, but notes especially that much agricultural improvement was brought into the city itself, and "except for a few congested centers, the town of the Middle Ages was not merely in the country but of the country: food was grown within the walls, as well as on terraces, or in the orchards and fields, outside." (24).

At the beginning of the twelfth century in Bologna and Paris, the university was founded, to "lay down the basis of a co-operative organization of knowledge on a regional basis: scholars flocked to these centers from every part of Europe, and in turn, their masters studied and taught at distant centers." Mumford sees this institution as a variation of the cloistered monastery, but of a much more active nature. As he says, "it made explicit, concrete, and systematic one of the enduring functions of the city: withdrawal from immediate practical responsibility and the critical reappraisal and renewal of the cultural heritage" (34). The unusual mandate of the university was its independence from the ethos of the market and the commerce of the city which gave it a special kind of authority comparable, in some sense, to that of the church.

A constant concern for the medieval city was increasing populations. We know that medieval towns rarely extended more than a half mile from their center. Other factors besides simple distance had to be considered: limitations of the water supply and local produce; limitations set by guild regulations which prevented uncontrolled settlement by outsiders; limitations of transport and communication. In general, these limitations were solved by simply building new independent towns and cities often close by. "The typical medieval town ranged in size from three or four hundred ... to forty thousand, which was the size of London in the fourteenth century...." (59). Thriving cities in Germany, Switzerland, and France in the fifteenth century were commonly no larger than ten to twenty thousand. According to Mumford the practice of overcrowding and overbuilding and suburban expansion did not begin until it became too difficult to build new cities.

If one were to ask why the late medieval city evolved into this new societal form, we would refer the reader to the three dimensions of our organic holistic theory. First, in terms of economic and environmental adaptation the "protected economy" of the medieval city was immensely superior to the insecure open country. Mumford maintains that the advantages of this new kind of "place"—the way it prepared persons

for "orderly economic effort, fostering skill by every variety of emula-
tion and gain"—were so numerous compared to the country that industry was not tempted to return to the country. There were still various
feudal restrictions, but life was much more predictable and orderly.

Second, while the artisans and merchants of various sorts may have
come to the city for environmental and economic reasons—because of its
protection, stability, and orderliness—the deeper meaning of life was not
primarily in work or economic gain; it was found within the church. As
Mumford notes, "Life was a succession of significant episodes in man's
pilgrimage to heaven: for each great moment the Church had its sacra-
ment or its celebration. Beneath the active drama was the constant chant
of prayer: in solitary or in company, men communed with God and
praised him. It was in such moments ... that one truly lived." (63). The
genius of the medieval city was the way it integrated deeper meaning
through the Church (its ritual, celebration, and pageantry) with stable
groups of parishioners in the form of households, guilds (and other sodalities), and a host of cross-linked organizations.

In a final passage, Mumford provides us with an eyewitness account
by one Albrecht Durer, who describes the Great Procession from the
Church of Our Lady at Antwerp. The stunning aspect of this description
is that it reveals how deeply economic, social structural, and meaning-making qualities of culture were integrated and balanced within this
society. As he says:

> ... all ranks and guilds had their signs, by which they might be
> known. In the intervals, great costly pole-candles were borne, and
> three long old Frankish trumpets of silver. There were also ... many
> pipers and drummers. All instruments were loudly and noisily
> blown and beaten.
>
> ... There were the Goldsmiths, the Painters, the Masons, the Fisher-
> men, the Butchers, the Leatherers, the Clothmakers, the Bakers, the
> Tailors, the Cordwainers—indeed, workmen of all kinds, and
> many craftsmen and dealers who work for their livelihood. Like-
> wise the shopkeepers and merchants and their assistants of all
> kinds were there. After these came the shooters with guns, bows,
> and crossbows, and the horsemen and foot-soldiers also. Then fol-
> lowed the watch of the Lord Magistrates. Then came a fine troop all
> in red, nobly and splendidly clad. Before them ... went all the reli-

gious orders and the members of some foundations, very devoutly, all in their different robes.... A very large company of widows also took part in the procession. They support themselves with their own hands and observe a special rule. (63-64)

Durer continues his litany of processors including "Wagons drawn with masques upon ships," "the Company of the Prophets," "scenes from the New Testament," "Three Holy Kings riding on great camels." And so the procession continues for more than two hours. Mumford comments that:

> the spectators are also the communicants and participants. They are engaged in the spectacle watching it from within, not from without; or rather, feeling it from within, acting in unison, not dismembered beings, reduced to a single specialized role. Prayer, mass, pageant, baptism, marriage, or funeral—the city itself was a stage for these separate scenes of the drama, and the citizen himself was the actor. (64)

We are intrigued by the imagination and creative impulses of local citizens to invent such institutions as chartered cities including markets, guilds, voluntary police functions, universities. After all these people were not R&D specialists or powerful corporate executives or leaders of great modern nations or philanthropic foundations who had experience in planning and executing such projects. And we in turn are discomforted by Mumford's observation that these creative popular institutions began to atrophy and fall away with the increasing wealth of individuals and the growing class/caste system. With the rise of the modern nation-state and commercial industrial cities, wealthy entrepreneurs and merchants endowed schools, financed asylums for the aged and orphaned, and accepted other such charitable responsibilities. And as the wealth increased along with the distance and segregation among the classes, the free chartered cities and towns began shrinking under the political domination of centralized and consolidated units of private corporate life. As Walter noted in Chapter Ten, with the new wealth from commerce and industry the rich became segregated from the middle and the poor. The poor are then cared for "at a distance" through concentrated factory-based jobs, privately financed asylums, orphanages, and the like.

In the end, Mumford announces that the "agglomerative city" in the modern Western context has failed—that is to say, modernity has failed. Modern people have created gigantic forms of "mechanical integration" but these have gone on side by side with "social disruption." What follows, he says, is "a crystallization of chaos" (7). Disorder hardens into slums and factories until there is an "exodus into the dormitory suburbs." The new and growing urban populations "lack the most elementary facilities … even sunlight and fresh air, to say nothing of the means to a more vivid social life" (8).

> The new cities grew up without the benefit of coherent social knowledge or orderly social effort: they lacked the useful urban folkways of the Middle Ages or the confident esthetic command of the Baroque period: indeed, a seventeenth century Dutch peasant, in his little village, knew more about the art of living in communities than a nineteenth century municipal councilor in London or Berlin. Statesmen who did not hesitate to weld together a diversity of regional interests into national states, or who wove together an empire that girdled the planet, failed to produce even a rough draft of a decent neighborhood. (8)

In short, the villager or resident of an earlier and more primal native town or city ends up knowing more about how to live within and sustain a genuine culture than the sophisticated resident of the commercial industrial conglomerate who lives apart within her/his isolated affluent cohort in the modern city, or even separated from the city amidst the manicured lawns and long driveways in the distant suburb or in the country estate.

A Theoretical Comparison of the Late Medieval City with the Modern Urban Conglomerate

In our holistic theory described in Chapter Ten we described three sets of cultural patterns placed along the primal-to-modern dimension of place. We will use this theoretical scheme to suggest significant contrasts between the late medieval orthogenetic native city and the modern commercial heterogenetic city or urban conglomerate.

Economic/Environmental Cultural Patterns

We can contrast the medieval city vs. the modern commercial system with respect to 1) *sense of place* (the importance of stable local communities *versus* the mobility and transiency of one's habitat); 2) *sense of vocation* (people engaged in work requiring significant skills and having a direct relationship with the tools they own and control *versus* a steep hi-erarchical system with many layers of specialization so that the worker is separated from the nature and quality of the final fruits of his/her work); and 3) *technology* (small easily accessible human scale technology *versus* complex large scale technology understood and controlled by a small elite of entrepreneurs and engineers).

1. *Sense of Place*. Most local medieval peoples had a profound and rela-tively stable sense of place connected to local churches, village life, guilds, sodalities, and agricultural lands. Nobility and clergy were, on the other hand, connected both to local places and more extensive re-gional places. In contrast, modern peoples are drawn toward a transient way of life based on perceived need for education, employment, and new opportunities for raising one's standard of living. Newly industrial-ized peoples are especially prone to migrate toward places where there are jobs when more self-sufficient modes of life dry up. Cities are espe-cially attractive because of their technologies and industries based on a fluid money economy. A superficial "popular culture" celebrates the in-stant global exchange of information and undervalues or repudiates face-to-face oral traditions characteristic of folk and religious culture.

2. *Vocation*. Most medieval villagers lived modest lives with little hope of mobility into affluence. Humble people of various vocations mingled with one another. The core vocations were connected with artisanry and agriculture, which were closely related to physical survival. Yet in native cities there was something of a "modern" balance that included a literati, an educated clergy, artists, merchants, and the like. Workers in modern industry or manufacturing, however, often have no sense that they are carrying out tasks that are necessary for the survival of the larger com-munity. They work for their own survival and self-interest. Members of the working and middle class are commonly driven by the desire for good jobs and money and hope of moving into higher classes. Yet the majority of people understand at some level that most will not arrive at the level of affluence depicted by what they learn in school or from mass media. Living simple frugal lives, as many do, is seen as a temporary "struggle" and is often associated with stagnation, failure, and the per-ceived or real threat of poverty.

3. *Technology*. In the medieval society there was constant technological innovation, but it was at a pace and level of complexity that was under-standable to common people within a biological time frame. Most voca-

tions still depended on skilled labor which could be learned from one generation to the next. In Modernity there is constant exponential change in the rate at which technical innovation happens, generated by complex sources of knowledge often within expensive laboratories that are inaccessible to most people. We have reached the point at the end of the 20th century where it was assumed that technological change would accelerate at a pace such that each individual would have to learn a new vocation or at least find a new way of making a living every five or six years.

4. *Segregation vs. Integration of Diverse Human Cohorts*. We assume that the range and variety of temperaments and talents of people in the medieval city as compared with the modern commercial industrial city were roughly similar. While we know that within medieval society there was much more gender segregation, there was undoubtedly greater integration among people with different temperaments, talents, and interests across work roles, family roles, religious roles, and civic roles. Artisans were not only the skilled creators of many artifacts, they often ran the shops in which the artifacts were sold. There they met the "high" and the "low" publics who needed to purchase their goods. Households were not only places where people did the essential "bread work" involved in the daily routine of life; it is where people practiced farming and artisanry and maintained shops or markets where goods and artifacts were created and sold.

Modern people do associate with a great variety of people, but only in the most superficial way. This is especially true of people in the higher socio-economic strata. High status business people, professionals, engineers, managers, etc. tend to live insulated from the common people, especially the working classes and the poor. And these high status people are, of course, the ones who make the most significant decisions and thus apparently live the most "significant" lives running and controlling, albeit in narrow and pragmatic ways, the major institutions of the system.

Medieval people obtained food grown in or near the city from local villagers—food that was then prepared for large households by kin or in-house servants. On the other hand, modern people go to the supermarket to purchase food. In such modern environments food is obtained by exchanging tokens of value (money), and those who do the purchasing or selling understand little of the actual skill, technology, effort, or resources required to grow, store, and transport it to the point where it can be sold and consumed. There are, of course, other settings which are required to make the supermarket function. Animals are slaughtered, cut up, and packaged and fruits and vegetables are grown, picked, frozen, canned, etc. But these activities happen in slaughter houses and packing plants quite invisible to the shopper. There is a disconnect between the consumer, the processor, the wholesaler, and the producer, and the specialized work that each does. No one really has any coherent sense of the complex process required to bring food to the point where it can be eaten and transformed into flesh and garbage.

CULTURAL PATTERNS
RELATED TO BONDING AND SOCIAL STRUCTURE

We can contrast the medieval city and the modern commercial system with respect to

- Types of Social Forms (families, work and religious settings, etc. *versus* individual/corporate institutions)
- Sources of Human Bonding (spousal relations, kinship, friendship and mutual aid *versus* contractual bureaucratic relations based on reciprocal responsibilities and duties)
- Expressions of Power (relational power within or among socially connected cohorts with the possibility of face-to-face negotiation to solve problems *versus* power as domination over highly segregated cohorts of humans with power based on differentials in affluence, merit, efficiency, and educational credentials).

Types of Social Forms. In the medieval city, common people could act out significant economic, social, and meaning-making aspects of their lives within a variety of primal-to-modern social forms which hold substantial significance for the individuals. In the more primal or mediating vital center we find nuclear and extended families, clans, and economic and religious sodalities. On the modern end of medieval society we have feudal contracts which define economic, civic and military relationships among the wealthy, the high nobility, and the central church hierarchy. Much of life, however, was actually controlled and made meaningful within immediate, intimate local settings in what we have called vital center or middle level institutions.

Social Bonding. The modern nuclear family as contrasted with the medieval household is considered a "non-productive" institution. From the point of view of modern economics, the work the modern family carries out yields nothing of "real" or monetary value, but only prepares people to do "productive" work in the corporate setting—or it simply allows people rest and recreation in between occasions of "real" work. Commonly in the modern system there is little overlap or connection between the intimate actions of family life and the more formal contractual self-interested relationships characteristic of work settings and consumer settings. The medieval household, on the other hand, was understood as a critical economic and social bonding unit in a society that transferred value through human relationships in work, in the barter of products, and in the exchange of money.

CULTURAL PATTERNS RELATED TO MEANING AND MEANING-MAKING

Within the framework of meaning and meaning-making, we consider patterns related to

- Sources of Personal Identity and Significance, (e.g., relational being *versus* individualistic essential being)
- Time (e.g., cyclical biological *versus* linear time)
- Experience/liturgy (e.g., "unseen" tacit/mystical experience *versus* one's cultural "story" versus pragmatic or practical problem solving).

1. *The Issue of Personal Identity and Significance.* Modernity views the person as a separate autonomous, "free" and ever changing individual. For modern people, "intrinsic being" or egocentric identity is commonly encultured and constantly reinforced. Modern people are "free individuals" born with blank slates and have the free choice to accept, resist and/or change past traditions and cultural patterns. With this encultured sense of free choice goes the assumption of independence and self-sufficiency. Any significant degree of dependence on anyone or anything may be seen as unseemly—a sign of "weakness."

The inhabitant of the medieval city was more likely to see the Self as defined in terms of relationships or connections: place and kin connections, religious connections, and vocational connections were sources of identity that often continued for a lifetime. Koestler's holon or part-whole sense of being is in many ways similar to relational being. One suspects that this was also a common form of experience in the medieval city, since the idea of the "whole" or the "holy" was a central metaphor in the Church. We assume that when a trope or metaphor is central to the culture it connects to other social experiences. So one is "part-whole" in a family, in a household, in a village, in a native city, and that "part-whole" understanding of being or reality gives one the self-significance associated with the whole, whether that be the whole family, the whole village, the whole native city, or the whole of the Christian Cosmos.

It is, perhaps, the religious feeling of relationality and the part-whole connection to the Christian cosmos which allowed the medieval individual to see her/his vulnerability and weakness as an admission that the ultimate weakness—mortality—was redeemed with the gift of being "within" or a "child of God." At any rate, we would guess that the medieval person experienced a more even balance in constructing meaning as a mix of relationality, part-whole, and simply being *intrinsically* and egocentrically "there" in contrast to the modern person.

2. *The Issue of Time.* Considering the issue of time, there seems little doubt that the medieval native had a more profound sense of eternal and cyclical or seasonal time than does the modern person. The Church was grounded in a multi-layered "chain of being" which began and ended in a conception of infinite time. The medieval person was also embedded in the vivid actuality of plant and animal life which lived and died and provided food in seasonal cycles. Human death was more visible, if not more common, than in our modern world and seen as a normal part of life, as part of living ,and was more immediately and directly experienced. The human life cycle was a salient part of one's identity, but we would not overly romanticize this point since humans do not easily escape from the centrality and salience of linear time, and the medieval person was probably no exception. On the other hand, the modern person is so deeply encultured within the ideology of technological reality and linear "progress" that it is often difficult to see eternal, cyclical or seasonal time as an important or significant aspect of her/his consciousness. Even those festivals and holidays that punctuate modern seasonal time are presumably celebrated as getting progressively "better" every year, e.g., higher sales figures with each succeeding holiday season. And without evidence of substantial visible progress, the modern person is compelled to work harder, "put in more time"—for unless one is moving "forward" or "upward" one seems to be standing still, on the edge of failure, or simply going "nowhere."

3. *Experience and Ritual*. Considering the issue of experience and ritual, we focus on the connection between what we earlier referred to as "emergent experience" from an "unseen world" versus self-directed, intentional, "conscious" objective experience. The medieval person commonly experienced the chant, the candles, and semi-darkness of the cathedral where an unseen "emergent reality" presumably entered the material body. There was, in fact, an unseen but vividly understood cosmos which included heaven and hell, purgatory and paradise. Likewise there were significant rituals through which these transcendent realities were made present, e.g., the holy Eucharist or communion.

By contrast, the modern person feels her/himself living largely within the immediate material world. Information comes from the material environment through the senses and reason interprets this information, or information comes into the culture from others who have already fathomed its meaning within the material world and are simply passing it on. Modern people, in short, are required to interpret meaning within the narrow band that runs between objective sense data and imaginative/rational inquiry and they tend to trust only those meanings that can be publicly and reliably confirmed and/or replicated. This, of course, diminishes the greatest of our living mysteries, e.g., birth, life, suffering, joy, death, and the manyness and layered qualities of the natural world that seem to come from some kind of transformed oneness. More subtle and inexplicable qualities of one's experience must be reduced to seemingly "understood explanations" which talk about particular rhetorical devices or categories of language that lead us toward vague non-material "realities." Thus, when we exhaust the material clarity in the modern positivistic secular mode of knowing, we can speak only in the uncertain language of "spirituality," "drama," "metaphor," "art," "poetry," or of the elegance and grandeur of the human "mind."

SUMMARY

In looking at these comparisons and contrasts between the medieval city and the modern commercial industrial conglomerate, we should keep in mind one of our central normative assumptions: organic or genuine culture is enhanced when it has an adequate set of places and cultural patterns along the primal-to-modern dimension within which to express itself. As we reflect on this assumption, we note that there is a tendency for societies which are moving from the village and orthogenetic city to the heterogenetic city or commercial-industrial conglomerate to increase their emphasis on modern patterns in all three cultural areas: the economic/environmental patterns, the social structural and bonding patterns, and patterns in meaning and meaning-making. *This creates a weakening of cultural patterns expressed in the vital mediating center.*

More specifically, as populations migrate in search of opportunities for work and material advantage within the economic/environmental cultural pattern, the sense of place is weakened. One does not stay long enough in one place to make it significant. In terms of vocation and technology, the artisan, the artist, and the homemaker lose significance as they replace or are replaced by people who work in corporate offices, factories, and warehouses, mines, and various forms of social service which stress efficiency and monetary pay rather than a vocational calling or personal job satisfaction. People work for money, for status, and the acclaim by others in their professions rather than for the less palpable goals we associate with "genuine culture."

From the point of view of social structure and bonding, the quality of human care and consideration in extended families, sodalities, and villages tends to diminish as the society becomes more modern. The self-sufficient productive and often exploitative individual is celebrated—the one who can manage her/his own life successfully. Modern people come to celebrate the rich and the famous of the society, regardless of what made people rich or famous in the first place resulting in the diminished importance of creating or sharing more primal bonds in the vital center. So expressions of friendship and mutual aid diminish.

With respect to meaning and meaning-making there is increasing modern emphasis on transforming concrete stories or narratives either into marketable media for sale to the millions or into abstract data which can be used to develop pragmatically effective ways of transforming them into marketable products. There is also the reverse tendency to consider any experience that cannot be directly transformed into a commercially exploitable product in the material world as something frivolous or simply "entertaining"—unless, of course, it can be "produced" as a movie or TV show and sold for profit. Then it is significant.

In what we have referred to as the organic society and the living place there is substantial balance and integration across all basic functional modalities. People live and spend time (and consider as having substantial importance) primal to modern activities within economic, social-relational, and meaning-making places. Settings which integrate in moderate degrees aspects of all three patterns of culture are seen as even more desirable, e.g., working and "living" in households; selling goods to and enjoying the company of customers within the market; participating in drama or music or liturgy with one's parishioners in a local holy place.

When these qualities of balance and integration within the vital center hold for social settings in which people live and work, we assume these places are more alive, dynamic, and consonant with our basic human nature. We assume that as such culture is also more stable and more kindly—more genuine—because it is consistent with the needs of our human condition.

NOTES

1. In each of the sections of this chapter—the evolution of place and the medieval city—we are developing a particular thesis based on two seminal essays rather than reviewing a broad range of literature from which to develop a critical synthesis. These essays are authored by Redfield and Singer and Mumford, the references of which are listed below.

2. Robert Redfield & Milton B. Singer, "The cultural role of cities," in *Peasants and Peasant Societies* Teodor Shanin, ed. (Middlesex, England: Penguin Books, 1971), 337; Lewis Mumford, *The Culture of Cities* (NewYork: Harcourt Brace Jovanovich, 1938).

3. Redfield & Singer, "The cultural role of cities," 341.

4. Ibid., 342.

5. Ibid.

6. Redfield and Singer present a rich and varied array of specific examples from Central America, Asia, Southern Europe, etc. to support their thesis which makes their theoretical model especially compelling and interesting.

7. Lewis Mumford, *The Culture of Cities*, 3-4.

8. Ibid., 4.

PART SIX

Reconsidering Prospects for Change

CHAPTER THIRTEEN

The Compatibility of Commercial Corporations and Middle Level Places

THE PROBLEMATIC NATURE OF MIXED SOCIAL FORMS

One premise of this work is that any significant successful effort to ameliorate the pathologies of modernity requires that two very different societal forms—the corporate organization and multi-level organic living places—coexist in balance within a single larger social system. The question is whether or not the cultural logic of the dynamic corporate form will inevitably dominate, distort, or eventually smother primal and mediating local forms and native cities that support them. There is currently much public discourse about the need for more local civic communal life within modern places, and it is often assumed that what we have called mediating places in the vital center can be sustained or somehow "folded" into the existing dominant corporate matrix.[1]

Within this "folding in" approach, corporate work places and schools, for example, can presumably be transformed with "homelike," more convivial atmospheres by adding day care and health care facilities, cafeterias, and gyms. Over the past two hundred years, countless communitarian experiments in the United States, motivated by a society dominated by corporate institutions, have failed. We must face the possibility that complex balanced forms of communal organization may not be viable within a modern industrial commercial system. While we may give lip service to strengthening primal or mediating social forms such as the extended family and the household or the neighborhood and village within the native city, there seems little serious effort to engage in serous or sustained efforts to make this happen.

To recapitulate our theory of the balanced center, the "multi-layered" local place is characterized by its rich organic complexity of social settings sustained by a genuine and balanced culture. In order for the primal or middle-level qualities of place, activity and work, and social bonding to come together, correlate, and integrate the world of the individual there have to be radical changes. For example, predatory corporations would have to restrain their temptation to grow in order to allow local businesses and artisans to participate and thrive in the economy. There would have to be less geographic mobility and transiency so that traditional forms of economic and personal association would have time to emerge gradually over time. Contractural associations would have to become more balanced by forms of association based on trust and on a degree of risk-based neighborly connectedness. Personal identity would have to come more from one's sense of place and association with the natural and personal environment rather than from having one's status based on occupational earnings or educational credentials. Time would have to become more balanced between the idea of linear progress and cyclical/seasonal/organic events in the lives of the humans and creatures who lived there. And finally, to temper our modern arrogance and zest for power there would have to be created what Mumford suggests are places of quiet humility and contemplation—beyond museums and libraries—in which the unconscious sensibilties of people might regularly feel the oneness of an emerging unseen reality as the source of the manyness of the material world.

When we contrast this living place with the modern corporate system, in the latter there are mainly four institutions: corporate product-centered work places, public or quasi-public contract-based consumer places, non-descript transitional places (e.g., sidewalks and streets), and private personal or family places. And there are sharply defined status and functional differences among these places. The essential distinction between the product-based corporate place and the multi-level set of pluralistic local places is the zealous drive of corporate places to define and enforce success economically within the narrow set of work places, work types, qualities of bonding, and qualities of meaning (pragmatic, technical, instrumental meanings). All activities outside of these limits tend to be bracketed and/or diminished as "one's own personal concern." Corporate work is the main course; one's personal egocentric life is the dessert; but there is no communal or civil middle interlude in which to negotiate the meaning of it all.

PULLMAN, ILLINOIS—THE QUICK FIX: AN EXPERIMENT IN COMPATIBILITY

As indicated in Chapter One, early responses to the increasing domination of industrial/commercial product centered corporations and the urban plcaces they created appeared with considerable energy in the United States shortly after the American Revolution and increased in intensity between the panic of 1837 through the Civil War. But the issue was and has generally been framed by social commentators in a more positive vein—as if the potential for serious incompatibility between corportion and local institutions was not really all that significant. It was assumed that criticisms and problems of this new system associated with the loss of communal associations, and artisan-based work, for example, were simply the price of progress and would somehow pass.

Paternalistic entrepreneurs apparently had little idea of the genie that was being uncorked from the bottle with the advent of the industrial factory and office complex as centers of the work environment, social relationships, and the culture of the community. They often framed problems of the new industrial-commercial order in terms of the need to devise connections between technology and industry on the one hand and community on the other. Such experiments began in early nineteenth century New England in Waltham, Lowell, and Lawrence, Massachusetts and in Manchester, New Hampshire where young men and women from nearby farms and villagers emigrated to the city to earn money to start a family when they had to leave the farm. When problems of poverty, unregulated growth, and sharp economic downturns began to happen and to hurt, there was often more confusion than outrage.

One of several self-conscious efforts to deal with the host of new problems that emerged at the end of the 19th century was an industrial-communal experiment undertaken by George Pullman near Chicago, where he constructed a full-blown community completed in 1884. Pullman believed, much as we have argued here, that real community had to be embodied within the overall conditions in which one lives, i.e., the physical environment and economy, the social structures and bonding within community, and the deeper cultural meanings and institutions that bring the physical environment and the relationships to life. And like many of the nineteenth century social experiments in community building, Pullman, Illinois was a response to the overwhelming ugliness, poverty, and chaotic world that Chicago had become. He sought a more genteel and dignified way of life for his workers.

James Gilbert describes Pullman's effort at creating this grand community:[2] "Into this enterprise," Gilbert writes, "[Pullman] the entrepreneur poured his hopes and aspirations for a reformed society. Here he fully articulated his faith that culture and enterprise could mutually reinforce each other for personal and social profit."[3]

> All the buildings, except the Greenstone Church, were constructed primarily of brick. Dominating the vast [industrial] works was the clock tower with a huge water tower and, close to the Illinois Central tracks and in full view of passing travelers, was the glass-plated observatory building housing the [great] Charles Engine. The large gates to the factory had substantial open spaces for billboards to announce company social and cultural events.

> The Florence Hotel ... dominated the central part of town ... to underscore the importance of visitations by guests.

> To the south rose the Arcade building [with] social and mercantile facilities.... [This represented the market motif of department stores in Chicago and foreshadowed the modern shopping mall.] Housing for workers consisted of brick row houses of differing quality and size. Those closest to the center, reserved for engineers and foreman, were the largest and most elaborate; those beyond the town center were less so.... Pullman constructed a model water and sewer system, whose compost was added to the profitable vegetable farm at the outskirts of the town. (150-152)

The streets were named after great inventors with whom Pullman associated with no reference to the employees of his works. There were no saloons, gambling or prostitution houses, cheap theaters, dance halls, or other institutions that might appeal to working class immigrants. There were no police stations or courts, orphanages or governmental institutions aside from post offices. The library was a centrally located and well-financed institution which focused on improvement rather than reading for enjoyment. The Pullman Band played concerts in the village during the summer.

Gilbert summarizes how the Pullman "community" would presumably fulfill the role of the ideal small town which George Pullman assumed was fully compatible with the industrial corporate place. "It contained all the institutions, a theater, library, stores, meeting places, athletics, savings bank, band, and religious and self-help organizations required for an ideal urban life" (154). It was designed to be the ideal mix of the virtues of the small town and the gentile environment of the city.

Yet despite this idyllic picture, it all came crashing down in 1893 with the onset of a major depression followed by a bitter strike. In Gilbert's words:

> Banning working-class culture from Pullman did not eliminate it, it only displaced it outside the town. Outlawing unions did not eliminate or even temper the resentments of workers. Franchising the lives of Pullman families in rented houses and planned cultural events did not, and could not, transform them into a [compliant] middle class. (162)

One is tempted to comment at this point that Pullman's top down totalitarian effort to elevate "common people" into a "higher culture" so that they could share the tastes and values of the moneyed elite was simply a more controlled version of our current advertising efforts to define success in terms of money, status, and the consumption of goods and services. The harsh fact was that with all of Pullman's moralistic ideals projected on his workers, the bottom line was making a profit manufacturing railroad sleeping cars. The more fundamental challenge for creating a balanced living place requires, perhaps, engaging people who are to live there to actually improvise and participate in the construction of their own indigenous local world in which there is no hard and fast "bottom line." Pullman rather simply gave them "his culture" just as modern R&D centers, marketing experts, housing developers, and Disney, Inc. package their understanding of "the good life" for contemporary people—one they believe will yield the greatest consumer satisfaction and profit for all.

Since Pullman, we have lived for a century in the United States searching for ways to sustain local middle level forms, such that they might thrive within the logic of the modern commercial industrial urban system. But when we think of communal forms, as did Pullman, we tend to refer to experiments in "total community." In this vein, we would note the substantial number and variety of intentional communitarian experiments and movements in the United States over the nineteenth and into the twentieth century, many of which were and are religiously based and most of which have failed.[4] It is important, however, to mention the continued success of the Amish, the Hutterites, and, of course, the Mormons who are, perhaps, the most successful of all these movements.

But despite its failure, the Pullman experiment does provide some focus for the questions we are posing here: Are there ways by which we can sustain or reclaim more complex balanced mediating places within the larger social units of a native city or even an urban conglomerate? Are there hopeful contemporary examples of anything like the organic naturalistic village-urban-complex illustrated in Mumford's description of the late medieval city?

PUTNAM'S STUDY OF CIVIC ENGAGEMENT IN ITALY

One response to this question comes in Robert Putnam's study of urban life in a number of cities in Italy between 1970 and 1990. Putnam and his associates were especially interested in the dramatic differences in economic growth and the effectiveness of government between cities in the North and the South in that country.[5] The broader historical context of the study—the revolutionary changes brought by modern Western industrialization—was similar to ours. As they say, the changes in these Italian cities involved "that colossal watershed in human history" in which "vast populations moved from land to factories," living standards increased dramatically, "[c]lass structures were transformed ... [c]apital stocks ... deepened ... [and e]conomic and technological capabilities multiplied."[6]

It is also important to note from the start that the study was prompted by a somewhat radical venture into political decentralization promoted by the central government in Rome which had, over a period of seven or eight years, given substantial new powers to local regional governments. In the summer of 1977, for example, "agreement was reached on a packet of regulations that dismantled and transferred to the regions 20,000 offices from the national bureaucracy, including substantial portions of several ministries, such as the Ministry of Agriculture, as well as hundreds of semipublic social agencies" (22).

Perhaps the most interesting finding of the study was that after decentralization the relationship between economic growth and the performance of public institutions came to be associated with what the study calls "civic engagement." This broader construct of "civic engagement" included the presence of egalitarian civic leadership, expression of and tolerance for strong views in politics and economics, and the presence of complex social networks of voluntary association, such as choral groups, which were often unrelated to economics or politics. These various civic cultural patterns in the North seemed to encourage mutual trust rather than individualistic opportunism. On this latter point the authors found that "[p]articipation in civic organizations inculcates skills in cooperation as well as a sense of shared responsibility for collective endeavors. Moreover, when individuals belong to 'cross-cutting' groups or local associations with diverse goals and members, their attitudes will tend to moderate as a result of group interaction and cross pressures" (90). Among these local associations they list sports clubs, cultural and scientific activities, music and theater, technical and economic activities, and health and social services.

Putnam and his associates were able to document dramatic differences in the "most civic" versus "least civic" communities studied:

> In the most civic regions ... citizens are actively involved in all sorts of local associations—literary guilds, local bands, hunting clubs, cooperatives, and so on. They follow civic affairs avidly in the local press, and they engage in politics out of programmatic conviction. By contrast, in the least civic regions ... voters are brought to the polls not on issues, but by hierarchical patron-client networks. An absence of civic associations and a paucity of local media in these latter regions mean that citizens there are rarely drawn into community affairs. Public life is very different in these two sorts of communities. When two citizens meet on the street in a civic region, *both* of them are likely to have seen a newspaper at home that day; when two people in a less civic region meet, probably *neither* of them has. More than half of the citizens in the civic regions have *never* cast a preference ballot in their lives; more than half of the voters in the less civic regions say they *always* have. Membership in sports clubs, cultural and recreational groups, community and social action organizations, educational and youth groups, and so on

is roughly twice as common in most civic regions as in the least civic regions.

So strong is the relationship [between civic engagement and institutional performance] that when we take the "civic-ness" of a region into account, the relationship we previously observed between economic development and institutional performance entirely vanishes. In other words, economically advanced regions appear to have more successful regional governments merely because they happen to be more civic. (98-99)

Putnam's findings qualify earlier theoretical assumptions borrowed from the nineteenth century German sociologist Tonnies, who claimed that traditional, small face-to-face communities are most likely to yield life satisfaction as opposed to modern, rationalistic, impersonal societies based on contract and self-interest. As Putnam says, "[t]his [earier] perspective leads readily to the view that the civic community is an atavism destined to disappear. In its place arise large, modern agglomerations, technologically advanced, but dehumanizing, which induce civic passivity and self-seeking individualism. [From this point of view] Modernity is the enemy of civility" (114).

Putnam's study comes to a somewhat different conclusion—that some forms of modernization "need not signal the demise of civic community" or what we would call the demise of a multi-level living place. In summary he states that:

Some regions of Italy have many choral societies and soccer teams and bird-watching clubs and Rotary clubs. Most citizens in those regions read eagerly about community affairs in the daily press. They are engaged by public issues, but not by personalistic or patron-client politics. Inhabitants trust one another to act fairly and to obey the law. Leaders in these regions are relatively honest. They believe in popular government, and they are predisposed to compromise with their political adversaries. Both citizens and leaders here find equality congenial. Social and political networks are organized horizontally, not hierarchically. The community values solidarity, civic engagement, cooperation, and honesty. (115)

According to Putnam, however, public life is quite different in the South:

Public life in these regions is organized hierarchically, rather than horizontally. The very concept of "citizen" here is stunted. From the point of view of the individual inhabitant, public affairs is the business of somebody else—*i notabili*, "the bosses," "the politicians"—but not for me.... Engagement in social and cultural associations is meager. Private piety stands in for public purpose. Corruption is widely regarded as the norm.... Laws (almost everyone agrees) are made to be broken, but fearing others' lawlessness, people demand sterner discipline. Trapped in these interlocking vicious circles, nearly everyone feels powerless, exploited, and unhappy. (115)

Putnam's findings concerning the quality of civic culture in limited geographic areas in the North and South of Italy provoke the reader to explore why such differences occur within a single country; why such a rich array of voluntary communal associations in the North which have either survived the past or sprouted anew and a paucity of such institutions in the South, when both were governed under a similar national policy of decentralization. In their search for the source of what we would call the "vital center," Putnam and his associates search in particular through the historical records of these two areas of Italy which leads them "to suspect that sociocultural factors are an important part of the explanation." As they say, "Civic traditions help explain why the North has been able to respond to the challenges and opportunities of the nineteenth and twentieth centuries so much more effectively than the South" (159).

Putnam and associates conclude their historical aspect of their findings with a striking observation regarding the importance of tradition and culture as sources of continued communal engagement:

Despite the whirl of change ... the regions characterized by civic involvement in the late twentieth century are almost precisely the same regions where cooperatives and cultural associations and mutual aid societies were most abundant in the nineteenth century, and where neighborhood associations and religious confraternities and guilds had contributed to the flourishing communal republics of the twelfth century. And although those civic regions were not especially advanced economically a century ago, they have steadily outpaced the less civic regions both in economic performance and ... in quality of government. The astonishing tensile strength of civic traditions testifies to the power of the past. (162)

As we reflect back on Mumford's description of the chartered city of the late middle ages and Putnam's description of civic communities in Northern Italy, we find important evidence for the importance of tradition, history, and cultural continuity in the midst of rapid change. When we recall Pullman's experiment in "community making" outside of Chicago in 1893 and the absence of any significant encultured tradition leading to the creation of Pullman's novel city, the possible viability of such a community seems almost absurd. At the end of the nineteenth century, American cities were caught in the storm of rapid industrialization and immigration. There are no roots of a long established civic tradition for the simple reason that these burgeoning industrial centers sprang into being often within less than a generation. Rather we find a culture of aggressive entrepreneurship and individualism on the part of corporate industry, a culture of weak government run by opportunistic, bought politicians, and often a culture of confusion and desperation on the part of immigrant workers and agencies concerned with their interests. American history tends to be marked by negotiations between profit-product-centered corporate power, governmental interests supporting moneyed interests, and workers' unions and citizens in local places who could muster very limited power. Ethnic/religious neighborhoods tended to become rather isolated refuges rather than engines of social reform. While Putnam makes the case that the beginning of the twentieth century in America marked a remarkable upturn in the creation of voluntary civic associations, it is difficult to find instances in which they significantly altered the momentum of corporate expansion and domination.

One thinks, for example, of the great Homestead Strike of 1892 in which the unionized steel workers, mostly of immigrant stock, sought some long term security and affiliation with the great Homestead mill into which they had poured so much of their lives. Here was an historical watershed in American history, a moment in which the powerful industrialists, Carnegie and Frick, had an opportunity to begin a new set of cultural relationships between workers and entrepreneur-owners. Yet despite Carnegie's earlier expressions of sympathy and support toward workers and unions, there was no historical record or tradition to carry these new relationships forward. In the Homestead confrontation, a critical opportunity was thus missed resulting in an armed battle and finally the total destruction of the great Homestead mill. While Carnegie (and

U.S. Steel) became the world's leading producer of steel over the next century, one wonders what damage was done to any hope of creating a cooperative tradition of relationships in America among local citizens and officials, workers, managers, entrepreneurs, and owners.

The lessons from Putnam's study of Italian urban civic life are profound and, we would argue, support two of our central conclusions. First, culture and tradition can lay the groundwork for new possibilities while at the same time perpetuating either positive aspects of the past or deep historical "errors." In the case of Northern Italy, the historical traditions helped sustain civic traditions in the midst of rapid industrialization and centralization, while in the South the errors of the past continued. And second, middle level economic, socio-political, and meaning-making institutions are critical for sustaining a strong civic culture. These include, for example: a) middle level aspects of economics in the form of decentralization, human scale, and the continued necessity of meaningful artisan type work; b) middle level aspects of human association which include both horizontal bases for power and varied economic, religious, recreational, and familial forms of association which are required to forge a link between volatile inward looking familistic social forms and larger, less personal governmental and corporate contractual forms of association; and c) middle level aspects of meaning which provide a mythic cultural story of place which transcends the limitations of instrumental pragmatic economic problem solving. The religious and artistic components were expressed in Northern Italy in the countless forms of association that allowed communities to thrive in ways beyond the utilitarian activities of productive work and product-centered selling and consuming.

HILLERY'S "VILL" OR NATIVE CITY: COMMUNITY AS A "PURPOSELESS" FORM OF HUMAN ORGANIZATION WHICH SUSTAINS BOTH FOLK AND COSMOPOLITAN CULTURE

In a comparative study of what he calls "communal organizations" George Hillery implicitly considers the question of the compatibility between the multi-level native city and conglomerate urban places. His work is closely related to Redfield's theory which proposes that the folk village and the orthogenetic or native city can be placed on a single continuum from folk culture to an urban cosmopolitan culture. Hillery studied nine "folk villages" and five "cities" in order to identify and compare similarities and differences between the village and city as generic social forms. He concluded that they can. In fact, they can be seen as a common socio-cultural form, which he names the "Vill." The Vill, he says, "is a more general model which is integrated around three basic characteristics: local space, cooperation, and family."[7]

In terms of social structure, the Vill (or village-and-city) is composed of more than separate individuals, since most individuals are attached to it through family membership. While this may be the major source of bonding in the folk village, in the city, family attachments are supplemented by relations among contractually bonded corporate groups. The Vill may thus be characterized as having two major kinds of cooperation: mutual aid and contracts. Mutual aid "emphasizes relationships that are more personal and diffuse. Contracts are more impersonal and the activities related to them are more rigid."[8]

The significance of Hillery's work for us is that he identifies empirically an essential "communal" type of organization defined in terms of the village-city composite—the Vill—which suggests that middle level social forms of place are compatible with the more complex contractual forms that characterize aspects of cities. Elaborating on what he means by the communal organization (beyond the characteristics of family, locality, and cooperation), he lists three other important but less obvious characteristics.

First, communal organizations lack explicit goals or self-conscious purpose. Paradoxically, although they are often the most meaningful places in which humans live, their meaningfulness does not rest on their serving some immediate focused identifiable "purpose." As Hillery says, the Vill

> ... first refers to a system of institutions formed by people who live together. The system has no specific goal. The reasons for living together are often no more than that of being born in a locality....

> [so] ... the migrant may enter a city specifically for a job, but he also marries, plays, goes to church, etc. (186)

> ... Communal organizations ... are heavily institutionalized systems which lack goals. They are related to each other principally in ever more inclusive levels, from households to neighborhoods to Vills to regions to nations. (189)

The fact that communal organizations have no overall focused purpose but rather share a set of deeply understood implicit "purposes" differs sharply from one of the requirements of the corporate organization which lives on the need for explicit goals as a rationale for their very existence.

Second, the communal organization always includes the family within a household place as a fundamental building block. The family or household place exists as a sustained voluntary social form in which people carry out a multitude of unpaid voluntary activities based on motives or habits of simple social bonding. Again, this is profoundly different from the corporate organization in which work is not voluntary but rather rewarded with various types of remuneration, usually under some form of contractual arrangement.

Third, as Redfield notes, the folk-urban connection is seen as a continuum rather than as separate societal types or societal types in opposition. Hillery makes it clear that "one cannot simply describe the city as the opposite of the folk society," (191) for the family exists as a strong unit in both forms, but families generally function with informal cooperation instead of the more rigid, formal contractual structures present in corporations. Obviously, corporate organizations commonly do not consist of familistic units but rather of individual units. While this may seem like such a common place that it is hardly worth mentioning, it is, in fact, one's empathy with the deep feelings for family and the loyalty to one's kin that connects folk culture with a cosmopolitan culture. Common folk and the elite alike marry, bear children, celebrate their good fortune and grieve when loved ones are sick, injured, or die. It is these perennial familistic dramas that bind the high born with the low born within a single community. In the sharply segregated strata of corporate hierarchies fraught with precarious power relationships, there are often few common joys or sorrows for all to share.[9]

THE PROBLEMATIC CONTINUITY OF FOLK PLACE TO CORPORATE ASPECTS OF THE NATIVE CITY: REVISITING THE HETEROGENTIC COMMERCIAL CITY

When we compare Hillery's Vill with Redfield and Singer's orthogenetic city, or Mumford's late medieval city, or our native city, we notice an overall continuity from village-to-city or village-within-a-city leading to a single, culturally coherent, multi-layered pluralistic set of places and relationships. In this conception, there is an historical continuum running from nuclear families to extended households to folk villages to preindustrial native cities to balanced contemporary native cities and finally to a limited corporate commercial complex. But when the Vill, or any type of communal organization, is required to relate to and in some sense compete within the framework of large modern urban conglomerates, the balance tips in the direction of a very different type of place and society. When this happens, we assume there is a radical discontinuity or disruption in a more balanced way of life.

As indicated by Berger and Neuhaus in Chapter One and Pietila in Chapter Ten, the stable-extended household, the quasi-religious sodality, the neighborhood/village, and the native town or city may well not thrive unless protected from the dominant preditory forces of self-interest commonly present in both amoral familism on the primal side and the egocentric individual and commercial contract-based corporations on the modern side. In the latter case, without some kind of legal, constitutional, customary or even military protection, local places can easily be transformed into bureaucratic political units serving only to administer functions for a distant central government (e.g., collecting taxes, welfare benefits, providing utilities and services such as water, electricity, police, courts, schools) which then provides patronage for politicians who serve the moneyed interests of corporate institutions. Or they may provide various forms of popular and/or high culture entertainment and diversion (museums, pop concerts, symphony orchestras, sports teams) which keep inhabitants "informed" and entertained.

But aside from the dynamic preditory nature of the corporate form, the overall economic and political structural factors in the modern economy work against the suvival of the Vill. The extended household is too place-based and kin-based to accommodate the corporate need for a mobile, migrating labor force. With the loss of stable families there is the loss of the sustained membership in local villages and native cities. Thus local places become simply repositories of isolated and transitory nuclear families. Villages which were once central to the activities of churches, small shops, businesses, and casual street life are too parochial, contained, and separated to serve large numbers of people efficiently, and are thus transformed into office parks, stadia, shopping malls, theaters, and warehouses. And as the overarching sovereign state replaces the traditional nobility of an earlier era and becomes totally secularized, its moral and religious functions (once overseen by a quasi religious king-leader or emperor in the preindustrial city) are transformed into a legal system managed by lawyers, lobbyists and legislators, and corporate philanthropists. In short, the city becomes mainly focused on commercial corporate development, jobs for pay, the production of goods and services, and the buying and selling of these goods.[10]

The issue of compatibility is finally confronted most starkly within Hillery's study and characterization of the modern "total institution" which has evolved out of earlier industrial forms.[11] Based on his observations in two prisons, two state hospitals, and a mental clinic, we are struck by the extent to which his description of these total institutions also applies to many other corporate settings such as public schools, boarding schools, universities, factories and offices.

Given Hillery's description, one is inclined to conclude that these "total" or "near- institutions" are akin to small totalitarian societies and that modern corporate environments generally are, for many workers, quite similar to such societies in the level of control exercised over worker behavior. Obviously, the level and quality of control is different for elite cohorts on the upper end of management as opposed to those on lower rungs of the hierarchy, but the invidious effect in a culture based on coercion, power, and control casts its influence over all those who participate in the system. Upper level management spends its time developing broad policies and strategies as a basis for controlling middle level management; middle level management spends its time creating bureaucratic rules by which to organize and control the lives of lower level supervisors and foremen; and lower level foremen and supervisors spend their time carefully watching the "workers."[12]

HISTORICAL REFLECTIONS ON CORPORATE-COMMUNAL COMPATIBILITY IN AMERICA

There are a number of other voices which, over the last century, have raised passionate concerns about the compatibility of local middle level institutions with the modern dynamic corporate urban complex in American society. A study discussing this issue was published by Jean Quandt in 1970 celebrating the work of a number of distinguished American public figures. She begins her work by noting that "it is generally assumed that the American mind [compared to such noted Europeans as Fourier, Owen, Maine, Spencer, Tonnies, Durkheim] was too individualistic, too devoted to the legacy of a natural rights philosophy to produce a serious theory of community. Nevertheless, such a theory did play a part in our intellectual history."[13]

Quandt then reviews "the writings of nine intellectuals and reformers of the Progressive period who came from small town America [along with] [t]heir formulation of the problem of community in the years after 1890." These figures included William Allen White, Frederic Howe, Jane Addams, Mary Parker Follett, John Dewey, Josiah Royce, Franklin Giddings, Charles Horton Cooley, and Robert Park. Quandt summarizes what these commentators saw when they looked out at the American landscape at the turn of the century. It was:

> ... the breakdown of the small close-knit group under the impact of urbanization and industrialization. A social organization based on family, neighborhood, and small-town solidarity was being replaced by one based on the more impersonal and tenuous ties of the market place. The division of labor, together with modern methods of communication and transportation, had created a physical unit based on the interdependence of parts, but a moral unity corresponding to this economic web had not yet emerged. So far technological changes had produced what Park and Dewey, borrowing a phrase from the English writer, Graham Wallas, called the Great Society—an urban, industrial order whose size and complexity precluded a sense of belonging.[14]

She then describes what these "progressive" intellectuals saw as the daunting and critical need for "[a] greater psychic and moral integration to match the increasing physical integration of society [which] is essential to the realization of their notion of community." As they saw it, to realize the promise of this new technological age, America needed to lay "the groundwork for that interpenetration of minds, that consciousness of and identification with the whole which characterized a sense of community." And this would be brought about by "modern communications [which] could create greater mutual understanding and common purpose [and t]hus their Great Society provided the material basis for its moral equivalent, the Great Community."[15]

Needless to say, within the time since these several scholars, writers, philosophers, and social reformers conceived of the Great Community as a moral extension to balance the Great Society, nothing like that has been realized. What we have seen instead, as illustrated by Hillery's work, is the move toward a totalitarian corporate monoculture and a new global commitment to industrialize and commercialize the planet into one vast enterprise.

This somewhat grim picture of Modernity as a set of commercial corporations bordering on total institutions gives one sober pause. We assume that at some point humans will rebel and attempt to reclaim living communal places. Perhaps it will be along the lines suggested by the regions in North Italy studied by Putnam or by the Scandinavian experiments to which Pietila alluded in Chapter Nine, which might provide local or regional peoples with more economic, social, and ideological independence from commercial corporate domination.

Rebellion and independence are, in fact, the major themes in *Resettling America: Energy, Ecology, and Community*, an anthology containing numerous case studies to illustrate the radical vision of a decentralized, regionalized America along the lines discussed in Putnam's Italian study. In one essay, David Morris deals with issues of localism and decentralization which are extensions of our own thinking above.[16] Morris lays out his concept for the new modern "self-reliant" city. He imagines using both city lands and surrounding green areas for the production of food and he makes a substantial case that city dwellers from the surrounding exurbs might well be able to produce from one-sixth to over half of their food needs.

While Morris's essay suggests the feasibility of a self-reliant city switching from a state of "neediness"—begging and bribing private corporations and state and federal governments to solve their economic problems—to a more independent posture, the arguments are narrowly economic. As Mumford suggests in his study of the Medieval city, when offered compelling economic incentives—stability of place, physical security for working artisans, stability of governmental relationships with nobility and clergy, there is rapid and permanent migration from the countryside to the city. But the forms of social bonding associated with village life and deeper modalities of meaning associated with powerful religious rituals and pageantry moderated the economic interests and created an integration among all three of our basic functional requirements of human nature. In short, it took more than economic self-interest. It took primal and middle-level social-bonding institutions and primal and middle-level meaning-making practices to transform medieval villages into nascent post-medieval city-states. This was also apparently the case in the regions of North Italy studied by Putnam. Unfortunately, Morris' conception of the new modern American City-State seems to stress social engineering and neglects issues of socio-political civic engagement, bonding, and meaning-making, and especially issues related to reclaiming some sense of metaphysical and social unity in the spiritual life of the local place.

In an earlier work on community in America, Thomas Bender proposes the thesis that local community and society can and do coexist throughout American history. The modern situation is somewhat different, he suggests, from the preindustrial period in that Americans no longer think of what we have been calling primary or middle level relationships as happening in any sustained physical place. Lasch summarizes Bender's argument and comments somewhat acidly on this optimistic vision of a continually transformed but presumably sustained presence of local communal relationships in America:

> [Bender] wants to argue that "community" and "society" can coexist and that we should think of them not as stages in an historical sequence but as contrasting "forms of interaction." Since "community" no longer has any territorial basis, however, it now has to rest on voluntary association. In the seventeenth century, "community as a place and community as an experience were one." In the nineteenth century, this linkage has shattered. Today the "experience" of community has to be found in the company of "family and friends," which satisfies the need for intimacy in a world governed by the impersonal dynamics of the market. The "coexistence of communal and non-communal ways" requires "multiple loyalties;" people have to "learn to live in two distinct worlds, each with its own rules and expectations."

The "coexistence" thesis is not new; in one form or another, it has figured in discussions of community from the beginning. It was the hope of sealing off private life as a protected sanctuary from the market that led nineteenth-century moralists to sentimentalize the domestic circle. The same desire to prevent the market from contaminating the "culture of the feelings," as John Stuart Mill called it, underlay the modern cult of art and artistic freedom. But the doctrine of segmented "spheres," whether it is conceived as a program of social reform or simply as a description of modern society, has always been open to insurmountable objections. The principle of "contract" has a tendency to invade the sphere of private life and to corrupt relationships based on "status."[17]

However one chooses to interpret Lasch's assessment of the future of local forms of communal organization and the possibility of a more balanced primal-to-modern culture, we have no doubt that we and Putnam and Quandt (along with her nine commentators almost a century ago) are asking the right question: Can local, face-to-face, middle level institutions persist and thrive in a modern corporate world, or will our lives be mainly "corporatized"—many in total or quasi-total institutions—such that what remains of local communal association happens on the run during an hour in the park with one's children or between a meal in a fast food restaurant, and shopping for football or soccer shoes?

Despite Putnam's hopeful findings in Italy, the rather sobering question we now face is the possibility that the cultural logic of these two social forms—pluralistic, multi-level, living places and contract-based corporate plases—may not be compatible, and the continued, unmodified or unbalanced form of the latter may well become increasingly dominant, destructive, and exploitative. As indicated earlier, the extreme example of exploitation is slavery. Less extreme examples echo from the past and persist, e.g., feudal domination of local villagers by a privileged nobility backed by military coercion; European domination of native peoples in once colonized countries all over the planet, which persists into the present; and the brutal treatment of formerly colonized native peoples by their own indigenous leaders following the example of their earlier Euro-American masters. However one sees the human capacity for self-interested exploitation of others, the condition is so common that it must be confronted in some theoretically plausible and practical way.

From our point of view, there are two overall visions for dealing with the current level of self-interested individualism and corporate greed. The first vision is stated in various ways within this work, but was articulated some one hundred years ago by Josiah Royce:

I should say today that our national [and now global] unities have grown so vast, our forces of consolidation have become so paramount that we, too, must flee in the pursuit of the ideal to a new realm. Freedom, I should say, dwells now in the small social group, and has its securest home in the provincial life. The province must save the individual.[18]

Quandt then adds:

> Royce was defending more than regionalism; he was, in fact, im-
> plicitly defending the small community. Although he put no upper
> limit on the size of a province—it could be a city, a county, or a re-
> gion so long as it was conscious of its unity. (156)

> ... The province, in Royce's view, was "the best mediator between
> the narrower interests of the individual" and the larger interests of
> the nation [and the planet]. It was the way to overcome the "*self-es-
> tranged spirit*," of the larger society. (156-157)

While sympathetic with Royce's local communitarian "provincial"
declaration, Quandt concludes her study with a radical shift in tone. She
argues that while it may be all well and good to begin one's transformation of Modernity to a more just and humane society in local places, "unless there is a fundamental change of priorities in the society as a whole,
decentralization will tend to perpetuate the conflicts and inequalities
which already exist." In short, shifting one's living and working environment from hierarchical, regimented corporate places to more informal middle level places will simply shift the locations in which the
fundamental problems of Modernity happen—problems of "poverty,
racism, and an environment which everywhere undercuts the physical
basis of community" (159).

Quandt's study and its approach to basic reconsiderations in how we
might understand transforming modern society is tremendously significant for us, since it frames in the clearest way the distinction between organic change and corporate change. As we argued in Chapter One,
simply stating issues in such fragmentary terms as poverty, racism, inadequate housing, personal and institutional violence, and economic exploitation and injustice suggests that we mobilize existing organizations
and/or create corporate movements to deal with such issues. And so, we
then generate the list of such movements, organizations, and political
parties (or parts of parties) and ameliorate the various pathologies of the
modern system within the same elite and hierarchical social structures
that caused the problems in the first place.

And so, we would first ask, how are these political parties and movements organized and what is their philosophical and cultural grounding? Are they not grounded in the same old cosmology that we have just
critiqued? They begin with "missions" and mechanistic corporate pur-

poses and objectives. They have hierarchical organizations with boards of directors on the top, professionals in the middle, and workers on the bottom. They communicate largely in scheduled meetings in corporate places in the meaning-making realm of rational interpretation and rhetorical persuasion. They are funded by governmental organizations, philanthropic organizations which skim money from parent profit-making companies, or by wealthy people who have very likely inherited their wealth from the same profit-making corporations a generation or two before.

To take one example of a reform-centered institution, the university, with which we are most familiar, the above scenario applies with few exceptions. As far as our experience goes, there are few examples of what we have called middle level places in the university except among stress-ridden students or junior faculty who come together in various ways for support groups or lunch to survive for the short time in their lives they are there. But, inevitably, it is these more informal places which are most profoundly remembered, not only for their social and cultural riches, but for enlightened moments of inspiration and real education.

Harking back to a variation of Marshall McLuhan's slogan, the medium may not be the whole message, but it is a significant part of it. The modern economic/environmental patterns of exploitation and contractual human bonding patterns condition how one thinks about creating new meanings for a more humane life for all, and these new meanings do not include rethinking the cultural logic of the corporate modus operandi. Basic change is too much for even the most idealistic enlightened liberal to stomach.

NOTES

1. See the work of Robert D. Putnam below on the sustainability of "civil places." For example,Robert D. Putnam, *Bowling Alone: The Collapse and Revival of American Community*, (New York: Simon and Schuster, 2000).

2. James Gilbert, *Perfect Cities: Chicago's Utopias of 1893* (Chicago: University of Chicago Press, 1991).

3. Ibid., p. 148.

4. See Rosabeth Kanter, *Commitment and Community: Communes and Utopias in Sociological Perspective* (Cambridge: Harvard University Press, 1972) on the longevity of such experiments and possible reasons for their failure.

5. Robert D. Putnam, Robert Leonardi, Rafaella Y, Nanetti, *Making Democracy Work: Civic Traditions in Modern Italy* (Princeton: Princeton University Press, 1993).

6. Ibid. p. 81.

7. George A. Hillery, Jr., *Communal Organizations* (Chicago: University of Chicago Press, 1968).

8. Ibid., p. 66.

9. A major contribution of Hillery's ambitious study is its clear empirical distinction between characteristics of the local Vill (the village-city continuum)and other modern institutions—the corporation, the "total institution," and the state, which are so different from it. The commercial industrial corporation and state have now come to dominate contemporary life to the point where "non-productive" institutions based on voluntary unpaid work and membership are increasingly marginalized. (Recall Pietila's findings on unpaid work in Chapter Eleven.) Based on the recent work of Korten below we briefly summarize and comment on the history and nature of the modern corporation and its relationship to the state, assuming that we all live and work in its midst and understand in some degree its presence from direct experience.

10. The corporate form of social organization flowered under the rule of British kings, who used it to explore new colonies and maintain control over them, often in distant places inhabited by non-European races and cultures. Such corporations were chartered by the crown and "granted monopoly powers over territories and industries that were considered critical to the English state" (55). From the beginning, this new form of social organization involved a contract between private entrepreneurial economic groups and the state, designed to exploit local peoples in distant places in the interests of the central government and wealthy people in the home land. In Korten's words: "The English Parliament, which during the seventeenth and eighteenth centuries was made up of wealthy landowners, merchants, and manufacturers, passed many laws intended to protect and extend these monopoly interests"(55). A central policy of the moneyed interests, which has persisted into the present day, was to control the administration of the corporation while exploiting, as much as possible, local natural resources, labor, and markets in the interest of maximizing profits for the owners at home.

The history of corporations in the United States followed substantially the pattern initiated in Britain. Throughout much of the 19th and early 20th centuries the American legal-governmental system developed constitutional privileges for corporations which finally granted them virtually the same rights as individual citizens. The consequences of this policy were dramatic. In the words of Korten: "The subsequent claim by corporations that they have the same right as any individual [including the right of free speech] to influence government in their own interest pits the individual citizen against the vast financial and communications resources of the corporation ..." (59). The free speech rights also gave corporations substantial control of media and its use for virtually unlimited merchandising of their products. Currently, for example, the internet medium allows commercial corporations to identify and target potential customers and buy and sell this information without the knowledge of the customer. A major purpose of free speech was thus transformed from a gift to citizens to discuss, negotiate, dispute, and construct purposes, activities, and cultural patterns for a shared civic life to a powerful elite force for promoting narrow instrumental corporate production and merchandising as the central purpose of modern culture and society. Thus newspapers and magazines, the telegraph, then radio and television and finally the internet have come to be used mainly as marketing instruments. David C. Korten, 1995, *When Corporations Rule the World*, (West Hartford, CT: Kumarian Press, 1995).

11. Note Erving Goffman's work on the "total institution," *Asylums*, (New York: Anchor Books, 1961).

12. For a discussion of the conditions prevailing in total institutions and compare them with what one might consider as normal or non-total corporate life, see below.

> *Comparing the Qualities of Activity in Total Institutions with Mainstream Industrial-Commercial Corporate Organizations*
>
> 1) Boundaries: The boundaries of total institutions are "pathologically sharp," which differ radically from the "vague" boundaries of folk villages and cities. (p.318) We would note that most corporate work places have similar sharp boundaries which often require workers to wear identification badges and report to and leave the property through designated gates at precise times, and punch time clocks.
>
> 2) Control of space and personal association: A sharp distinction is made between inmates or patients and staff or professional workers. The former are carefully monitored to control the spaces they occupy. This is also true of many corporate places. A sharp distinction is commonly made between students and staff as opposed to faculty and administration in schools and universities. Likewise a sharp distinction is made between "executives," "middle management," and "workers" in commercial or industrial settings.
>
> 3) Control of activities: Inmates and patients are carefully supervised. There is normally a hierarchy of staff. Mainstream corporate activities generally are supervised and controlled by those higher on a status hierarchy. In folk villages and cities, those who are not in corporate institutions are normally free to control what they are doing within the framework of communal norms. A common metaphor for "free time" within modernity is only when one is "on the street." Prisoners, for example, go "back on the street" after incarceration.
>
> 4) Recruitment, entrance, and discharge: There are sharp rituals providing for the conditions of entrance and exit. The admissions process

in prisons and hospitals is highly organized, bureaucratic, and carefully supervised. There must be appropriate space "available." This is also true of corporate institutions. One must be formally "hired" and "discharged." There must be "jobs" available. People do not wander casually within corporate space without official sanction.

5) Historical continuity: Today's corporate institutions in the form of large factories, offices, schools, warehouses, and large businesses are thus only about 300 years old within the modern era. At an earlier time, large sailing vessels were probably one of the first factory-warehouse corporate institutions.

6) Loyalty and hostility toward various segments of the system: A major problem of the total institution, e.g., the prison, is the necessity of monitoring the feelings of people on the lower end of the institution to assure that problems of disloyalty or hostility do not get out of hand. This is also an issue in corporate places: how to keep the workers happy and productive. Labor unions and "personnel" officers are institutional responses by both managers and workers to control problems of disloyalty. Commonly those who show overt dissatisfaction with the corporation are considered "trouble makers" and metaphorically "fired" (discharged) or disciplined.

7) Homogeneity and heterogeneity of roles: There is a basic distinction between inmates and patients (those on the bottom of a pyramid subject to custodial power), and a complex hierarchy of staff and professionals who are empowered to manage those on the bottom as well as each other and to make sure that all are kept under control. This is similar to large corporations generally, which have a complex hierarchy of roles with different privileges, powers, and responsibilities controlled from the top down. The result of this hierarchy is the distancing of people on the upper end from people at the lower end. This distancing then leads to a quality of "impersonality" which dampens the natural human empathy commonly seen in more primal face-to-face relationships. When people meet outside of these corporate relationships in the village or the city, the informal relationships may be difficult to reclaim.

8) The absence of family and explicit friendships: Both total institutions and corporate institutions are based on the judgment and support of actions of work-oriented separate individuals. Support or influence by family or friends may be seen as "biased" interference from partisans. Note, for example, the suspicion in schools that parents might exercise too much control if allowed open access to the school building.

9) Value of people and material things is generally based on the extent to which they contribute to economic profitability: The value of an individual within a total institution is based on his/her contribution to the maintenance of the institution. The employment of prison guards and

professional staff is predicated on having inmates. Patients in hospitals are needed for similar reasons. In corporate institutions the workers at all levels have to demonstrate their value to the maintenance and/or profitability of the institution. A major source of stress is the fact that one's value may rise or fall independent of anything that one does. One can be an excellent nurse, but if the number of patients declines, one's participation in the organization may be "terminated"—one is no longer needed. One may be an excellent machine tool worker, but if technology or customer tastes change, one's skills may no longer be needed. By way of example, one has only to think of the contemporary effort to transform schools, once conceived as humane personal extensions of family life, into efficient corporate training places characterized by "objective" supervision for "accountability" and credential-based testing procedures. Rather than being the center of local cultural, family life, and community activity, schools are becoming high stress training grounds to keep corporate and local economies "competitive." There is the "essential school" movement which limits schooling to training for narrow, academic competence. There is increasing interest in "full service schools" patterned after the total institution. Such full service schools will thus employ a comprehensive complement of human service professionals from ordinary teachers to social workers to medical personnel to truant officers and police and will presumably be in a position to remedy every possible deficiency that might prevent students from performing adequately in school, and, more importantly, in the work place later in life. Parents are invited in as clients or guests; not as full members of such schools.

13. Jean B. Quandt, *From Small Town to the Great Community: The Social Thought of Progressive Intellectuals*, (New Brunswick, NJ: Rutgers University Press, 1970), p. 3.

14. Ibid., p. 17.

15. Ibid., p. 20.

16. David Morris, "Self-Reliant Cities: The Rise of the New City States" in *Resettling America*, Gary J. Coates, ed. (Andover, MA: Brick House Publishing Co., 1981).

17. Christopher Lasch, *The True and Only Heaven*, p. 165. Reference to Bender's book: Thomas Bender, *Community and Social Change* (Baltimore: Johns Hopkins Press, 1978).

18. Quandt, *From Small Town to the Great Community*, p. 156.

CHAPTER FOURTEEN

Letting Go

THE TITANIC

As a way of summing up this work, we ask the reader to think of the Titanic as a metaphor for Modernity. Imagine that such a ship has been constructed and is the most luxurious and modern vessel ever built. It is the incarnation of the Celestial City. It is fast, unsinkable, indestructible and undergoing constant technical improvements. There is a long waiting list of passengers from all over the world who want to experience "sailing on the Titanic." This mighty vessel is a microcosm of the affluent society in which it was built. It is a gigantic masterpiece of modern technology. It carries all the necessities of life as well as the luxuries of a modern civilization. It also carries the diverse representatives of the human family that helped build it—men, women, the poor and rich, the servants and the masters, professionals and entertainers, celebrities and common people. Of course, the passengers are segregated in different quarters and treated with different degrees of civility, respect, and material support. The ship requires extraordinary resources to run. But it would appear to be a monument to modern technology and provide a glimpse of the ultimate in the good life.

At some point, however, there are hints that the ship has serious problems. A complete computer analysis is run and the findings are disconcerting. Apparently under shifting seismic conditions a tidal wave may burst forth causing the ship to founder and even sink. It is also difficult to provide security against acts of terrorism by radical groups who see it as a symbol of over consumption and environmental waste. Occasional threats have already been received. As security analysts have commented, "Remember Lockerbie!"

This book might be considered a rather long and complicated critique of the "Titanic Problem." In our analysis, some have begun to find errors in the construction of this marvelous vessel we call Modernity and suspect that it may need radical repair, reconstruction, or even be discontinued altogether. How would people so devoted to the technology, genius, and achievement of this great vessel respond to such a conclusion?

Some might simply say that the Titanic cannot possibly be defective in any real fundamental way. A few technical failures or close calls or security problems are not grounds for rethinking or redoing the whole ship. People with such a turn of mind might well say "find the problems and fix them." Enlightened engineering can solve any of these problems. Don't scrap it; simply make it more modern. Get better radar, more life jackets and life boats, more air tight compartments above the water line, better trained personnel to run it. Give the third class passengers better quarters, or perhaps switch away from ocean liners and build more progressive ships, like hydroplanes. But there is the disquieting thought that haunts the engineers and the owners: What if at some point the ship were at sea far from any port and a disaster struck—an outbreak of some uncontrollable virus or bacteria, the threat of a terrorist bomb, or the eruption of an underground volcano triggering a tsunami?

Then there are those more circumspect policy analysts who would look at the larger picture and argue that the Titanic is only one rather superficial product of a technological age and as such has little to do with addressing the "real" problems of the modern condition. According to this argument, what is most needed is a change in our priorities and, as Quandt suggests above, work on issues less related to the efficiency, speed, and luxury of our way of life and worry more about improving the basic living conditions of humanity around the world, e.g., conditions of poverty, racism, medical care, and education. Worry less about the viability of luxury liners, supersonic airplanes, and resort hotels and more about improving our ability to trust each other, participate and work together, and actively engage in solving our chronic economic and social problems. When this happens we won't be distracted and obsessed with "fixing the Titanic" but rather with fixing our society.

With this point of view in mind we return to Putnam's work and the concept of civic engagement or "social capital," discussed in Chapter Thirteen.[1] In his analysis Putnam reviews American civic and communitarian institutions created at the beginning of the twentieth century when, he argues, an enormous amount of creative "social capital" was created to deal with the serious problems of inequality, poverty, economic dislocations and stresses related to the vast migrations of people around the globe, as well as the violence from labor discontent, fear of revolutionary movements, and even war. As he says,

> Institutions of civil society formed between roughly 1880 and 1910 have lasted for nearly a century [and i]n those few decades the voluntary structures of American society assumed modern form. Essentially, the trends toward civic disengagement reviewed in ... this book register the decay of that structure over the last third of the twentieth century.

> For all the difficulties, errors, and misdeeds of the Progressive Era its leaders and their immediate forebears in the late nineteenth century correctly diagnosed the problem of a social capital or civic engagement deficit.

> ... My message [here] is that we desperately need an era of civic inventiveness to create a renewed set of institutions and channels for a reinvigorated civic life that will fit the way we have come to live. Our challenge now is to reinvent the twenty-first century equivalent of the Boy Scouts or the settlement house or the playground or Hadassah or the United Mine Workers or the NAACP.[2]

Aside from some rather general encouragement to make "America's workplace ... more family-friendly and community congenial," "to spend less leisure time sitting in front of glowing screens and more time in active connection with our fellow citizens," and "ensure that ... significantly more Americans will participate in (not merely consume or appreciate) cultural activities from group dancing to songfests to community theater to rap festivals,"[3] Putnam talks little about what it would take to move a modern society toward the profound reenculturation required to effect such a change. One wonders how he might persuade his fellow policy specialists to reconsider saving (or scuttling) the Titanic and turn their attention to reconstructing more community-based down to earth social capital.[4]

From our point of view, this pragmatic policy-oriented response to the Titanic problem, i.e. efforts to replenish "social capital" and "make progress" in resolving basic social problems through increased social and political engagement, looks mainly at the *symptoms* of the illness. The focus is on educating, persuading, and enlightening people to a heightened level of awareness so that they might be moved to act in the immediate present rather than living through the long process of reenculturation required to undo the destructive habits that caused the problems in the first place. From this policy point of view, as rational people we carefully define objectives and mount the relevant personnel and resources to achieve them. We then assume that changing older encultured patterns of thought and action is really no different from constructing such complex pieces of technology as sky scrapers, space stations, or missile defenses. We fix social problems like we fix machines—with technological skills and corporate management.

We see this choice of a technically based problems approach over an organic culture-based approach as having had limited success. We would emphasize, however, that achieving even short term humanitarian goals in such fields as health care, education, and adequate housing, for example, is well worth the effort when it alleviates the pain of those most affected by the deficiencies in the current system. Unfortunately, we think it unlikely that these reforms will yield long term gains in dealing with the chronic destructive cultural patterns we first presented in Chapter One.

THE INTERRELATED PATTERNS OF HUMAN CULTURE AND THE DIFFICULTY OF CHANGE

Here we restate three aspects of culture and then discuss how they relate to the inherent difficulties of social change. First, as humans we live in places in which we construct a variety of relatively stable cultural patterns to provide us with some degree of order and predictability for our comfort and survival. Second, these patterns may be seen as layers of encultured human potential which interrelate and connect with one another and add up to something like an integrated unitary system we call "culture." (The layers or overall patterns we have discussed in this work relate mainly to: a) the physical and technological creation of skills and vocations and the construction of tools, artifacts, and machines to modify the environment within which we live; b) the patterned ways humans engage with and relate to one another in groups; and c) the construction of meaning and modes of communication.) If applied to individuals, we might say that a culture, like a person, has a certain integrated "personality."

The issue we have confronted arises when a "personality" or "type" of culture (as a whole) becomes dysfunctional and we seek to change it. As with individual personalities, it is extremely difficult to change cultures for at least two reasons. First, layers of culture are in considerable degree integrated; like those of an individual personality, i.e., they fit together and reinforce one another. It is difficult to change any single significant pattern without affecting all patterns. And second, like psychotherapy, the deeper "memories" of culture are not accessible to more superficial techniques of conscious learning. In Chapter Six, Masters, for example, sees important aspects of our conscious behavior as based on unconscious perceptions mediated and organized by prestructured neurological processes. Likewise, the current understanding of enculturation presented by Schweder and Shorr suggests that the learning of deep cultural patterns has neurological concomitants which are difficult to reverse or change. These insights lead us to question again the extent to which our modern optimistic sense of human freedom, choice, rationality, and self-control is really justified.

CULTURAL CHANGE AND RECLAIMING THE FULLNESS OF EXPERIENCE

Given the difficulties faced by the engineering of planned programs for cultural change, we suggest turning our attention toward reclaiming or getting in touch with earlier primal forms of consciousness. That is, instead of beginning by identifying social problems or cultural errors as they manifest themselves in the stress of everyday life (as we did in Chapter One), why not reexamine, at least theoretically, the "embryological" unconscious beginnings of our distorted and unbalanced dualistic culture? Why not probe the nature and source of these dualisms? For example, instead of seeing ourselves as living in the duality of a human world vs. natural world, or in a dualistic world of self vs. others, or in the duality of rational pragmatic meaning vs. metaphorical aesthetic meaning, why not search for a way of apprehending a "oneness" or a mediating center between such dualities? Unless we can reclaim this sense of unity or a middle ground to connect these dualities, we will continue to express but a small measure of our larger human potentiality by focusing on and emphasizing, as we do now, only the modern end of our contemporary culture.

Our assumption is that these unbalanced, one-sided cultural patterns distort the content of our unconscious psyche and we lose our capacity for actually perceiving or discriminating what it means to function in a balanced living place. We lose our capacity for humane conscious judgment because we actually can no longer "hear" or "see" the destructive elements that surround us. For example, we become deaf to the roar of the twelve lane superhighway and blind to the black tarmac that invades so much of our physical reality. How to regain our ability to see and hear and touch and feel the dominant presence of the living world around us rather than the machines?

Below we present some theoretical speculations about how we might think about regaining the gift of primal perception and in so doing lay the groundwork for our own thinking about deep cultural change.

OWEN BARFIELD'S THEORY OF INITIAL PERCEPTION OR "ORIGINAL PARTICIPATION"

The critical juncture in how we understand the beginning of primal experience is when "inner/outer" reality come together—between the inner reality of the living organism (in this case a human being) and the reality outside of our skin. In the simplest terms, we might speculate that the inner reality of mind/brain/sense organs acts as a kind of elaborate movie camera by which it can record what is happening on the "outside." This model is quickly dashed when we recall that what is "outside," if we are to believe the theory of modern physics, is, in fact, nothing more than waves and particles that carry information between "nature" and the human organs of sensation and mind/brain. Most of what we perceive as "outside" is constructed within our own bodies.

We would here note our earlier distinction between our notion of "nature-in-an-open-universe" or NOUS and "nature" used in the more common sensical way as the "natural environment" or the natural world "out there." In this latter sense, each being or organism is responsive to a range of aspects of the "natural world" which constitutes its "environment." Each organism has what von Uexkull calls an "Umwelt" or a range of possible perceivable sensibilities.[5]

Owen Barfield uses the rainbow as his most telling example to point out that organisms construct a particular world from a repertory of particles and waves provided by the "outside" of nature interacting with the "inside" of the organism. Without the perceiving human organism, for example, there would be no rainbow—only light waves or particles. Barfield calls this particle world the "unrepresented." What is "represented" to our human sensibilities are the particles plus the response of the human senses/body/mind. And that which humans commonly take to be the actual world are the cultural representations that groups or societies agree upon, which Barfield calls "collective representations." From this point of view, it is important to realize two things about perception: 1) We must not confuse the perceptions with their cause. As he says, "We do not hear undulating molecules of air. We hear sound." And 2) we do not perceive anything with our sense organs alone but with a great part of the whole human being—including our mental habits, memory, imagination, feeling, will.[6]

Barfield is suggesting that before we actually identify things or figures or sounds in the world around us, there is an interactive synthetic process in which particles of some sort trigger and provide the information for what later becomes the intelligible world. This momentary interactive synaptic occasion Barfield names "original participation." To "participate" the rainbow would be to actually perceive (consciously or unconsciously) the magical micro second when the photons of light from the outside interact with the neurons within us to create the rainbow within. It is this initial perceptual participation from which the organism will later construct figures or objects in the "outer world." As stated above, much of the information that it is participating in this construction is provided by the organism.

Barfield then asks the question: Although modern people are generally unaware of this unperceived interactive synaptic moment in which the inner-outer world connects before we actually "glimpse reality" as an "objective" world of figures "out there," was this always the case? That is, was there a time earlier in history when people could consciously feel or experience the synaptic moment of primary perception? He then begins a set of speculations in which he argues that some contemporary "primitive societies" as well as societies living in earlier periods of history have actually been able to apprehend this preverbal preconceptual interactive process and engage in "original participation."

He suggests, for example, that the capacity of "primitive people" to apprehend spirits, ghosts, and see animals as totems or living spirits connected to the lineage of their clans may be understood, not as superstitious inventions or imaginative stories, but rather as real collective socially shared representations. Supporting this claim, he quotes commentaries by the anthropologist Levy-Bruhl and the sociologist Durkheim as well as presenting etymological evidence from the earlier writings of archaic societies in Greece, Rome, and Medieval Europe.[7]

In summary, Barfield's speculations regarding the primal emergence of human experience are essentially three. First, he reminds us that our perception of the world is an interactive synaptic process between a micro-particle "natural" world of electrons/waves/photons, etc. "out there" and a micro-organic world within the perceiver.

Second, he suggests that various societies (some contemporary "primitive" peoples as well as archaic societies in the past) have, as a group, been able to apprehend and later recall this moment of original participation or "proto-awareness" when the energy and forms generated by nature were triggering potential throbs of experience within the human mind (psyche). This explains why humans in some societies experience the spirits of animals as if they were both within and outside of them during moments of ritual and high energy release.

Finally, he argues that human consciousness evolves just as the rest of the universe evolves. So the world we "perceive" today is understood by most of us as having a different quality of consciousness from the world humans perceived a thousand years ago. Consciousness has evolved within the last four or five hundred years such that modern "scientific" people have increasingly lost this capacity to apprehend the primary experience of original participation and remember it.

Below we move from Barfield's efforts to describe and support the idea that humans once experienced a vaguely conscious "proto-experience" of the inner-outer quality of reality[8] toward a related theory of direct perception suggested by an anthropologist, James Ingold, and a biologist, Timothy Gibson.

INGOLD'S AND GIBSON'S THEORY OF DIRECT PERCEPTION

In a position similar to that of Barfield, Ingold[9] and Gibson[10] also suggest that humans, as do other living organisms generally, experience direct connections to the outer world by what they call "direct perception." Like Barfield, Ingold takes us back to the instant when the living organism "senses" or perceives something in the natural world. (In our terms it would be the beginning of the "unseen world.") In the evolution of the organism its *umwelt* has developed a set of archetypal relations within the "outer" world of nature which move it to act in an automatic adaptive way. It is assumed that for most organisms few things or objects are perceived in simply a neutral way. Organisms, Ingold argues, tend to react to most "things" in the "external world" as if they already had preloaded adaptive meanings, i.e., they have an immediate positive or negative valence. He uses the stone as an example. The stone, he says, may serve as a place of concealment for the crab, as a hammer to break snail shells for the thrush, and as a weapon for a threatened human. The interaction between the data of the stone perceived by the crab and the perceptual mechanism of the crab give the stone a tropic (cathected or "loaded") quality or a particular "given" meaning. That is, the stone is "loaded" with meaning so that the crab may respond by concealing itself. Ingold also suggests that for animals the "given" includes not only the meaning (e.g., concealment) but also an action or connected reaction chain. So organisms are to some degree prewired with "Environment-Perception-Reaction" chains. The natural world presented to the *umwelt* of the organism (i.e., the potentiality of sensory-action mechanisms) provides a limited set of schema or metaphors which afford adaptive meanings or action possibilities so they can respond appropriately. So, for the crab, the stone is a metaphor for a shield or hiding place; for the thrush it is a metaphor for a hammer; for the human it is a metaphor for a weapon.

Ingold then suggests that humans, unlike many other animals, do see much of the world "as raw [or neutral] material, awaiting the imposition of form and function … [whereas for other] animals which lack the linguistically grounded, symbolic intelligence of human beings, the environment simply cannot exist" as fundamentally separated from the organism.[11] However, he qualifies this distinction between humans and animals saying that although humans have a much larger potentiality for seeing objects in the world as having a neutral "separated-from-environment" status (versus a connected and a loaded relational status for other organisms), that is, in fact, not the way things commonly appear in our everyday life. As he says, "No more than other animals can human beings live in a permanently suspended condition of contemplative detachment. If the animal is always and immediately 'one with its life activity,' so is the human for much (if not all) of the time."[12] He continues:

> life is given in engagement, not in disengagement; or as Whitehead remarked, 'from the moment of birth we are immersed in action, and can only fitfully guide it by taking thought.' Ecological anthropology, dealing as it does with human relations with the environment in the life process, must take the condition of active

engagement as its starting point. We have therefore to overturn the Cartesian prioritization of cognition over action, or thought over life. Only by so doing can the dualism of culture and nature be replaced by the synergy of person and environment.[13]

The Ingold-Gibson view of perception is a major departure from some common contemporary cognitive views of how humans make sense in the world which hark back to Locke and assume that data are sensed by the neutral receptive human, who then constructs an interpretive rational adaptive understanding of what is going on in the environment as a basis for appropriate action.

The Ingold-Gibson theory assumes rather that nature provides intelligible resources or "affordances" which connect with the unconscious needs of organisms. The living and non-living elements of nature are thus connected and related to the requirements of a living environment. They provide patterns already grounded in nature that have a tropic or "given" connection with the organism, which, in fact, control in some degree which patterns nature has made available for them to perceive. Thus perception is not a static tableau; it is a dance with many partners. Common observations of nature provide us with an infinite range of examples, e.g., the bird's direct perception of a twig which is instantly seen as useful for building a nest; the honey bee's instant connection with particular flowers as a source of food; the human's direct perception of another human as a source of sexual gratification.

DIRECT PERCEPTION AND CULTURAL CHANGE

The implications of Barfield's theory of original participation and of the Ingold-Gibson theory of direct perception along with Shweder's and Shorr's analysis of the unconscious basis of encultured patterns of action and meaning are profound. As Ingold says, "The cultural construction of the environment is not so much a prelude to practical action as an (optional) epilogue."[14] That is, culture begins with many of the substantive sources for meaning already built into our psyche. In Ingold's terms, we relate to the world directly, both to our social human world and to the "natural" physical world. This more direct relationship between environment and perceptual participation by the organism is implied by our earlier idea of "ground" presented in Chapter Five. The "ground" is the territory that mediates information coming from the void, from the "external" material world, and from the structures within the organism. It is a time/space within which meaning and "beings" are first formed. It is an occasion in which "tropic" reactions happen; where the organism and environment respond to their mutual interests.

It is after this point, as Neville suggests in Chapter Four, that the natural spontaneous preconscious or unconscious imaginative processes of the human psyche begin to spin various interpretive possibilities for what the "tropic" reaction might mean for the fullness of human life. And it is even later, after the emergent processes of perceiving and imagination have happened that experience breaks into consciousness and we are actually aware of trying to interpret or make sense out of our initial perceptions. It is in this later phase when interpretation interacts with a more conscious process of imagination that we apprehend the idea of choice among alternative modes of belief and action. As Barfield argues, the various qualities of consciousness (and unconsciousness) required for this whole complex process of "experiencing" nature or the world has evolved over thousands of years of human history. So it would be accurate to say that while the world of the twentieth century is embedded in a different reality from the world of the tenth century, humans carry within them primal capacities for perception that link them with these earlier realities. And it is when these primal capacities are "forgotten" for a time that we run the risk of losing the fullness of our humanity.

It is at this point that we return to Shweder's argument presented in Chapter Three that humans from different cultures live in different "actual" realities. That is, if reality is construed not as "the objective world out there" but rather as the nexus of the inner world of the culturally conditioned organism and the outer world of nature (which may be seen as part-realities), then humans have the capacity in some degree to create different "objective" types of "living" or "dead" places. And we can imagine that cultures which can apprehend or feel the presence of spirits of ancestors or the spirits of rivers and mountains or the spirits of the land are not simply constructing metaphorical stories but are constructing a living reality. In this sense, we would argue that basic cultural change is not invented initially by conscious pragmatic "thinking" or action of the moment, but rather by living out the potentialities of silent unconscious "participations" as they connect over long periods of time during which one hears the subtle voices of the surrounding environment. In this sense, we experience culture and cultural change before we are conscious of it or think of it. Or to repeat what Ingold says, "The cultural construction of the environment is not so much a prelude to practical action as an (optional) epilogue."[15]

THE SILENT VOICES OF THE LIVING PLACE

Perhaps one of the most problematic ideas for modern people to grasp is the possibility that important qualities of "consciousness" come at various levels—from Barfield's "original participation" and preconscious perception—to unconscious mediation of images and symbols—to the stream of consciousness that generates imaginative stories—to the self-conscious realization of a world "out there," etc. Even the categorical nature of the term consciousness (implying that we are "truly aware" of the world around us) implies that we should be suspicious of the dimly felt left-over "other" "consciousnesses." From the time of Freud, for example, the unconscious or subconscious has often been considered as having no independent "reality" of its own but is rather a backwash containing only the residue of earlier threatening repressed memories.

If we take seriously Ingold and Gibson's theory of direct perception and our understanding of the important influence of deep culture over our unconscious processes, we would conclude that what is perhaps needed to transform Modernity into a more balanced culture is to find ways of speaking to our "less than conscious" reality, ways that would allow us in some degree to "let go" of that limited view of experience in which we associate what is "really real" with only the vivid materialistic "things" that can be publicly measured, counted, and controlled. Letting go of this narrow view of reality and embracing what Northrop sees as the full aesthetic dimension of direct experience appears to be profoundly threatening. If we allow modern science fiction to create this fuller view of experience, more often than not stories, movies, and TV, filled with criminals, murder, police violence, wars, betrayal, unrestrained passion, blood and guts in hospital operating rooms, various forms of mutilation and dying, car chases, crashing airplanes, sinking ships provide our unconscious world with a source of negative fantasies designed to give us bad thoughts or bad dreams and impel us to do bad things. We are thus not inclined to think of these more primal layers of perception, imagination, and dreaming as a great aesthetic and moral gift, as a source of positive adaptation in our evolutionary trip down through the ages of our planetary survival and finally as the silent connection with living place.

If we view our ability to sense these earlier phases of unconscious experience as a gift, the question then is how to nourish or reclaim it. Our thesis here is that basic qualities of a genuine or authentic culture somehow fit together under auspicious circumstances to create a living place. Such places have many layers along the primal to modern dimension, and what is critical are the middle level connecting institutions in the vital center. It is these that are needed to generate the depth and honesty and intensity of conversation, ritual, and action among human and non-human neighbors in sacred and contemplative settings over the time required to build and sustain living places—neighborhoods in native cities—that will foster more direct forms of perceiving and imagining and relating. The various levels of place described in Chapter Nine would have to be modified to effect any significant change. It is not enough to construct "planned neighborhoods" in which friends and neighbors move in and out every two or three years. It is not enough to have clubs and singing groups and Girl Scouts if people cannot, in considerable degree, create a strong set of civic institutions which prevent these forms of "social capital" from simply being tokens of superficial corporate conviviality and small talk. And perhaps most of all, there has to be a detoxification of the oppressive distractions and noise from the ever present internal combustion engines, TV sets, airplanes, telephones, and advertising that drown out the organic texture of our natural world. For it is the less "developed" natural world which connects its affordances to our preconscious sensibilities and which signal to our unconscious and conscious ways of being that we are really human and not some kind of pseudo-machine.

We need to recall and reclaim Emerson's layers of soul quoted in Chapter Three where he talks about the range of our vocations and artisanship, the range of our social relationships, the range of our artistic expression, and in the range of our life cycle. We need unsegregated groups of the young and old to feel the affordances of the organic life cycle, the limits of our mortality , and the vision of death and perennial being. We need stillness and prayer and meditation to feel the voices of the silent source, the split-second voices of the nature-organism's "original participation" in which we "participate" in nature bringing reality into being and seeing it though its many transformations until it reaches satisfaction within us and passes on to create another being.

In summary, we need to develop a sustained set of cultural patterns which may, in some mysterious way, allow us to experience ourselves and the world around us closer to the critical moment of oneness when the outer and the inner are still in touch. We need to experience not only the voices of emerging life but to feel in our being the cycles of life, death, and regeneration, for it is impossible to imagine transforming the most serious error of Modernity—its assumption of unrelenting "immortal" sustained progress—without grasping some unconscious feeling for the inevitability of decline and death, and regeneration for all levels of being from the muon to the atom to humans, to a whole society, to the planet, and to the universe.

This latter mood of living and "letting go" is vividly illustrated by the Taoist principle of Wu Wei or "subtle action" and is appropriate and important for anyone who seeks to participate, maintain, or reclaim the vital center of genuine culture we have discussed here. As John Blofeld presents this principle:

> A dedicated Taoist is one who seeks to live as closely in accord as possible with nature. From the outset, this involves contemplation of nature's ways, recognition of fitness, and perception that all of them are 'good' in the sense of being essential to the pattern as a whole. Depart from them and chaos and destruction loom! To go along with nature effortlessly, as does a fish or a master artisan, is to swim with the current, to let one's knife slip along the grain. Wu Wei, a cardinal principle of Taoists, literally means 'no action,' but not in the sense of sitting all day like a dead tree stump or a block of stone; rather it means avoiding action that is not spontaneous, acting fully and skillfully by all means but only in accordance with present need, being lively when required but never over strenuous and certainly not strained, eschewing artfully calculated action and every activity stemming from a profit motive. A plant in need of sunlight bends towards the sun instinctively, effortlessly, its movement economically and wholly without calculation but none the less effective. So should it be with man. Free from greed, free from strain, a stranger to anxiety and care, the sage takes whatever action is needed, stopping the very moment his objective is attained, and, far from congratulating himself with success, puts it out of mind as soon as it is done.[16]

There is, of course, a vast literature on levels of consciousness and the meaning of obsessive control and letting go. Much of this comes from Eastern thought through both Western and Eastern eyes. But there are valuable works in traditional academic philosophy.[17] In summary, we are saying that one cannot alter the deeper cultural pathologies in modern places—our anxious concern over "having enough," our fear of being "insignificant," our fear of loing control, our fear of losing our grip on who we really are—simply with top down programs in policy-making, education, therapy, or with social and political movements organized and run by specialized elite professionals operating out of think tanks or universities who are paid to solve the problems of "other people" who live "somewhere else."

We are saying that we must begin by reclaiming or creating living places and renewing genuine cultures both without and within our own being and in the oneness where that being seems to belong. This effort will require many of us to quiet the noise of much of our immediate modern reality and enter continuing, sustained, and significant living places in which we can participate and negotiate and engage simply what in the moment of our history seems right and meaningful. This may be within a household, within a neighborhood, within a church, within a garden, in a back yard, with a sick friend, or simply lost in the reverie of the moment. But these various places must be connected in some degree to the sustained vital center of a living place in order to have a significant impact on our lives. These places must also provide what Ingold and Gibson refer to as the natural affordances that stimulate the unconscious structures which will move us from the drive toward unlimited progress to the subtle balance between the more primal and modern aspects of our being. One thinks back to Mumford's description of the medieval city with its "affordances" of smells and sounds and texture of the nature/human mix—the animals, the land, the bricks and buildings, the manure and hay, the work of artisans and the prayers of priests and common pious people, and perhaps most important of all—the opportunity for quiet reflection all around.

We believe that one begins to reconsider and alter the errors of our modern way when we refrain from blocking out the primal sounds of the wind and the animals and the voices of friends and let their affordances transform our unconscious cultural patterns so that they can give voice to the subtle messages of story, of art, of music, of sport and ritual. For these cultural inventions, which we perceive consciously, must come from deep inside—first in the form of vaguely apprehended feelings seeping out from one's unconscious flowing body. Only then can these feelings be transformed into artifacts and habits of genuine culture. It is when we can hear the deaf presence of these "feelings" and their connection to the blind images that are later revealed to our conscious world that we may begin to find our neighborly place and a new balance between the logic and power of the corporate machine and the deeper logic of one's own being which stretches from the outer cosmos through the vital center to ones own inner light.

We might end this work with words from Emerson who lived his lifetime of almost 80 years in a neighborly place, in Concord, at the very early stages of that great machine revolution which resulted in what we now call Modernity. Emerson said:

> A Person will worship something—have no doubt about that. We may think our tribute is paid in secret in the dark recesses of our hearts—but it will out. That which dominates our imaginations and our thoughts will determine our lives, and our character. Therefore, it behooves us to be careful what we worship, for what we are worshipping we are becoming.[18]

As Emerson says, be careful of the tribute paid in the dark shadows in the recesses of our hearts—for what we are worshipping we are becoming. And we would add: To stand outside of the living place as a calculating spectator to manufacture, to manage, to sell, to consume, to discard and to trash the infinite quantity and variety of products we now create is to risk becoming simply part of a great machine that creates more of these products. Better to find, to be within, to be part of, and to celebrate, no matter how elusive, the complex organic experience of the continuing coming into being of a local living place—and thus engage in the process of becoming a householder in a family, a neighbor in a village, and a citizen in a native town or city, not as a casual visitor but as an artisan or an artist with an abiding and continuing communal vocation. Better to experience brief moments of becoming one with nature, one with one's neighbor, and one with the silence of the All and know that we will never be alone. Never.

Notes

1. For an elaboration of this position see Putnam's *Bowling Alone: the Collapse and Revival of American Community*. In this work Putnam recovers the term "social capital" from a 1916 article on rural education written by L.J. Hanifan by which the author means "those tangible substances [that] count most in the daily lives of people: namely good will, fellowship, sympathy, and social intercourse among individuals and families who make up a social unit.... (p.130) (Lydia Judson Hanifan, "The Rural School Community Center," *Annals of the American Academy of Political and Social Science* 67 (1916): 130-138).

2. Robert Putnam, *Bowling Alone*, pp. 400-401.

3. Ibid., pp. 406 - 411.

4. We would also refer here to the work of another policy analyst, Francis Fukuyama, author of *The Great Disruption: Human Nature and the Reconstitution of Social Order* (New York: Simon & Schuster, 1999.) whose methodological approach to social issues is similar to Putnam's *Bowling Alone*. Fukuyama opens his book with a theme similar to our own, i.e., substantial evidence for the mounting pathology of modernity in the United States over the past 50 years (increases in violent crimes, lowered fertility, increasing divorce rates, increasing births to single mothers, decreasing trust among high school seniors, etc.) but concludes with anecdotal evidence that America has "turned the corner" and in his terms, "the Great Disruption [of the second half of the twentieth century] has run its course." (p. 271) His faith in what he explicitly calls "human nature" rests on the assumption that humans so passionately crave social order that they can and will regenerate the "social capital" to solve the current problems of the modern system. As compared with our own critique and vision of the future, his time frame is radically shorter—something in the order of fifty years—and his sense of history is considerably more optimistic. As he says, "Our only reason for hope is the very powerful innate human capacities for reconstituting social order. On the success of this process of reconstitution depends the upward direction of the arrow of history." (p. 282) Putnam apparently shares this optimism. Unlike Gordon Kaufman's reminder of the potential for tragic episodes in human history presented earlier, there is no serious consideration of such a potential by either of these scholars.

5. J. von Uexkull, "The theory of meaning," translated by B. Stone and H. Weiner from *Bedeugtungslehre*, T. von Uexskull, ed., *Semiotica* 42 (1982 / 1940), pp. 25-82.

6. Owen Barfield, *Saving the Appearances*, 2nd edition. (Hanover, NH: University Press of New England, 1965), p. 20.

7. Ibid., pp. 41-42.

8. While Barfield assumes that modern humans have lost their capacity for "original participation," he speculates that something like it—what he calls "final participation"—may be reclaimed though the process of imagination.

9. Tim Ingold, "Culture and the Perception of the Environment," in *Bush Base: Forest Farm*, Chapter Three, edited by Elisabeth Croll and David Parkin (London, Routledge, 1992), pp. 39-55.

10. J. J. Gibson, *Reasons for Realism: Selected Essays of James J. Gibson*, edited by E. Reed, & R. Jones (Hillsdale, NJ: Lawrence Erlbaum, 1982), p. 412.

11. Ingold, *Culture and the Perception of the Environment*, p. 43.

12. Ibid., p. 44.

13. Ibid., p. 44.

14. Ibid., p. 52.

15. Ibid.

16. John Blofeld, *Taoism: The Road to Immortality* (Boulder, CO: Shambhala, 1978), p. 10.

17. We would note especially the classic work of Goethe, Whitehead, Steiner, Jung, Barfield, Eliade, Wiilber, Hillman, and Neville, and on and on.

18. Ralph Waldo Emerson, "A person will worship something" (In *Singing the Living Tradition*, A hymnal compiled by the Unitarian Universalist Association (Boston: Beacon Press, 1993) Selection 563.

Bibliography

Aberle, D. F., Cohen, A., Levey, M., Sutton, F. (1950). The Functional Prerequisites of a Society. *Ethics*, 60.

Albanese, C. L. (1977). *Corresponding Motion*. Philadelphia: Temple University Press.

Alexander, C. (1979). *A Timeless Way of Building*. New York & Oxford: Oxford University Press.

Alexander, C. (1977). *A Pattern Language*. New York: Oxford University Press.

Appadurai, A. *Modernity at Large: Cultural Dimensions of Globalization*. Minneapolis: University of Minnesota Press.

Ariyaratne, A. T. (1982). *In Search of Development: The Survodaya Shrama Dam Movement's Effort to Harmonize Tradition with Change*. Moratuwa, Sri Lanka: Sarvodaya Press..

Banfield, E. C. (1958). *The Moral Basis of a Backward Society*. New York: The Free Press.

Barfield, O. (1965). *Saving the Appearances: A Study in Idolatry*. New York: Harcourt Brace Harvest Book.

Basso, K. H. (1987). Stalking with Stories: Names, Places and Moral Narratives Among the Western Apache. In *On Nature*. Daniel Halpern (Ed.). San Francisco: North Point Press.

Bateson, G. (1972). *Steps to an Ecology of Mind*. San Francisco, CA: Chandler.

Behrendt, R. R. (1970). Socio-cultural development up to the present time and our place in it. In *Readings in Social Evolution and Development*. S. N. Eisenstadt (Ed.). Oxford: Pergamon Press.

Bellah, R. N., Madson, R., Sullivan, W. M., Swidler, A., Tipton, S. M. (1985). *Habits of the Heart: Individualism and Commitment in American Life*. New York: Perennial Library (Harper & Row).

Bender, T. (1978). *Community and Social Change*. Baltimore, MD: Johns Hopkins Press.

Benedict, R. (1934). *Patterns of Culture*. New York: The New American Library: Mentor.

Benedict, R. (1934). Anthropology and the Abnormal. *The Journal of General Psychology*, 10(1).

Benet, S. (1970). *The Village of Viriatino: An Ethnographic Study of a Russian Village from Before the Revolution to the Present*. Garden City, NY: Anchor Books.

Berger, P. L. & Neuhaus, R. J. (1977). *To Empower People: The Role of Mediating Structures in Public Policy*. Washington, DC: American Enterprise Institute for Public Policy Research.

Berry, W. (1981). People, Land and Community. *People, Land and Community*, Collected E. F. Schumacher Society Lectures. H. Hannum (ed.). New Haven & London: Yale University Press.

Berry, T. (1988). *The Dream of the Earth*. San Francisco: Sierra Club Books.

Bidney, D. (1967). *Theoretical Anthropology*. 2nd edition. New York: Schocken Books.

Blasi, J. (1986). *The Communal Experience of the Kibbutz*. New Brunswick, NJ: Transaction Press.

Blofeld, J. (1978). *Taoism: The Road to Immortality*. Boulder, CO: Shambhala..

Boff, L. (1995). *Ecology and Liberation*. Maryknoll, NY: Orbis Books.

Bohm, D. (1980). *Wholeness and the Implicate Order*. London: Routledge and Kegan Paul.

Bookchin, M. (1982). *The Ecology of Freedom*. Palo Alto, CA: Cheshire Books.

Borish, S. M. (1991). *The Land of the Living: The Danish Folk High Schools and Denmark's Non-violent Path to Modernization*. Nevada City, CA: Blue Dolphin.

Bradley, N. L. (1999, Fall). Aldo Leopold. *Wild Earth*.

Callicott, J. B. (1999). *Beyond the Land Ethic*. Albany, NY: SUNY Press.

Coates, G. (1981). *Resettling America: Energy, Ecology and Community*. Andover, MA: Brick House.

Couclelis, H. (1995). Bridging Cognition and Knowledge. *Rethinking Knowledge*. R. F. Goodman & W. F. Fisher (Eds.). Albany, NY: SUNY Press.

Critchfield, R. (1960). *Villages*. Garden City, NY: Anchor Books.

Critchfield, R. (1994). *The Villagers*. New York: Anchor Books.

Csikszentmihalyi, M. (1960). *Flow*. New York: Harper and Row.

Cyberhood vs Neighborhood. *Utne Reader*. March-April 1995.

Daly, H. E., Cobb, J. B. (1991). *For the Common Good: Redirecting the Economy Toward Community, the Environment, and Sustainable Future*. Boston: Beacon Press.

Degler, C. N. (1991). *In Search of Human Nature*. New York: Oxford University Press.

Dewey, J. (1939). *Freedom and Culture*. New York: Capricorn Books.

Diamond, S. (Ed.). (1960). *Primitive Views of the World*. New York: Columbia University Press.

Diamond, S. (1974). *In Search of the Primitive*. New Brunswick, NJ: Transaction Books.

Durrell, L. (1957). *Bitter Lemons (Cyprus)*. New York: Dutton.

Eastman, C. (1971). *Indian Boyhood*. New York: Dover.

Emerson, R. W. (1940/1940). *The Selected Writings of Ralph Waldo Emerson*. Brooks Atkinson (Ed.). New York: The Modern Library.

Erickson, K. T. (1976). *Everything in its Path*. New York: Simon & Schuster.

Fromm, E. (1944). Individual and Social Origins of Neurosis. *American Sociological Review, IX*.

Fromm, E. & M. Maccoby. (1970). *Social Character in a Mexican Village*. Englewood Cliffs, NJ: Prentice Hall.

Fukuyama, F. (1999). *The Great Disruption: Human Nature and the Reconstitution of Social Order*. New York: Simon & Schuster.

Gans, H. (1962). *Urban Villagers: Group and Class in the Life of Italian-Americans*. New York: The Free Press.

Gibson, J. J. (1979). *The Ecological Approach to Visual Perception*. Boston: Houghton-Mifflin.

Gilbert, J. (1991). *Perfect Cities: Chicago's Utopias of 1893*. Chicago: University of Chicago Press.

Goffman, Erving. (1961). *Asylums*. New York: Anchor Books.

Goldschmidt, W. (1966). *Comparative Functionalism*. Berkeley: University of California Press.

Goldweiser, A. A. (1936). Loose Ends of Theory on the Individual Pattern and Involution in Primitive Society. *Essays in Anthropology*. R. H. Lowie (Ed.). Berkeley, CA: University of California Press.

Goodman, P. & P. (1947). *Communitas, Means of Livelihood and Ways of Life*. New York: Vintage.

Gould, S. J. (1997, June 26). The Pleasures of Pluralism. *The New York Review of Books*. XLIV, (11).

Guha, Ramachandra. (1996). Lewis Mumford, the Forgotten American Environmentalist: An Essay in Rehabilitation, in *Minding Nature*. D. Macauley (Ed.). New York: The Guilford Press. pp. 209-228.

Hall, E. T. (1976). *Beyond Culture*. Garden City, NY: Anchor Books.

Hanifan, L. J. (1916). The rural school community center. *Annals of the American Academy of Political and Social Science*, 67.

Havel, V. (1989, 1990). *Living in Truth*. London: Farber and Farber.

Hawken, P. (1975). *The Magic of Findhorn*. New York: Bantam.

Hawkin, P. (1993). *The Ecology of Commerce*. New York: Harper Collins.

Henry, J. (1959, April). Culture, Personality and Evolution. *American Anthropologist*, 61(2).

Hillery, Jr., G. A. (1968). *Communal Organizations*. Chicago: University of Chicago Press.

Hollingshead, A. B. (1975) *Elmtown's Youth* and *Elmtown Revisited*. New York: Wiley.

Homans, G. C. (1942). *English Villagers of the Thirteenth Century*. New York: Harper Torchbooks.

Ingold, T. (1993). Globes and Spheres: The Topology of Environmentalism. *Environmentalism: The View from Anthropology*. K. Milton (Ed.). New York: Routledge.

Inkeles, A. & Smith, D. H. (1974). *Becoming Modern*. Cambridge, MA: Harvard University Press.

Janicke, M. (1990). *State Failure : The Impotence of Politics in Industrial Society*. University Park: Pennsylvania State University Press.

Johnson, M. (1987). *The Body in the Mind*. Chicago: University of Chicago Press.

Kanter, R. M. (1972). *Commitment and Community: Communes and Utopias in Sociological Perspective*. Cambridge, MA: Harvard University Press.

Kaplan, A. (1977). *The Pursuit of Wisdom*. Beverly Hills, CA: Glencoe Press.

Kaufman, G. D. (1993). *In Face of Mystery*. Cambridge & London: Harvard University Press.

Kinkade, K. A. (1973). *Walden Two Experiment: The First Five Years of the Twin Oaks Community*. New York: William Morrow.

Koestler, A. (1979). *Janus*. New York: Vintage Books.

Korten, D. C. (1995). *When Corporations Rule the World*. West Hartford, CT: Kumarian Press.

Kurtzweil, R. (1999). *The Age of Spiritual Machines*. New York: Viking Press.

Lakoff, G. (1987). *Women, Fire, and Dangerous Things*. Chicago: University of Chicago Press.

Langer, S. (1948). *Philosophy in a New Key: A Study in the Symbolism of Reason, Rite, and Art*. New York: Penguin Books.

Lantz, H. R. (1958). *People of Coal Town*. Carbondale, IL: Southern Illinois University Press.

Lasch, C. (1991). *The True and Only Heaven: Progress and its Critics*. New York: Norton.

Lenski, G. (1970). *Human Societies*. New York: Norton.

Liebow, E. (1967). *Tally's Corner: A Study of Negro Street Corner Men*. New York: Little, Brown and Co.

Linton, R. (1955). *The Tree of Culture*. New York: Little, Brown and Co.

Living Together: Sustainable Community Development. *In Context: A Quarterly of Human Sustainable Culture*. (29). Summer 1991.

Luke, T. (1991, Summer). Community and Ecology. *Telos*.

Macdonald, C. (1994, June). An Energy/awareness/information Interpretation of Physical and Mental Reality. *Zygon*, 29(2).

Maryanski, A. & Turner, J. H. (1992). *The Social Cage: Human Nature and the Evolution of Society*. Stanford: Stanford University Press.

Masters, R. (1993). *Beyond Relativism*. Hanover, NH: University Press of New England.

Mazur, A. & Robertson, L. S. (1972). *Biology and Social Behavior*. New York: The Free Press.

McLaughlin, C. & Davidson, G. (1985). *Builders of the Dawn: Community Lifestyles in a changing world*. Summertown, TN: Book Publishing Co.

Meadows, D. H. & Donella, H. (1972). *The Limits of Growth*. Washington, DC: Potomac Associates.

Meadows, D. H. & Donella, H. (1992). *Beyond the Limits*. Post Mills, VT: Chelsea Green.

Mandelbaum, D. G. (1949). Selected Writings of Edward Sapir. *Language, Culture and Personality*. Berkeley & Los Angeles: University of California Press.

Mitchell, J. H. (1984). *Ceremonial Time: Fifteen Thousand Years on One Square Mile*. Garden City, NY: Anchor Books.

Mollison, B. (1990). *Permaculture: A Practical Guide for a Sustainable Future*. Washington, DC: Island Press.

Moore, W. E. (1963). *Social Change*. Englewood Cliffs, NJ: Prentice-Hall.

Morris, D. (1981). Self Reliant Cities: The Rise of the New City States, in *Resettling America*. G. J. Coates (Ed.). Andover, MA: Brick House Publishing Company.

Muir, D. (2000). *Reflections in Bullough's Pond: Economy and Ecosystem in New England*. Hanover, NH & London: University Press of New England.

Mumford, L. (1938). *The Culture of Cities*. New York: Harcourt Brace Jovanovich.

Mumford, L. (1964). *The Pentagon of Power*. New York: Harcourt Brace Jovanovich.

Myrdal, J. (1965). *Report From a Chinese Village*. New York: Pantheon.

Neville, R. C. (1989). *Recovery of the Measure*. Albany, NY: SUNY Press.

Nisbet, R. A. (1953/1969). *The Quest for Community*. New York: Oxford University Press.

Northrop, F. S. C. (1946). *The Meeting of East and West*. NewYork: Macmillan.

Odin, S. (1982). *Process Metaphysics and Hua-yen Buddhism*. Albany, NY: SUNY Press.

Oliver, D. W. (1976). *Education and Community: A Radical Critique of Innovative Schooling*. Berkeley, CA: McCutchen.

Orr, D. (1992). *Ecological Literacy*. Albany, NY: SUNY Press.

Palmer, P. (1998, September). The Grace of Great Things: Reclaiming the Sacred in Knowing, Teaching and Learning. *The Sun: A Magazine of Ideas*, Issue 273.

Parsons, T. (1951). *The Social System*. New York: The Free Press.

Percy, W. (1954). *The Message in the Bottle*. New York: Farrar, Straus & Giroux.

Pietila, H. (1997) The Triangle of the Human Economy: Household-Cultivation-Industrial Production: An Attempt at Making Visible the Human Economy in Toto. *Ecological Economics*, 20.

Piore, M. J. & Sabel, C. F. (1984). *The Second Industrial Divide: Possibilities for Prosperity*. New York: Basic Books.

Priestly, J. B. (1964). *Man and Time*. London: Aldus Books.

Putnam, R. D. (2000). *Bowling Alone: The Collapse and Revival of American Community*. New York: Simon & Schuster.

Putnam, R. D., Leonardi, R, & Nanetti, T. Y. (1993). *Making Democracy Work: Civic Traditions in Modern Italy*. Princeton: Princeton University Press.

Quandt, J. B. (1970). *From Small Town to the Great Community: The Social Thought of Progressive Intellectuals*. New Brunswick, NJ: Rutgers University Press.

Redfield, R. (1956). *Peasant Society and Culture*. Chicago: University of Chicago Press.

Redfield, R. (1956). *The Little Community*. Chicago: University of Chicago Press.

Redfield, R. & Singer, M. B. (1971). The Cultural Role of Cities. *Peasants and Peasant Societies*. T. Shanin (ed.). Middlesex, England: Penguin.

Reinventing the Village. *Utne Reader* May/June 1992. p. 51.

Richardson, E. A. (1988). *Strangers in This Land: Pluralism and the Response to Diversity in the United States*. New York: The Pilgrim Press.

Riesman, D. (1950). *The Loney Crowd*. New Haven: Yale University Press.

Sahlins, M. (1976). *Culture and Practical Reason*. Chicago: University of Chicago Press.

Schectman, M. (1996, December). The Story of the Mind: Psychological and Biological Explanations of Human Behavior. *Zygon*, 31(4).

Schumacher, E. F. (1973). *Small is Beautiful: Economics as if People Mattered*. New York: Perennial Library (Harpers).

Searle, J. R. (1999, April 8). I Married a Computer. *New York Review of Books*. 46(6).

Service, E. (1962/1971). *Primitive Social Organization*. 2nd Edition. New York: Random House.

Sessions, G. (1995). *Deep Ecology for the 21st Century*. Boston: Shambhala.

Sheldrake, R. (1988). *The Presence of the Past*. New York: New York Times Books.

Sherburne, D. (Ed.). (1966). *A Key to Whitehead's Process and Reality*. Chicago: University of Chicago Press.

Shore, B. (1996). *Culture in Mind*. New York: Oxford University Press.

Shweder, R. A. (1991). *Thinking Through Culture: Expeditions in Cultural Psychology*. Cambridge, MA: Harvard University Press.

Smith-Bowen, E. (1954). *Return to Laughter*. Garden City, NY: Anchor Books.

Snyder, G. (1990). *The Practice of the Wild*. Berkeley, CA: North Point Press.

Spiro, M. E. (1956). *Kibbutz: Venture Into Utopia*. Cambridge: Harvard University Press..

Stein, M. R. (1960). *The Eclipse of Community: An Interpretation of American Studies*. Princeton, NJ: Princeton University Press.

Stein, M. R. (1960). Anthropological Perspectives on the Modern Community. *Primitive Views of the World*. S. Diamond (Ed.). New York: Columbia University Press.

Suzuki, D. & Knudtson, P. (1992). *Wisdom of the Elders*. New York: Bantam Books.

Swimme, B. (1985). *The Universe is a Green Dragon*. Santa Fe: Bear and Company.

Swimme, B. & Berry, T. (1992). *The Universe Story*. San Francisco: HarperCollins.

Thomas, W. & Znaniechie, F. (1960). Three Types of Personality. *Images of Man*. C. Wright Mills (Ed.). New York: George Braziller.

Thomas, W. L., Sauer, C. O., Bates, M. & Mumford, L. (Eds.). (1956). *Man's Role in Changing the Face of the Earth*. Chicago: University of Chicago Press.

Todd, J. & Jack, N. (1994). *From Eco-Cities to Living Machines: Principles of Ecological Design*. Berkeley: North Atlantic Books.

Toulmin, S. (1990). *Cosmopolis*. Chicago: University of Chicago Press.

Turnbull, C. M. (1961). *The Forest People: A Study of the Pygmies of the Congo*. New York: Touchstone.

Tyack, D. & Cubin, L. (1995). *Tinkering Toward Utopia*. Cambridge, MA: Harvard University Press.

Wallace, A. F. C. (1970). *Culture and Personality*. 2nd Edition. New York: Random House.

Walter, E. V. (1988). *Placeways: A Theory of Human Environment*. Chapel Hill, NC: University of North Carolina Press.

Waters, F. (1963). *Book of the Hopi*. New York: Penguin.

Weatherford, J. (1964). *Savages and Civilizations: Who will survive?* New York: Crown.

What is Enough: Fulfilling Lifestyles for a Small Planet. In *Context: A Quarterly of Human Sustainable Culture*, 26. Summer 1990.

Whitehead, A. N. (1925). *Science and the Modern World*. New York: Macmillan.

Whitehead, A. N. (1933). *Adventures of Ideas*. New York: The Free Press.

Whitehead, A. N. (1948/1974). *Science and Philosophy*. New York: Philosophical Library.

Wigginton, E. (1986). *Sometimes A Shining Moment: The Foxfire Experience*. Garden City, NY: Anchor Books.

Wilson, E. O. (1978). *On Human Nature*. Cambridge, MA: Harvard University Press.

Wilson, E. O. (1998). *Consilience*. New York: Knopf.

Working Communities. *Rain*. 14(2). Winter/Spring 1992.

Wylie, L. (1957) *Village in the Vaucluse: An Account of Life in a French Village*. New York: Harper Colophon.

Zablocki, B. (1971). *The Joyful Community*. Baltimore, MD: Pelican.

Zerzan, J. (1998, September). Enemy of the State. *The Sun: A Magazine of Ideas*. Issue 273.

Zeusse, E. M. (1979). *Ritual Cosmos*. Athens, OH: Ohio University Press.

About the Authors

Dr. DONALD W. OLIVER is a native New Englander. He was a professor at the Harvard Graduate School of Education teaching philosophy, curriculum, and community studies for more than four decades. He has published two previous books, *Education and Community* (1976) and *Education, Modernity and Fractured Meaning* (1989). His immense love and passion for local culture and small places made his teaching unique. With his students, he shared immense intellectual and conversational talents. Donald shared his robust tenor voice, gracing schools, hospitals, and many choir lofts and congregations in Unitarian parishes in and around Boston, and was often accompanied by his wife Polly, a musician, choir director, and church organist.

JULIE G. CANIFF received her doctorate in 1999 at the Harvard Graduate School of Education. Her research is focused on the cultural epistemology of "success," as articulated by different generations within a distinct cultural group. Her recent publication, *Cambodian Refugees' Pathways to Success*, is a ten-year ethnography of three families who value the extended family, the Cambodian community, and their Buddhist traditions as fundamental to their concept of what it means to be a successful person. Dr. Caniff is currently a Clinical Lecturer in the Extended Teacher Education Program at the University of Southern Maine. She works with graduate students who have chosen to leave successful mainstream careers and enter the field of teaching in Maine's public schools.

JOUNI KORHONEN holds a Ph.D. in environmental management from the University of Jyväskylä, Finland, and is currently working as an Associate Professor at the University of Joensuu Department of Economics, Finland. He serves as a member of the editorial board of the *Journal of Corporate Social Responsibility and Environmental Management* and has published on corporate social responsibility and industrial ecology in several international journals, including *Sustainable Development, International Journal of Sustainable Development and World Ecology, International Journal of Environmental Technology and Management, Ecological Economics, Journal of Cleaner Production* and others. Currently, Jouni Korhonen heads an Academy of Finland research project, Regional Industrial Ecosystem Management (RIEM).

For Further Reading on Holistic Education

OTHER TITLES IN THE FOUNDATIONS OF HOLISTIC EDUCATION SERIES PUBLISHED BY THE FOUNDATION FOR EDUCATIONAL RENEWAL

- *Caring for New Life: Essays on Holistic Education* by Ron Miller
- *Education for Awakening: An Eastern Approach to Holistic Education* by Yoshiharu Nakagawa
- *Unfolding Bodymind: Exploring Possibility Through Education,* edited by Brent Hocking, Johnna Haskell, and Warren Linds
- *"Under the Tough Old Stars": Ecopedagogical Essays* by David Jardine
- *Holistic Education: Pedagogy of Universal Love* by Ramón Gallegos Nava
- *Nurturing Our Wholeness: Perspectives on Spirituality in Education,* edited by John (Jack) Miller and Yoshiharu Nakagawa

BOOKS FROM OTHER PUBLISHERS AVAILABLE FROM GREAT IDEAS IN EDUCATION

- *What Are Schools For? Holistic Education in American Culture* by Ron Miller
- *New Directions in Education: Selections from Holistic Education Review,* edited by Ron Miller
- *Insight-Imagination: The Emancipation of Thought and the Modern World* by Douglas Sloan
- *Designing and Implementing an Integrated Curriculum* by Edward T. Clark, Jr.

FOR MORE INFORMATION CONTACT THE FOUNDATION AT P.O. BOX 328, BRANDON, VT 05733-0328.
1-800-639-4122.
HTTP://WWW.GREAT-IDEAS.ORG
HTTP://WWW.PATHSOFLEARNING.NET